First Children's Encyclopedia

REVISED EDITION
Editor Ishani Nandi
Assistant editor Debangana Banerjee
Art editor Shipra Jain
Senior editor Shatarupa Chaudhuri
DTP designer Bimlesh Tiwary
Managing editors Laura Gilbert, Alka Thakur Hazarika
Managing art editors Diane Peyton Jones,
Romi Chakraborty
CTS manager Balwant Singh
Producer Nicole Landau
Producer, pre-production Francesca Wardell
Publisher Sarah Larter
Publishing director Sophie Mitchell
Art director Stuart Jackman
Jacket editor Ishani Nandi
Jacket designer Kartik Gera
Consultants Carole Stott, Jack Challoner,
John Woodward, Susan Kennedy

ORIGINAL EDITION
Editors Penny Smith, Lorrie Mack,
Caroline Stamps, Lee Wilson
Project Art Editor Mary Sandberg
Designers Laura Roberts-Jensen, Lauren Rosier
Publishing Manager Bridget Giles
Art Director Rachael Foster
Production Editor Siu Chan
Jacket Designers Natalie Godwin,
Laura Roberts-Jensen

This edition published in 2015
First published in Great Britain in 2010 by
Dorling Kindersley Limited
80 Strand, London, WC2R 0RL

A CIP catalogue record for this book
is available from the British Library.

ISBN 978-0-2412-0676-8

Printed and bound in Malaysia

A WORLD OF IDEAS:
SEE ALL THERE IS TO KNOW

www.dk.com

Contents

Using this book

The First Children's Encyclopedia is divided into ten colour-coded chapters so you can see what you are looking for at a glance.

In these pages, you can find a country and discover its major features, look at culture and history, and observe wildlife and ecosystems. You can also explore the world of science – from how technology works to what's going on inside the human body. Enjoy a thrilling journey!

Our world

People and society

History of people

Human body

The living world

Ecosystems and habitats

Age of the dinosaurs

Science and technology

Planet Earth

The Universe

What's what on a page?

The pages of this book have special features that will show you how to get your hands on as much information as possible! Look out for these.

The **Picture Detective** will get you searching through each section for the answers.

The living world

The living world

Our amazing world is filled with millions of species, or types, of living thing. They can be as big as elephants or so small that you have to look through a microscope to see them.

Spider

Animals
The animal kingdom is made up of vertebrates (animals with a backbone) and invertebrates (animals without a backbone).

Coral reef, home to a variety of living organisms

Mammals, birds, reptiles, amphibians, and fish are vertebrates.

Deer

Micro-organisms
Micro-organisms are very tiny – each of them is made up of a single cell. This amoeba has been magnified more than 100 times.

Sunflower

Fungi

Dragonfly

Snake

Insects, such as butterflies, are invertebrates.

Plants
Plants cannot move around like animals. To survive and grow, they have to make their own food. Plants provide food for many animals and fungi, too.

Signs of life
Living things share some characteristics. They all need food and water. They also grow, reproduce, and adapt to their environment.

Fungi
Fungi (like toadstools, mushrooms, and moulds) are neither plants nor animals, but they're more like plants than animals.

Tree frog

The living world

Picture detective
Look through the Life Science pages and see if you can identify the pictures below.

Turn and learn
Types of animal: **pp. 126-127**
How plants work: **pp. 148-149**

122

Which group of animals has the most members?

123

Invertebrates – they make up 97 per cent of all animal species.

Turn and Learn buttons tell you which pages to turn to in order to find more information on each subject.

There is a question at the bottom of each page...

hands on

Want to try something for yourself? Then look at a "hands on" tip.

Detailed captions tell you more about a subject.

Hands on circles tell you how to get stuck in and try an experiment for yourself.

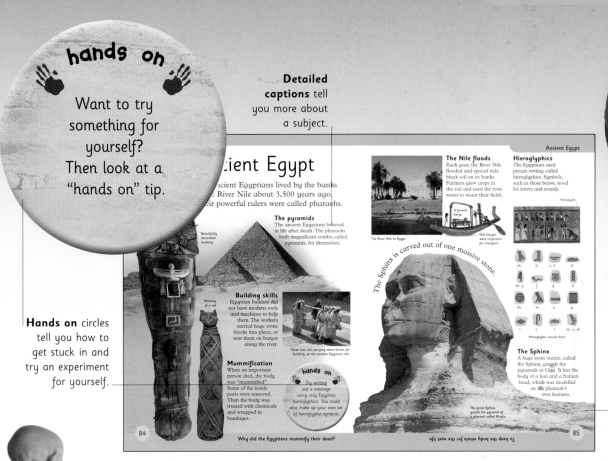

Ancient Egypt

The ancient Egyptians lived by the banks of the River Nile about 3,500 years ago. Their powerful rulers were called pharaohs.

The pyramids
The ancient Egyptians believed in life after death. The pharaohs built magnificent tombs, called pyramids, for themselves.

Beautifully decorated mummy

Mummy of a cat

Building skills
Egyptian builders did not have modern tools and machines to help them. The workers carried huge stone blocks into place, or sent them on barges along the river.

These men are carrying stone blocks for building, as the ancient Egyptians did.

Mummification
When an important person died, the body was "mummified". Some of the inside parts were removed. Then the body was treated with chemicals and wrapped in bandages.

hands on
Try writing out a message using only Egyptian hieroglyphics. You could also make up your own set of hieroglyphic symbols.

84

Why did the Egyptians mummify their dead?

The Nile floods
Each year, the River Nile flooded and spread rich, black soil on its banks. Farmers grew crops in the soil and used the river water to water their fields.

The River Nile in Egypt

A funeral barge

Nile barges were important for transport.

Hieroglyphics
The Egyptians used picture writing called hieroglyphics. Symbols, such as those below, stood for letters and sounds.

Hieroglyphs

Hieroglyphic sound chart

The Sphinx is carved out of one massive stone.

The Sphinx
A huge stone statue, called the Sphinx, guards the pyramids at Giza. It has the body of a lion and a human head, which was modelled on the pharaoh's own features.

The great Sphinx guards the pyramid of a pharaoh called Khufra.

85

To keep the body whole for the next life.

Ancient Egypt

Stunning photographs show you what the captions describe.

Colour coding identifies each chapter at a glance.

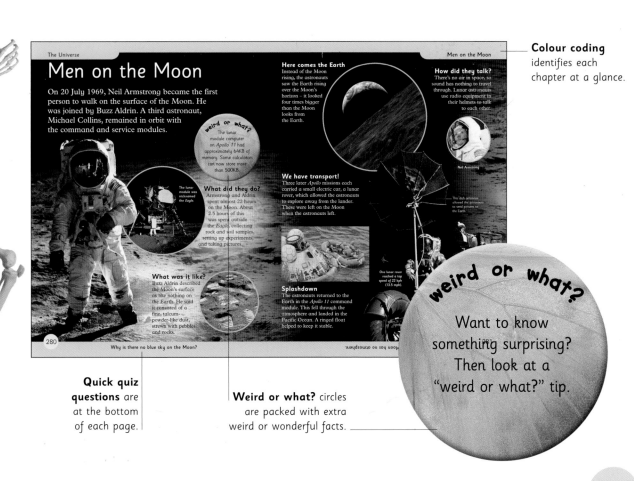

The Universe

Men on the Moon

On 20 July 1969, Neil Armstrong became the first person to walk on the surface of the Moon. He was joined by Buzz Aldrin. A third astronaut, Michael Collins, remained in orbit with the command and service modules.

weird or what?
The lunar module computer on Apollo 11 had approximately 64KB of memory. Some calculators can now store more than 500KB.

The lunar module was nicknamed the Eagle.

What did they do?
Armstrong and Aldrin spent almost 22 hours on the Moon. About 2.5 hours of this was spent outside the Eagle, collecting rock and soil samples, setting up experiments, and taking pictures.

What was it like?
Buzz Aldrin described the Moon's surface as like nothing on the Earth. He said it consisted of a fine, talcum-powder-like dust, strewn with pebbles and rocks.

Here comes the Earth
Instead of the Moon rising, the astronauts saw the Earth rising over the Moon's horizon – it looked four times bigger than the Moon looks from the Earth.

We have transport!
Three later Apollo missions each carried a small electric car, a lunar rover, which allowed the astronauts to explore away from the lander. These were left on the Moon when the astronauts left.

Splashdown
The astronauts returned to the Earth in the Apollo 11 command module. This fell through the atmosphere and landed in the Pacific Ocean. A ringed float helped to keep it stable.

One lunar rover reached a top speed of 22 kph (13.5 mph).

How did they talk?
There's no air in space, so sound has nothing to travel through. Lunar astronauts use radio equipment in their helmets to talk to each other.

Neil Armstrong

This dish antenna allowed the astronauts to send pictures to the Earth.

280

Why is there no blue sky on the Moon?

Moon has no atmosphere.

Men on the Moon

weird or what?

Want to know something surprising? Then look at a "weird or what?" tip.

Quick quiz questions are at the bottom of each page.

Weird or what? circles are packed with extra weird or wonderful facts.

Our world

Land covers a third of planet Earth, and water and ice cover the rest. We divide the land into seven main chunks, called continents. The sea is divided into five major areas, called oceans.

North America

Pacific Ocean

Atlantic Ocean

Earth's crust

Inside the Earth

The inside of the Earth is made of hot, mobile rock that slowly swirls about like thick treacle. We live on a thin, solid crust, a bit like the crust of a pie.

South America

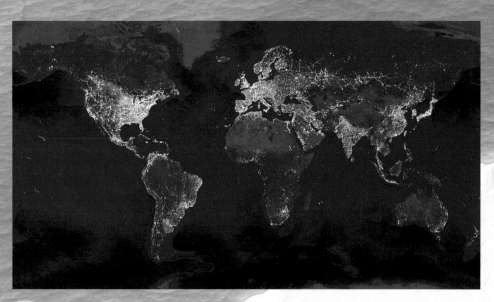

Where people live

This picture of the Earth at night was taken by a satellite in space. The bright bits are made by lights on the surface. They show where the world's big cities and towns are.

How long would a trip around the Equator take at walking speed?

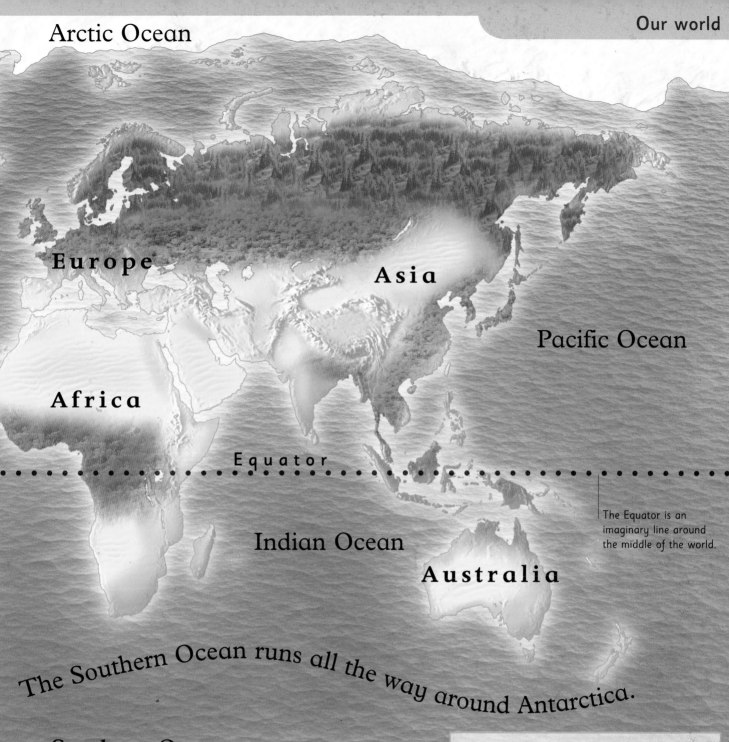

Arctic Ocean

Europe

Asia

Pacific Ocean

Africa

Equator

The Equator is an imaginary line around the middle of the world.

Indian Ocean

Australia

The Southern Ocean runs all the way around Antarctica.

Southern Ocean

Antarctica

Can you find...

The smallest continent?
The continent of Australia is also the world's biggest island.

The most crowded continent?
Around 4.4 billion people live in Asia.

The biggest ocean?
The Pacific Ocean is as big as all other oceans put together.

Seven continents

North America, South America, Europe, Asia, Africa, Australia, and Antarctica are the Earth's continents. Sometimes, people call Europe and Asia one continent (Eurasia).

About a year (without stopping for a rest).

The Arctic

The North Pole is the northernmost point of the globe, and around this is an area called the Arctic. The Arctic is mostly ocean. In its centre is a gigantic lump of floating ice that never completely melts. Further out are the northern tips of the continents and the huge island of Greenland.

Arctic people

The people of the Arctic live in the icy lands surrounding the Arctic Ocean. The weather is too cold for growing crops, so they get all their food from animals. They survive by fishing, herding reindeer, and hunting seals and whales.

An imaginary line called the Arctic Circle marks the outer edge of the Arctic region.

Alaska

Prudhoe Bay

Beaufort Sea

Arctic tern

Moose

Canada

Queen Elizabeth Islands

Ellesmere Island

Ptarmigan

● Thule

Polar bear

Greenland

8

Who was the first person to reach the North Pole?

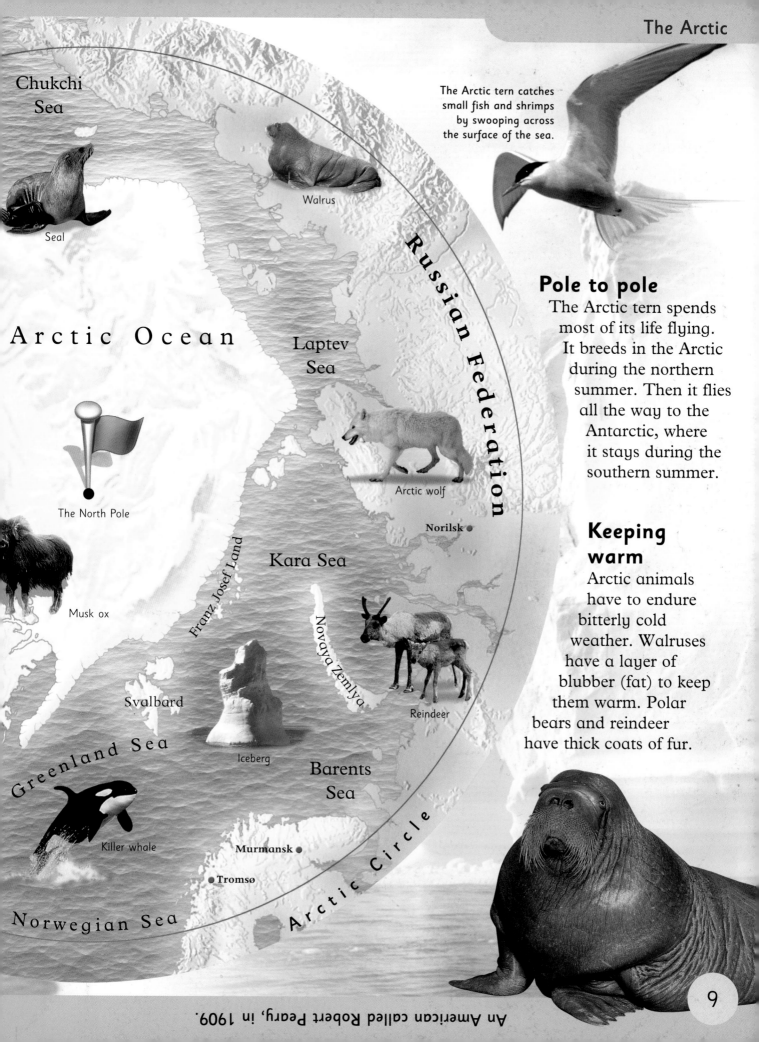

Chukchi
Sea

Seal

Walrus

The Arctic tern catches
small fish and shrimps
by swooping across
the surface of the sea.

Arctic Ocean

Laptev
Sea

Russian Federation

The North Pole

Musk ox

Franz Josef Land

Kara Sea

Novaya Zemlya

Arctic wolf

Norilsk

Reindeer

Svalbard

Iceberg

Greenland Sea

Killer whale

Barents
Sea

Murmansk

Tromsø

Arctic Circle

Norwegian Sea

Pole to pole

The Arctic tern spends
most of its life flying.
It breeds in the Arctic
during the northern
summer. Then it flies
all the way to the
Antarctic, where
it stays during the
southern summer.

Keeping
warm

Arctic animals
have to endure
bitterly cold
weather. Walruses
have a layer of
blubber (fat) to keep
them warm. Polar
bears and reindeer
have thick coats of fur.

9

An American called Robert Peary, in 1909.

Canada and Alaska

Canada is the second-largest country in the world, and Alaska is the largest of all the US states. Despite their huge sizes, both places have small populations, because much of the land is covered in thick forest or frozen for most of the year.

Ellesmere Island

Queen Elizabeth Islands

Banks Island

Victoria Island

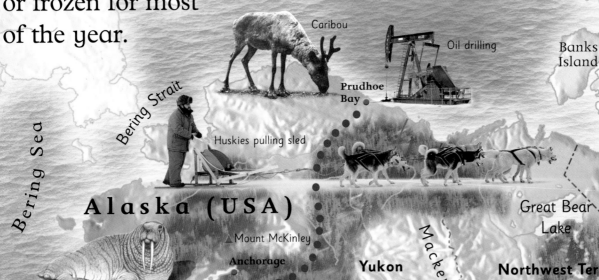

Caribou

Oil drilling

Prudhoe Bay

Bering Strait

Bering Sea

Huskies pulling sled

Alaska (USA)

Mount McKinley

Walrus

Anchorage

Valdez

Fur seal

Salmon

Yukon

Whitehorse

Juneau

Great Bear Lake

Musk ox

Northwest Territories

Yellowknife

Mackenzie Mountains

British Columbia

Grizzly bear

C

Totem pole

Rocky Mountains

Alberta

Saskatchewan

Edmonton

Mountie (policeman)

Timber

Trans-Alaska Pipeline System

The USA's largest oil-drilling area is in Alaska. A huge overground pipeline, 1,287 km (800 miles) long, carries the oil from Prudhoe Bay to the port of Valdez.

Pacific Ocean

Vancouver Island

Vancouver

Victoria

Calgary

Reg

Calgary skyline

Canadian Prairies

U S A

Which is the tallest mountain in North America, at 6,168 m (20,237 ft) high?

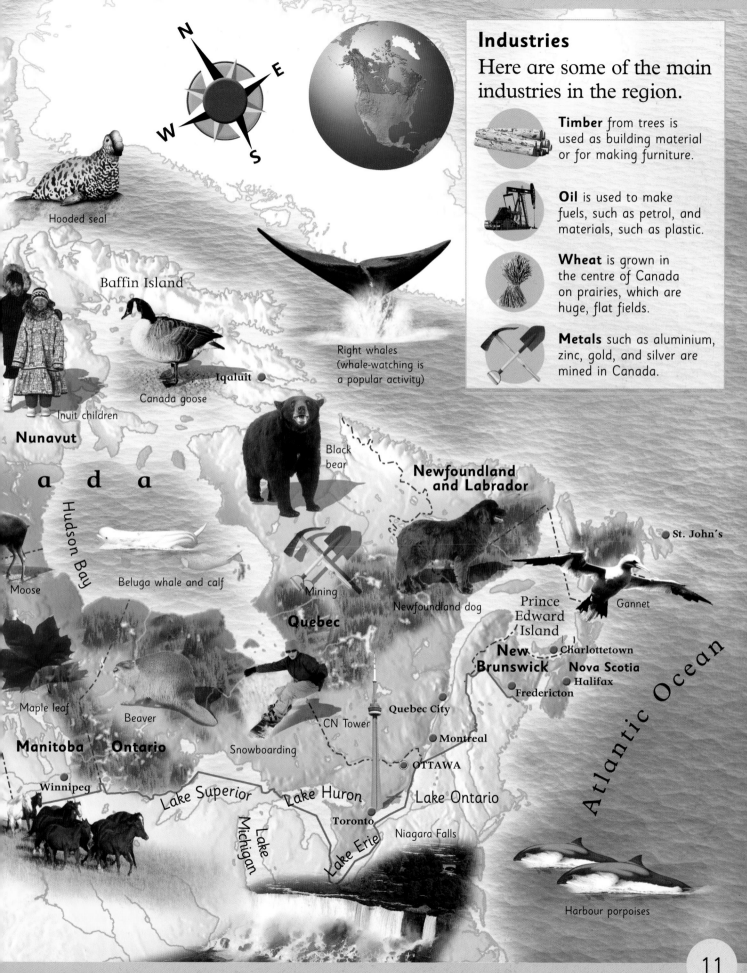

N **E** **W** **S**

Industries

Here are some of the main industries in the region.

Timber from trees is used as building material or for making furniture.

Oil is used to make fuels, such as petrol, and materials, such as plastic.

Wheat is grown in the centre of Canada on prairies, which are huge, flat fields.

Metals such as aluminium, zinc, gold, and silver are mined in Canada.

Hooded seal

Baffin Island

Inuit children

Nunavut

Canada goose

Iqaluit

Right whales (whale-watching is a popular activity)

Black bear

Newfoundland and Labrador

St. John's

a d a

Hudson Bay

Moose

Beluga whale and calf

Mining

Newfoundland dog

Gannet

Quebec

Prince Edward Island

New Brunswick

Charlottetown

Nova Scotia

Halifax

Fredericton

Maple leaf

Beaver

Snowboarding

CN Tower

Quebec City

Montreal

OTTAWA

Manitoba **Ontario**

Winnipeg

Lake Superior

Lake Huron

Lake Ontario

Toronto

Lake Michigan

Lake Erie

Niagara Falls

Atlantic Ocean

Harbour porpoises

Mount McKinley (Denali).

United States of America

The United States of America is an enormous country made up of 50 states. There are mountains, deserts, forests, wetlands, and vast plains in the USA.

Technology industry
Seattle
Grizzly bear (brown bear)
Bisons
Miss
Olympia
Washington
Columbia River
Helena
Salem
Montana
Mount Rushmore National Memorial
Oregon
Boise
Idaho
Skiing in the Rockies
Rocky Mountains
Wyoming
Golden Gate Bridge
Great Salt Lake
Cheyenne
Carson City
Mountain lion
Salt Lake City
Wheat harvesting
San Francisco
California
Nevada
Utah
Denver
Colorado
HOLLYWOOD
Road runner
Hollywood Hills
Los Angeles
Monument Valley
Santa Fe
Death Valley National Monument
Arizona
New Mexico
Colorado River
Sonoran
Phoenix
Desert
Socorro space telescope
Gila monster

Pacific Ocean

Hawaii

One of the USA's 50 states is a group of eight volcanic islands in the Pacific Ocean. This state is called Hawaii.

Kauai
Niihau
Honolulu
Oahu
Molokai
Lanai
Maui

Hawaii

Mount Kilauea, on the main island of Hawaii, is the world's most active volcano.

N
W E
S

Rio Grande

M e x i c o

Which is the only US state not shown on this map?

Canada

Here, you can see 49 of the 50 states of the USA. Alaska is thousands of kilometres away, to the northwest of Canada.

Blueberries

Lake Superior

Bismarck
North Dakota

Minnesota

Lake Huron

Lake Ontario

Augusta

Maine

Vermont

New Hampshire

New York

Boston

Wisconsin

Massachusetts

Rhode Island

Connecticut

Pierre

South Dakota

Dairy farming

Lake Michigan

Michigan

Detroit

Lake Erie

Statue of Liberty

New York

New Jersey

Iowa

Chicago

Indiana

Ohio

Pennsylvania

Harrisburg

Delaware

Nebraska

Raccoon

Sears Tower, Chicago

American football

Maryland

WASHINGTON, DC

West Virginia

Virginia

The Capitol building, Washington, DC

Lincoln

Illinois

St. Louis

Ohio River

Topeka

Missouri

American bald eagle

Kentucky

Tennessee

Appalachian Mountains

Raleigh

North Carolina

Kansas

Great plains

Oklahoma City

"Tornado Alley"

Arkansas

Mississippi River

Country music

South Carolina

Oklahoma

Little Rock

Mississippi

Alabama

Atlanta

Georgia

Montgomery

Kennedy Space Center

Atlantic Ocean

Dallas

Oil wells

Louisiana

Baton Rouge

Paddle steamer

Tallahassee

Texas

New Orleans

Florida

Jazz music

Everglades

Dolphin-watching

Miami

Cowboy

Gulf of Mexico

American alligator

Sonoran Desert

Prickly pear cactus

Tijuana

USA

N

W

S

Gulf of California

Baja California

Cattle

Rio Grande River

Armadillo

Gulf of Mexico

Sierra Madre Occidental

Monarch butterflies

Boojum tree

Los Mochis

Sierra Madre Oriental

Monterrey

Mariachi

La Paz

Brown pelican

Grey whale

Agave

Mexico

Atlante statue at Tula

Pacific Ocean

Guadalajara

MEXICO CITY

Vera

Metropolitan Cathedral

Acapulco

Mexico and Central America

Mexico and Central America form a natural bridge linking the USA to South America. The north of Mexico is dry and dusty. As you travel south, the weather gets rainier and the land becomes greener, with lush rainforests covering mountains and volcanoes.

Did you know?

Coffee beans and bananas are Costa Rica's most important crops.

Chocolate was first made in Mexico, from the seeds of the cacao tree.

Sugar cane from Central America and the Caribbean is used to make sugar.

14

West Indies

To the east of Central America is a chain of tropical islands called the West Indies. The weather here is warm all year, but hurricanes can strike in summer.

Bahamas

NASSAU

HAVANA

Cuba

Palm trees

Pineapple

Atlantic Ocean

Lesser Antilles

Haiti

Dominican Republic

PORT-AU-PRINCE

SAN JUAN

Puerto Rico

SANTO DOMINGO

Jamaica

KINGSTON

Greater Antilles

Caribbean Sea

Dominica

St Lucia

Barbados

Yacht

Frigatebird

PORT-OF-SPAIN

Trinidad and Tobago

Flamingos

Chichén Itzá

El Castillo

Coral reef

Green turtle

Olmec head

Macaw

Belize

●BELMOPAN

Grapefruit

Shrimp

Guatemala

Honduras

TEGUCIGALPA

GUATEMALA CITY

El Salvador

SAN SALVADOR

Bananas

Panama Canal

The man-made Panama Canal links the Atlantic and Pacific Oceans. About 12,000 ships pass through it every year, making it one of the world's busiest waterways.

Nicaragua

Lake Nicaragua

MANAGUA

Panama Canal

Spider monkey

Costa Rica

SAN JOSÉ

PANAMA CITY

Panama

Toucan

South America

A vast chain of mountains runs the length of this continent. On its western side is the world's driest desert. On the east is the biggest rainforest.

Equator walkabout

The Equator is an imaginary line around the Earth's middle. If you walked non-stop, it would take you a month to cross just the South American part of it, which is more than 2,347 km (1,458 miles) wide.

Bananas

Brazil nuts

Belém

CAYENNE

PARAMARIBO

French Guiana

Suriname

GEORGETOWN

Guyana

Capybara

Brazil

Brasília Cathedral

Angel Falls

Equator

Amazon Rainforest

Manaus

River Amazon

CARACAS

Venezuela

Orinoco

Jaguar

Parakeet

Cartagena

Agrias butterfly

Colombia

BOGOTÁ

Ecuador

QUITO

Condor

Machu Picchu

Peru

Bolivia

La Paz

Lake Titicaca

Andes Mountains

Arequipa

LIMA

Pacific Ocean

What is the highest mountain in the Andes?

Oil rig

BRASÍLIA

Football

São Paulo ● Rio de Janeiro

Sugar Loaf Mountain

Atlantic Ocean

Green turtle

Gaucho

Paraguay

Bolivian Indian

ASUNCIÓN

Llama

Argentina

Uruguay

MONTEVIDEO

BUENOS
AIRES ●

Pampas

● Bahía Blanca

Chile

Atacama Desert

Andes Mountains

Aconcagua
6,960 m
(22,837 ft)

Valparaíso ●
SANTIAGO ●

Pampas grass

Sheep farming

Patagonia

Magellan
penguins

Mackerel

Can you find...

The world's highest capital?
La Paz, Bolivia, is 3,632 m
(11,916 ft) above sea level.

The world's highest waterfall?
Angel Falls in Venezuela
measures 979 m (3,212 ft)
from top to bottom.

The world's driest town?
Arica in Chile's Atacama Desert
has an annual rainfall of zero!

Cape Horn
The southern tip of South
America is called Cape
Horn. The seas around
it are so stormy that
hundreds of ships have
been shipwrecked there.

Cape Horn

Aconcagua, which is 6,960 m (22,834 ft) high.

Africa

Africa is a vast, sun-baked continent, famous for its amazing wildlife. In the north and south are hot deserts. Between the deserts are swampy rainforests and grasslands full of wild animals.

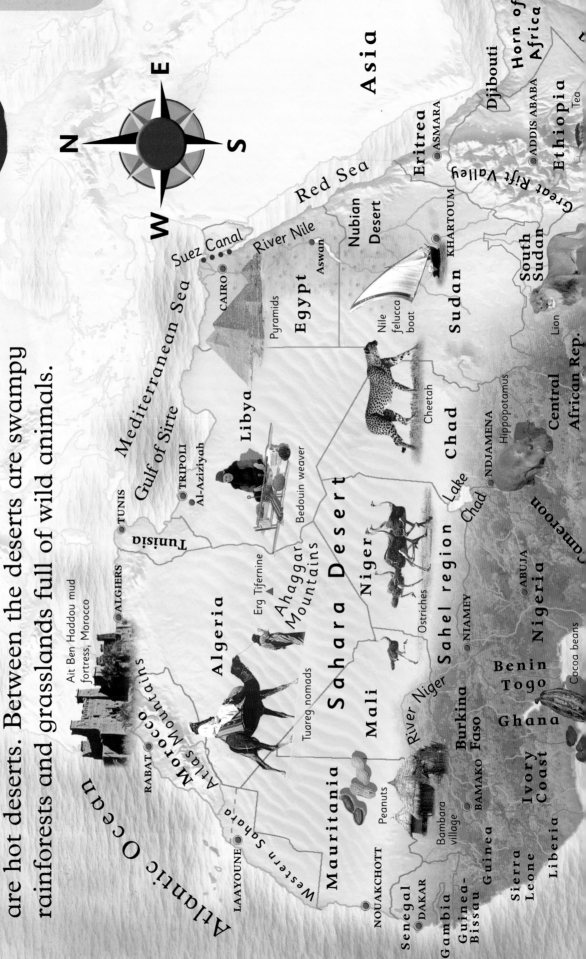

Asia

Horn of Africa

Djibouti

ADDIS ABABA

Ethiopia

Tea

Eritrea

ASMARA

Great Rift Valley

KHARTOUM

Red Sea

South Sudan

Nubian Desert

Sudan

River Nile

Aswan

Lion

Suez Canal

CAIRO

Egypt

Pyramids

Nile felucca boat

Mediterranean Sea

Cheetah

Hippopotamus

Central African Rep.

Gulf of Sirte

Libya

Chad

Lake Chad

NDJAMENA

Cameroon

TRIPOLI

Al-Aziziyah

TUNIS

Tunisia

Bedouin weaver

Niger

NIAMEY

ABUJA

Nigeria

Cocoa beans

ALGIERS

Erg Tifernine

Ahaggar Mountains

Sahara Desert

Sahel region

Benin

Togo

Ait Ben Haddou mud fortress, Morocco

Algeria

Ostriches

River Niger

Burkina Faso

Ghana

RABAT

Morocco

Atlas Mountains

Tuareg nomads

Mali

BAMAKO

Ivory Coast

Atlantic Ocean

Western Sahara

Mauritania

Peanuts

Bambara village

Guinea

Sierra Leone

Liberia

LAAYOUNE

NOUAKCHOTT

Senegal

DAKAR

Gambia

Guinea-Bissau

How long is Africa from north to south?

MOGADISHU

Kenya

●NAIROBI

●KAMPALA

Lake
Victoria

Rwanda

Burundi

S e r e n g e t i

Masai herder

●DODOMA

Mount Kilimanjaro

Tanzania

Dhow sailing boat

Lemur

Madagascar

●ANTANANARIVO

Mozambique Channel

Chameleon

Malawi

Elephant

Great Rift Valley

Mozambique

MAPUTO●

PRETORIA●
Swaziland

Ndeble
Lesotho
house

●LUSAKA
Zambezi
River

Zambia

Zimbabwe

Victoria Falls

Zebras

Angola

Dem. Rep.
of Congo

●KINSHASA

Lowland
gorilla

Rep. of
Congo

Gabon

Equatorial
Guinea

●LUANDA

River Congo

Hornbill

Giraffe

Namibia

●WINDHOEK

Namib Desert

Botswana

Kalahari Desert

Springbok

Tin and
copper
mining

South Africa

●Cape Town

Cape of Good Hope

Oil rig

Atlantic Ocean

Madagascar

The island of Madagascar
is home to tree-dwelling
animals called lemurs.
They have faces like cats
but bodies like monkeys.

Can you find...

The highest point in Africa?
Mount Kilimanjaro in Tanzania
is 5,895 m (19,341 ft) tall.

**One of the world's
highest sand dunes?**
Erg Tifernine in the Sahara
is 400 m (1,300 ft) tall.

**One of the hottest places
on Earth?** Al-Aziziyah, in
Libya, has had temperatures
of 58°C (136.4°F).

The Suez Canal

This canal is a man-made waterway
that runs from the Red Sea to the
Mediterranean. It provides a shortcut
for ships travelling from Europe to Asia.

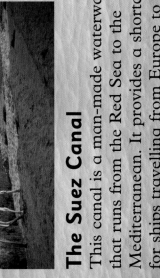

Savannah wildlife

Much of Africa is covered by a
type of grassland called savannah.
Huge herds of grazing animals live
on the savannah, as well as lions,
hyenas, and cheetahs.

About 8,000 km (5,000 miles).

Scandinavia

The northernmost part of Europe is Scandinavia – a region of dense pine forests, snowy mountains, and craggy coastlines.

Russian Federation

Arctic Ocean

North Cape

Sami man with reindeer

Wolf

Sauna

River Kemijoki

Oulu

Lapland

Gulf of Bothnia

Fishing trawler

Tromso

Mining

Lynx

Grey seal

Sweden

Kjolen Mountains

Puffin

Norwegian Sea

Atlantic Ocean

Iceland

Iceland is a volcanic island in the far north Atlantic Ocean. It has hundreds of hot springs and geysers.

Greenland Sea

Church of Hallgrímur

Vatnajökull (Ice sheet)

Geyser

REYKJAVÍK

20

Finland

Rainbow-trout

Cathedral, Helsinki

HELSINKI

Gulf of Finland

Åland Islands

STOCKHOLM

Golden eagle

City Hall, Stockholm

Gotland

Lake Vänern

Lake Vättern

Rune stone

Öland

Baltic Sea

Swedish glass

Bornholm

N
W **E**
S

The Øresund Bridge

The Øresund Bridge links Copenhagen in Denmark to Malmö in Sweden. There are three parts to the bridge – an underground tunnel, an artificial island, and a bridge over the sea. Together, they are 16 km (10 miles) long.

Gothenburg

COPENHAGEN
Malmö
Øresund Bridge

Little Mermaid statue, Copenhagen

Denmark

Dairy farming

LEGO®

Pig farming

Herrings

North Sea

Faroe Islands

Tórshavn

These islands are part of Denmark. They lie halfway between Iceland and Scotland.

Stave church

▲ Mount Galdhøppigen 2,469 m (8,100 ft)

Cross-country skiing

Norway

OSLO

Oslo Fjord

Sculptures in Vigeland Park, Oslo

Nord Fjord

Sogne Fjord

Bergen

Hardanger Fjord

Bokna Fjord

Stavanger

UK and Ireland

The United Kingdom is made up of England, Scotland, Wales, and Northern Ireland. Ireland is a separate country. Most of the people in the UK and Ireland speak English as their main language.

The royal family

England and Scotland had separate royal families until 1603, when they joined together to form the United Kingdom. Queen Elizabeth II is the current Head of State.

Shetland Islands

Orkney Islands

• Thurso

Red deer

Outer Hebrides

Skye

Highland cow

Mull

Loch Ness Monster

Aberdeen •

Grampian Mountains

Ben Nevis
1,343 m (4,406 ft)

Scotland

River Forth

Glasgow •

• Edinburgh

Edinburgh Castle

Bagpiper

North Sea

Angel of the North

• Newcastle upon Tyne

Giant's Causeway

Northern Ireland

What is the name of the Queen's official residence in London?

North Sea oil rig

Yacht

Norfolk Broads

Cambridge

Big Ben

Dover

LONDON

Eurotunnel to France

Middlesbrough

Kingston upon Hull

England

Brighton

Royal Pavillion

English Channel

France

Pennines Mountains

Football

Birmingham

Oxford

River Thames

Isle of Wight

Lake District

Blackpool Tower

Manchester

Crufts dog show

River Severn

Stonehenge

Portland Bill Lighthouse

Liverpool

Snowdonia

Cambrian Mountains

Wales

Cardiff

Exmoor

Exeter

Dartmoor

Isle of Man

Douglas

Irish Sea

Sheep

Surfing

Eden Project

The Eden Project, Cornwall

These giant greenhouses are home to lots of plants from different areas of the world. People can visit here to learn how important nature is to the future of the planet.

Guinness

DUBLIN

Land's End

Isles of Scilly

Galway Cathedral

Ireland

Blarney Castle

Cork

N E S W

Galway

Jaunting car

The Low Countries

Belgium, the Netherlands, and Luxembourg are called the Low Countries because much of their land is at or below sea level. They are also sometimes called Benelux — the first letters of BElgium, NEtherlands and LUXembourg.

Avocet

West Frisian Islands

Wadden Sea

Ice-skating

Cattle

Netherlands

Cycling

Horse

Germany

Tern

Lelystad

Flevoland

IJsselmeer

Windmill

River Rhine

Arnhem

Clogs

Dairy industry

AMSTERDAM

Tulips

Rotterdam

North Sea

The Hague

Barge

Antwerp Cathedral

Cubic Houses

Fishing

Natural and man-made dams in these areas stop floods from the sea.

Herring

Bruges City Hall

Bruges

Ostend

N
E
S
W

By what other name is the Netherlands sometimes called?

Did you know?

Brussels is the capital of Europe. It is the centre of the European Union and home of the European Parliament.

900 windmills along the Netherlands' coast help to keep the land drained.

Wooden clogs were first invented by Dutch workmen 600 years ago.

France

Lace

Chocolates

BRUSSELS

The Atomium

Belgium

Charleroi

Crystal

Liege

Beer

River Meuse

Deer

Ardennes Forest

Wild boar

Luxembourg

Vianden Castle

LUXEMBOURG

Amsterdam
The tall houses lining the canals of Amsterdam were built by rich spice merchants hundreds of years ago. Each one is unique, and many are crooked because they are built on marshy land.

Holland.

France

France is the biggest country in western Europe. Its capital is the city of Paris, site of the Eiffel Tower. France is famous for its scenic countryside, which is dotted with sleepy villages and fairytale castles called châteaux.

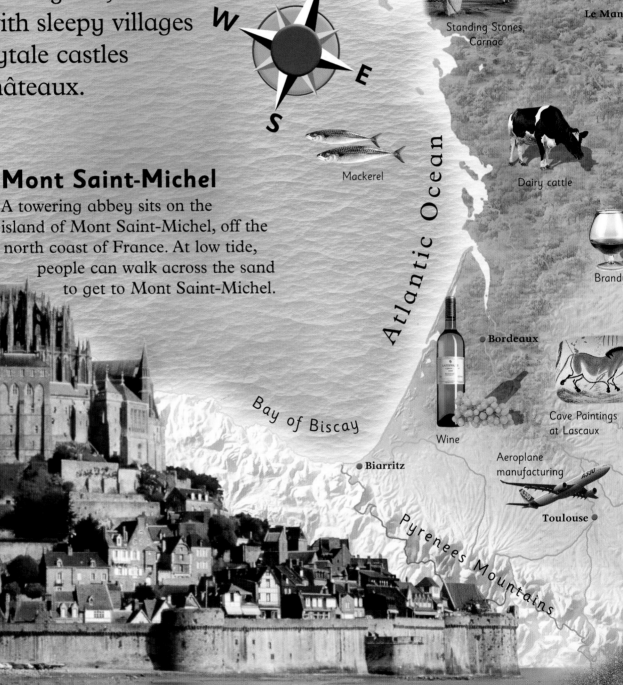

English Channel

Breton woman

Mont Saint-Michel

Part of the Bayeux Tapestry

Rennes

Le Mans

Standing Stones, Carnac

Mackerel

Dairy cattle

Atlantic Ocean

Brandy

Bordeaux

Wine

Bay of Biscay

Cave Paintings at Lascaux

Aeroplane manufacturing

Biarritz

Toulouse

Pyrenees Mountains

Mont Saint-Michel

A towering abbey sits on the island of Mont Saint-Michel, off the north coast of France. At low tide, people can walk across the sand to get to Mont Saint-Michel.

Where in France would you find pink flamingos and wild horses?

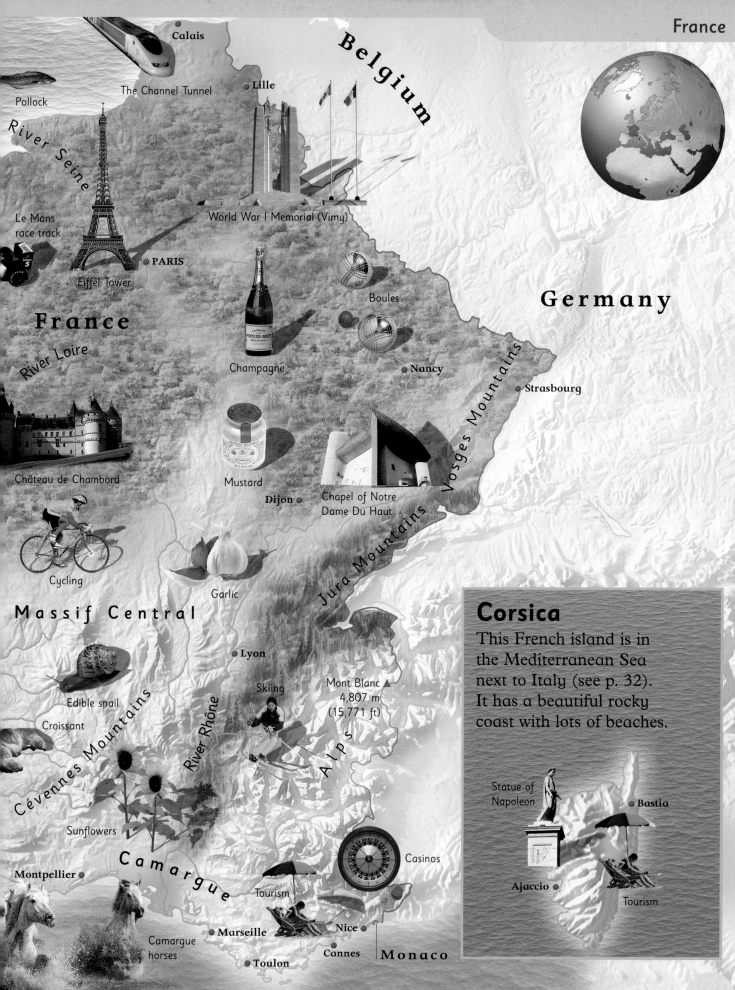

Pollock

River Seine

Calais

The Channel Tunnel

Lille

Belgium

Germany

World War I Memorial (Vimy)

Le Mans race track

PARIS

Eiffel Tower

France

Boules

River Loire

Champagne

Nancy

Strasbourg

Vosges Mountains

Château de Chambord

Mustard

Dijon

Chapel of Notre Dame Du Haut

Jura Mountains

Cycling

Garlic

Massif Central

Corsica

This French island is in the Mediterranean Sea next to Italy (see p. 32). It has a beautiful rocky coast with lots of beaches.

Edible snail

Croissant

Lyon

Skiing

Mont Blanc
4,807 m
(15,771 ft)

Alps

Cévennes Mountains

River Rhône

Statue of Napoleon

Bastia

Sunflowers

Casinos

Camargue

Montpellier

Ajaccio

Tourism

Tourism

Marseille

Nice

Cannes

Monaco

Camargue horses

Toulon

The marshes of the Camargue.

Germany and the Alps

The north of Germany is low and flat, but the land gradually rises towards the south. Switzerland and Austria lie at the heart of the Alps – Europe's tallest and most spectacular mountains.

Berlin Wall

A long wall used to divide the city of Berlin into communist and western halves. In 1989, the people of Berlin tore the wall down and reunited the city.

Poland

N E S W

River Oder

Rügen

Stork

Lake Müritz

Brandenburg Gate

●BERLIN

Chemical Industry

Zwinger Palace

Halle

Leipzig

Fehmarn

Kiel Canal

●Kiel

Heidschnuche sheep

Volkswagen car

River Elbe

Red deer

River Elbe

Hamburg

●Bremen

Hanover

Wheat

Germany

North Sea

Container ship

Dairy cattle

Cologne Cathedral

River Rhine

Düsseldorf●

Which composer was born in Salzburg, Austria, in 1756?

Czech Republic

France

Austria

VIENNA

Spanish riding school

Lake Neusiedler

Mountain climbing

Graz

Austrian Alps

Snowboarding

Chamois goat

Thuringian Forest

Bohemian Forest

River Main

River Danube

Linz

Mozart

Salzburg

Lake Chiemsee

Bavarian Alps

Innsbruck

Liechtenstein

Nuremberg

Oktoberfest

Munich

Swabian Alps

River Danube

Zugspitze
2,962 m
(9,718 ft)

Marmot

Frankfurt skyline

Frankfurt

Mannheim

Heidelberg

Mercedes

Stuttgart

Ulm

Neuschwanstein
Castle

Lake Constance

VADUZ

Davos

Alpine horn

Black Forest

River Rhine

Freiburg

Cheese

Zurich

Swiss army knife

Switzerland

Swiss Alps

BERN

Chocolates

Wine

River Rhône

Matterhorn
4,478 m
(14,692 ft)

Geneva

Spain and Portugal

Spain and Portugal are in the sunny southwest corner of Europe. Together they make up a region called the Iberian Peninsula.

Mountain biking

Santiago

León

Santiago Cathedral

Coal mine

Dolphin

Oporto

Salamanca

Clay cockerel (symbol of Portugal)

Coimbra

Windmill

River Tagus

Azores
These Portuguese islands are in the Atlantic, about a third of the way to the USA.

Azores

Ponta Delgada

Atlantic Ocean

Portugal

Belem Tower

LISBON

Sheep

Badajoz

Madeira
The Portuguese island of Madeira is famous for making a rich type of wine also called Madeira.

Madeira

Funchal

Packaged fish

Flamenco dancer

Canary Islands
These seven Spanish islands are off the west coast of Africa.

Lanzarote

Santa Cruz de Tenerife

Fuerteventura

La Palma

Tenerife

Gran Canaria

Canary Islands

Seville

Tourism

Algarve

Lagos

Faro

Lynx

Baetic

Crayfish

Wind surfing

Gibraltar

30

Which is the rainiest city in Spain?

France

Guggenheim Museum
• **Bilbao**

Basque Country

Mountain goat

Andorra

ANDORRA LA VELLA ○

Pyrenees

Skiing

Wild boar

Iberian Mountains

• Valladolid

Spain

Rioja wine

River Ebro

Barcelona •

Sagrada Família Cathedral, Barcelona

Roman aqueduct

N

W   E

S

Balearic Islands

○ **MADRID**

Royal Palace

Bull-fighting

Paella

Sardines

Minorca
Mahón •

Majorca
• **Palma**

Valencia

Albacete •

Oranges

Ibiza
• **Ibiza**

Formentera

Mediterranean Sea

Andalusian horse

• Alicante

Costa Blanca

River Guadalquivir

Guitar

Andalusia

Mountains

• Granada

Olive oil

Costa del Sol

• **Malaga**

• **Cartagena**

Majorca
The Spanish island of Majorca is one of Europe's top tourist destinations. Its rugged coast has lots of beautiful beaches.

Jet ski

Santiago.

Italy

Italy is shaped like a boot, with the top in the Alps and the toe swimming in the Mediterranean Sea. The Apennine mountains run like a bone down the leg.

Skier

Dolomites

Lake Garda

Mountain goat

A l p s

Milan

Wine

Turin

Ferrari

River Po

Venice

Venetian gondola

Tagliatelli carbonara

San Marino

Bologna

Leaning Tower of Pisa

Pisa

Florence

Florence Cathedral

Moped

Fishing boat

Tuna

Italian lakes

There are 23 lakes in the lake district in northern Italy. Lake Garda is the biggest, and a popular place to sail and windsurf.

How many islands make up Malta?

Octopus

Crab

Wine

Taranto

Olives and olive oil

Italy

Sheep

Oranges

Cast of a body at Pompeii

Almonds

▲ Mount Vesuvius
● **Pompeii**

Naples

Squid

Amalfi

Messina

Pizza

Vatican City

Apennines

ROME ●

The Colosseum (Rome)

Mount Etna

Syracuse

SICILY

Palermo

Noto Cathedral

Malta

● VALLETTA

Scuba diving

Agrigento

Temple of Castor and Pollux

Lemons

Mediterranean Sea

Can you find...

Europe's largest volcano? Mount Etna in Sicily is also Europe's most active volcano.

The world's most wonky tower? The Leaning Tower of Pisa is a campanile, or bell tower.

Where the first pizza was made? A baker in Naples invented the pizza in the 1800s.

Sardines

Tourism

SARDINIA

Wild boar

● Cagliari

Amalfi

33

Seven – people live only in three: Malta, Gozo, and Comino.

Central Eastern Europe

The countries in this region were under communist rule until the 1990s. Today, they are modern nations with thriving industries. Traditional farming continues in the rural areas.

Baltic Sea

Canoeing

Mazury Lakes

European bison

Market Square, Warsaw

Lublin

River Vistula

Sugar beet

Skiing

Chemical industry

WARSAW

Kielce

Kraków

Gdansk

Torun

Gingerbread

Lodz

Wheat

Cattle farming

Koszalin

Potato farming

Poznan

Poland

Szczecin

Windmill

Mining

Pig farming

River Oder

Wroclaw

Ship building

Hradec Králove

Charles Bridge

River Elbe

Karlovy Vary

PRAGUE

Plzen

G e r m a n y

Did you know?

The Polish town of Torun is well known for its **gingerbread**.

Budapest is split by the Danube. Buda is on one bank, Pest on the other.

The snow-white **Lipizzaner horse** is bred in Slovenia.

What ingredient makes Hungarian goulash spicy?

High Tatra Mountains

This mountain range lies in Poland and Slovakia, and forms part of the Carpathian Mountains. The highest peak is 2,655 m (8,711 ft) high.

High Tatra Mountains

Spišský Hrad Castle

Nyíregyháza

Tokay wine

Debrecen

Parliament, Budapest

Eger

Szeged

Horse riding

Slovakia

Painted Easter eggs

Wooden house

BRATISLAVA

Gyor

BUDAPEST

Hungary

Goulash

River Danube

Pécs

Osijek

Czech Republic

Brno

Škoda

Wine

LJUBLJANA

ZAGREB

Croatia

Slovenia

Austria

Lipizzaner mare and foal

Rijeka

Dinaric Alps

Dalmatian

Split

Dubrovnik

Tourism

Adriatic Sea

Romania

Pilsner lager

Paprika.

N E S W

35

Eastern Europe

The countries of eastern Europe lie between the Baltic Sea and the Black Sea. They were part of the Soviet Union, but became independent states in 1991.

Hill of Crosses

This sacred site in Lithuania is visited by lots of pilgrims every year. They leave crosses on the hill to show their devotion to Christianity.

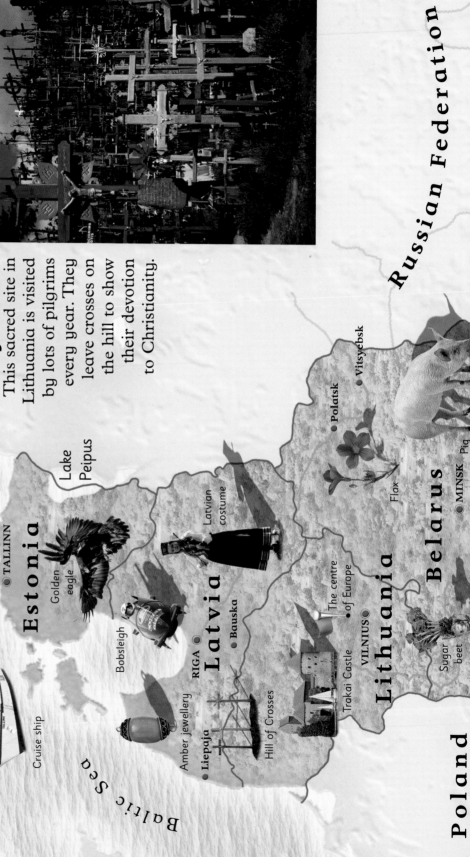

Russian Federation

Lake Peipus

TALLINN

Estonia

Golden eagle

Cruise ship

Bobsleigh

Baltic Sea

Amber jewellery

Liepaja

RIGA

Latvia

Bauska

Latvian costume

Hill of Crosses

Trakai Castle

The centre of Europe

VILNIUS

Lithuania

Sugar beet

Flax

Polatsk

Vitsyebsk

Belarus

MINSK

Pig

Poland

What are the Baltic States?

Coal mining

● **Donetsk**

Sea of Azov

● Kerch

White geese

Kharkiv ●

River Dnieper

● **Dnipropetrovsk**

Sunflowers

Crimea

● Yalta

St Andrew's Church

Wheat

Black Sea tourism

Swallow's Nest Castle

● **Chernihiv**

KIEV ●

Wooden church

Gymnastics school

Black Sea

● Homyel

Mushrooms

Chernobyl ●

Mammoth fossils

● Odessa

Ukraine

● **CHISINAU**

Wooden Moldovian gateway

Pripet Marshes

Moldova

Potatoes

Mink

Ukranian folk dancers

Chernivtsi ●

● Lviv

Carpathian Mountains

Romania

Can you find…

Ukraine's oldest creatures? Mammoths lived in Europe 10,000 years ago.

The plant used to make linen? Flax is a major crop of Belarus. Its fibres are made into linen clothes.

Europe's largest marshland? The Pripet Marshes cover 270,000 sq km (104,000 sq miles).

Estonia, Latvia, and Lithuania – the countries bordering the Baltic Sea.

Southeast Europe

The mighty River Danube winds its way across southeast Europe, forming a natural border between Romania and Bulgaria. Further south are the scattered ruins of the cities of ancient Greece.

Black Sea

River Danube

Carpathian Mountains

Wolf

Bran Castle, Transylvania

BUCHAREST

Natural yoghurt

Varna

Burgas

Ruse

Satu Mare

Wild boar

Romania

Sibiu

Transylvanian Alps

Parliament Palace

Pleven

Alexander Nevsky Cathedral

Kazanlak

Folk dancers at Kazanlak Festival of Roses

SOFIA

Bulgaria

Rose

Timisoara

BELGRADE

Serbian Kebabs

Traditional Serbian costume

Serbia

Grapes

Goat

Macedonia

SKOPJE

PRISTINA

Kosovo

Banja Luka

Bosnia and Herzegovina

SARAJEVO

Dinaric Alps

Statue in Liberation Square, Sarajevo

Mostar

Montenegro

PODGORICA

Oranges

Tourism

Adriatic Sea

What is Greece's most important crop?

N
E
W
S

Turkey

Rhodes

Sponge

Lesbos

Chios

Dolphin

Aegean Sea

Cyclades Islands

Tourism

Knossos Palace

Heraklion

Crete

Salonika

Olive oil

Greece

ATHENS

Ceremonial soldier from Athens

Parthenon

Peloponnese

Pindus Mountains

Greek coffee

Greek vase

Patras

Zakynthos

Cephalonia

Greek church

Mediterranean Sea

Albania

Bouzouki

Watermelon

Octopus

Sailing ship

Can you find...

A sponge? Old-fashioned bathroom sponges are the skeletons of dead sea creatures.

Yoghurt? People in Bulgaria eat lots of yoghurt because they think it helps them live longer.

Greek coffee? Greek people make coffee by boiling ground coffee in a tiny pan of water until it foams.

Chios Island in the Aegean Sea

Olives.

Russia and Central Asia

The Russian Federation spans two continents –
Europe and Asia. To its southwest are the
eight independent countries of
Central Asia and Caucasia.

Barents Sea

Harp seal

Murmansk

Icebreaker ship

Kara Sea

Kaliningrad

St Petersburg

Pskov

Velíky Novgorod

Kirov ballet

Vorkuta

Norilsk

St Basil's Cathedral

MOSCOW

Kirov

Ural Mountains

River Ob

S i b

Russian matryoshka dolls

Elk

Crimea

River Volga

Chess

Magnitogorsk

R u s s i a n

Black Sea

Caucasus Mountains

Georgia

Uralsk

Orsk

Omsk

Grozny

Sturgeon caviar

Baikonur Cosmodrome

Novosibirsk

TBILISI

ASTANA

Wheat

Armenia

YEREVAN

Baikonur

Aral Sea

Zhezkazgan

Azerbaijan

BAKU

K a z a k h s t a n

Caspian Sea

Uzbekistan

Lake Balkhash

Turkmenistan

Kyzyl Kum Desert

Cotton

ASHGABAT

TASHKENT

BISHKEK

Almaty

Iran

Samarqand

Kyrgyzstan

DUSHANBE

Tajikistan

Gur-Emir Mausoleum, Samarqand

Afghanistan

Where is 90 per cent of Russia's tea grown?

Arctic Ocean

Brent geese

Pevek

Reindeer

Nenet people

Walrus

River Lena

Verkhoyansk

Yakut people

Kamchatka Peninsula

eria

Wolf

Yakutsk

Magadan

Okhotsk

Sea of Okhotsk

Brown bear

Salmon

N

W   E

S

Timber

Mining

Diamond

Federation

Bratsk

Trans-Siberian railway

Khabarovsk

Lake Baikal

Irkutsk

Freshwater seal

Siberian tiger

China

Vladivostok

Walkabout
Russia is the world's widest country. It would take more than two months to cross if you walked non-stop from west to east. It is more than 5,074 km (3,153 miles) wide.

A shrinking lake
The Aral Sea, once one of the largest lakes in the world, has today shrunk by about 90 per cent. Massive amounts of water have been drained for use on Uzbekistan's cotton fields, stranding fishing boats.

Did you know?

Caviar from the Caspian Sea is so expensive it is known as "black gold".

Lake Baikal is the world's deepest, and largest, freshwater lake.

Verkhoyansk, in Russia, is the world's coldest town. In January 1885, the temperature fell to -68 °C (-90 °F).

41

Georgia

Middle East

This part of the world is hot and dry, with large deserts. Three of the world's great religions began here.

Istanbul

Blue Mosque   ANKA

Turke

Mediterranean Sea

NICOSIA
Cyprus

Sculpt
menorah
Jerusale

Mecca

The holiest place for Muslims is the Ka'ba, a cube-shaped shrine in Mecca. Muslims face the Ka'ba when they pray and try to visit it at least once in their lifetime.

World's first skyscrapers

Thousands of years ago, the people of Yemen built some of the tallest mud-brick buildings in the world. They could be up to 11 storeys high. Usually, people lived on the upper floors, and kept animals and goods on the lower storeys.

Fruits of the desert

Farmers can grow crops only in the wettest parts of the Middle East.

Figs are soft, sticky fruits that can be dried to make them last longer.

Olive trees are grown for their fruit, which are mostly pressed to make oil.

Dates are the fruit of palm trees, which grow by rivers and in oases.

Which country produces 65 per cent of the world's hazelnuts?

Black Sea

Caspian Sea

Whirling dervish dancer

Head of Zeus

▲ Mount Ararat
5,165 m (16,945 ft)

Syria

BEIRUT

Lebanon

Figs

Olives

DAMASCUS

BAGHDAD ●

●TEHRAN

Turquoise

Iran

Chador, traditional
dress for women

Chicken kebab

AMMAN
Jordan

RUSALEM

Israel

Iraq

Falconry

Marsh Arab
reed house

Kuwait

KUWAIT
CITY

The Gulf

Persepolis palace

Ancient city
of Petra

Oasis

Bahrain

Qatar

Oman

Gulf of Oman

Red Sea

Mecca

Oil

DOHA

ABU DHABI

United
Arab Emirates

MUSCAT ●

RIYADH ●

Saudi Arabia

Oil refinery

Mecca

Coral reefs grow
along the coast
of the Red Sea,
where the water
is warm and clear.

Arabian desert

Camels

Frankincense tree

Desert oryx

Oman

Oil tanker

N

W   E

S

Yemen

● SANA'A

Arabian Sea

Southern Asia

This region is made up of five important countries. India is the biggest – with a population of more than a billion.

Elephants on parade
During the festival of Puram in southern India, 101 elephants march through the town of Trichur in a grand parade.

Bangladesh

Tea picking

Imphal

DHAKA

Nepal

River Ganges

River dolphin

Cow

NEW DELHI

Agra

Rickshaw

River Narmada

Golden Temple

India

Taj Mahal

Camels

Snow leopard

Afghanistan

KABUL

ISLAMABAD

Multan

Lapis lazuli

Herat

Decorated lorry

Quetta

Pakistan

Tomb of Muhammad Ali Jinnah

Dancer

Hyderabad

Karachi

Green turtles

44

Coconut tree and coconut

Andaman Islands (India)

Nicobar Islands (India)

Bay of Bengal

Fishing boat

• Cuttack

N E S W

Common lobster

Herring

Raipur

Nagpur

Tiger

• Vijayawada

• Chennai

Thresher shark

Snake charmer

• Jaffna

Sri Lanka

• Mumbai

Indian elephant

Calicut

Kathkali Dancer

• Trichur

Kandy Tea leaves

COLOMBO

The monsoon

Southern Asia is normally hot and dry, but every summer it pours down for weeks. This rainy season, called the monsoon, helps farmers grow crops, such as rice.

Arabian Sea

Tuna fish

Can you find...

Lapis lazuli? This precious stone was once used to make brilliant, sky-blue paint.

An Indian dancer? Classical dancers use movements of their bodies to tell ancient stories.

Ganges river dolphin? This dolphin is almost blind and finds its way in muddy water by sound.

The ashes are to be scattered in a river.

Southeast Asia

Southeast Asia is hot and rainy all year round. There are thousands of islands, and many are covered by thick rainforests and towering volcanoes.

Floating market
The city of Bangkok is riddled with canals. Traders sell their goods from boats and shoppers paddle by to look for bargains.

Elephant

China

Myanmar (Burma)

NAYPYIDAW

Rubies

Thai dancer

HANOI

Laos

VIENTIANE

Thailand

BANGKOK

Angkor Wat

Cambodia

PHNOM PENH

Tapir

Vietnam

Ho Chi Minh City

Sampan boat

South China Sea

Pearl in a shell

Orchid

Tiger

KUALA LUMPUR

Petronas Twin Towers

Sultan Omar Ali Saifuddin Mosque

Brunei

BANDAR SERI BEGAWAN

Malaysia

Sumatra

Singapore

Padang

Indo

Orang-utan

Borneo

Coconut

Rafflesia

JAKARTA

Java

Shadow puppet

46

What is the largest lizard in the world?

Can you find...

A very rare kind of ape?
Orang-utans live only
in Borneo and Sumatra.

**An animal with tusks that
grow through its face?**
The babirusa is a kind of pig.

**The world's largest
flower?** Rafflesia grows to
nearly 1 m (3 ft) wide.

N
W E
S

MANILA

Rice cultivation

Vinta boats

Philippines

Cebu

Water
buffalo

Davao City

Pacific Ocean

Tuna

Rice paddies

The wet climate is ideal for growing rice.
Farmers plant it in flooded fields called
paddies, which are sometimes built like
steps in the sides of hills.

Celebes Sea

Moluccas

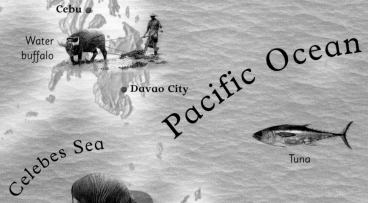

Babirusa

Nutmeg

Sulawesi

Ambon

Jayapura

New Guinea

Conch shell

Toraja house

e s i a

Papua New
Guinea

Asmat warrior

DILI

Komodo dragon

East Timor

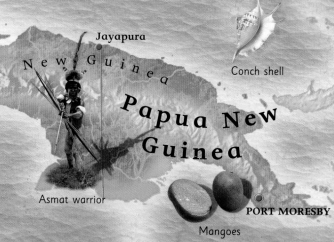

Mangoes

PORT MORESBY

The Komodo dragon. It can grow to 3 m (10 ft) long.

China and neighbours

Well over one billion people live in China – that's one fifth of the world's people. Next door, Mongolia has the fewest people for its size.

Terracotta Army
This army of statues in Xi'an was made more than 2,000 years ago to guard the tomb of Qin Shi Huang, China's first emperor. The statues were rediscovered in 1974.

Chinese opera
Chinese opera has lots of singing, acting, and acrobatics. Make-up is used to show the type of character being played.

Altay •

• Yining

• Urumqi

• Turpan   Ham

• Kashi

Ibex

K2
▲ 8,611 m (28,250 ft)

Yak

T i b e t

Potala
Palace

Bhairabnath
Temple

H i m a l a y a s

Lhasa

KATHMANDU
Mount Everest

N e p a l   THIM
Bhutar

Can you find...

The world's tallest mountain? Mount Everest is 8,850 m (29,035 ft) tall.

The world's most crowded place? Hong Kong has 6,000 people per sq km (2,300 per sq mile).

China's hottest place? Turpan has recorded temperatures of up to 47 °C (117 °F).

What is the world's second-tallest mountain?

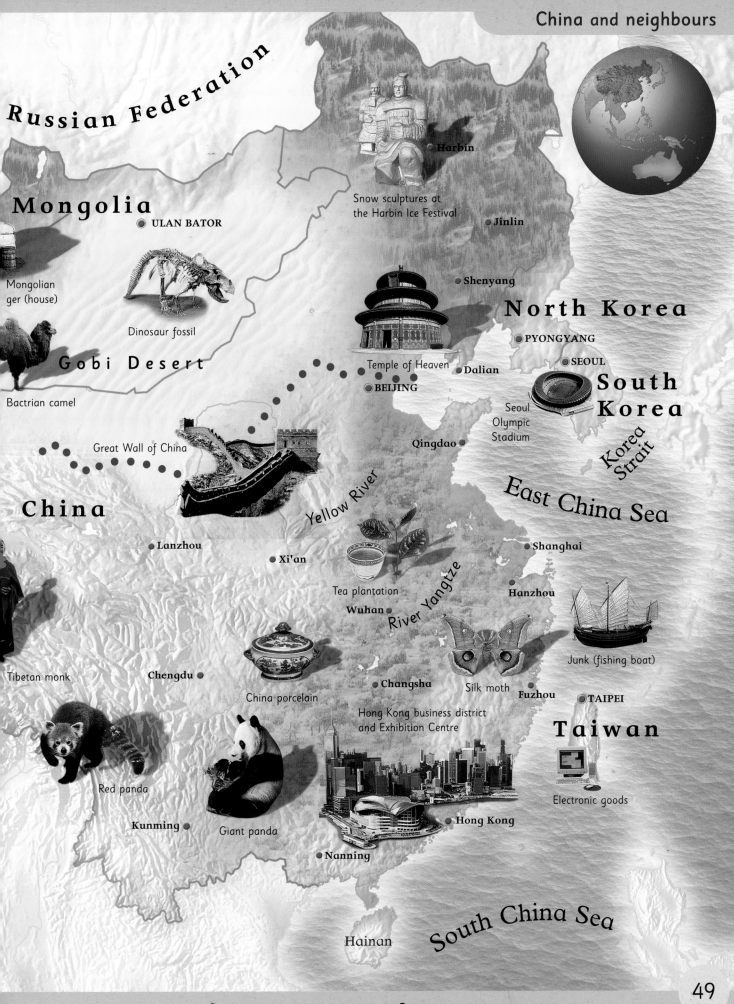

Russian Federation

Mongolia

● ULAN BATOR

Mongolian ger (house)

Dinosaur fossil

Gobi Desert

Bactrian camel

Great Wall of China

China

● Lanzhou

● Xi'an

Tibetan monk

Red panda

● Kunming

Giant panda

China porcelain

● Chengdu

● Harbin

Snow sculptures at the Harbin Ice Festival

● Jinlin

● Shenyang

Temple of Heaven

● BEIJING   ● Dalian

North Korea

● PYONGYANG

● SEOUL

South Korea

Seoul Olympic Stadium

Korea Strait

● Qingdao

East China Sea

Yellow River

● Shanghai

Tea plantation

● Hanzhou

River Yangtze

● Wuhan

Silk moth

● Changsha

● Fuzhou

Junk (fishing boat)

● TAIPEI

Taiwan

Electronic goods

Hong Kong business district and Exhibition Centre

● Hong Kong

● Nanning

South China Sea

Hainan

49

K2 in the Himalayas. It is 8,611 m (28,250 ft) tall.

Japan

Japan is made up of four large islands and several thousand small ones. Most of the country is mountainous. The biggest cities are near the coast, where the land is flat.

Kuril Islands

Steller's sea eagle

Japanese crane

Hokkaido

Pollock

Sapporo

Snow monkey

Aomori

Apples

Ou Mountains

Sushi

Cups for rice wine

Honshu

Sea of Japan

N E S W

Snow and ice festival

An ice festival takes place every February in the town of Sapporo. People carve towers of ice into temples, sculptures, or replicas of famous buildings.

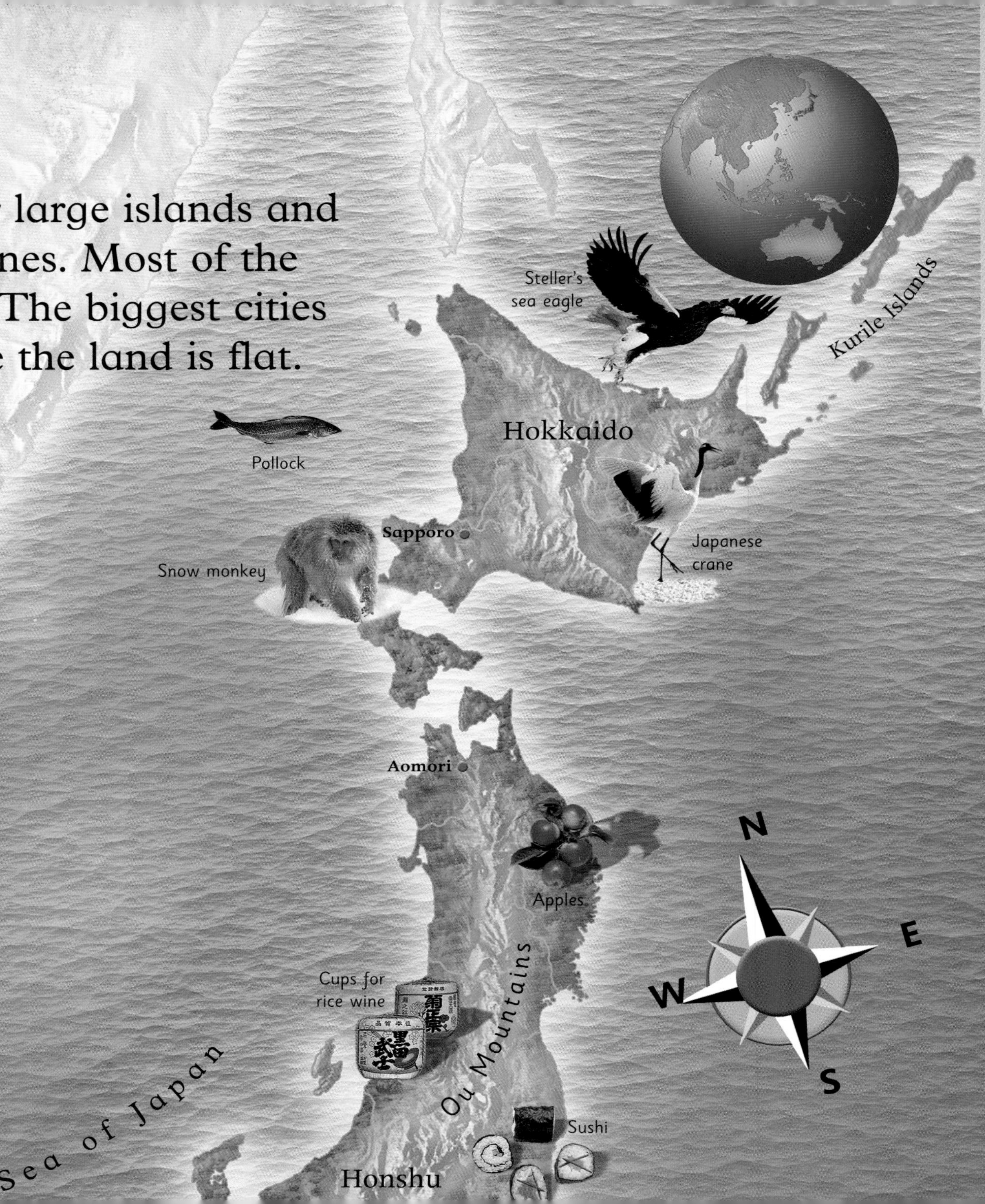

50

Toys and gadgets
Japan makes lots of electronic goods, such as computer games, televisions, and robot pets.

Robot dog

Ogasawara Islands

Volcano Islands

Kabuki theatre

Izu Islands

Mount Fuji 3,776 m (12,388 ft)

Nagoya Castle

Pearl in shell

Nagoya

Pacific Ocean

Tokyo skyline
Japan's capital city, Tokyo, is crowded and lively. Its skyscrapers are designed to sway slightly, which protects them from falling during earthquakes.

Geishas

Chugoku Mountains

Kyoto

Osaka

Bullet train

Shikoku

Matsuyama Castle

Shinto shrine

Oki Islands

Hiroshima

Sumo wrestlers

Kyushu

Bonsai tree

Iki

Fukuoka

Nagasaki

Pottery

Octopus

East China Sea

Ryukyu Islands

Sakishima Islands
These small tropical islands lie far to the south of the rest of Japan.

Ishigaki

Iriomote

Yonaguni

Okinawa

KEY COFFEE

Australia

Australia is the world's smallest continent, but it is a huge country. Most Australians live on the coast, far from the vast, dusty deserts that make up the outback.

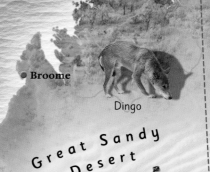
Saltwater crocodile

Darwin

Boomerang

Broome

Dingo

Port Hedland

Great Sandy Desert

Tanami Desert

Northern Territory

Emu

Uluru (Ayer's Rock)

Iron ore

Road train

Musgrav

Western Australia

Camel

Great Victoria Desert

South Australia

Poisonous animals

More poisonous animals live in Australia than in any other country.

 The male **platypus** has a poisonous spur on each of its back ankles.

 A **box jellyfish**'s stings can kill and cause terrible pain that lasts for weeks.

 Taipans are the world's deadliest snakes. A bite can kill in 30 minutes.

 Sea snake venom can kill a child, but bites from these shy snakes are rare.

 Cone shells are sea snails with deadly stings. The venom causes suffocation.

 Funnel-web spiders can bite through a fingernail and stop a person's heart.

 The tiny **blue-ringed octopus** can paralyse and kill a person with its bite.

Geraldton

Kalgoorlie

Perth skyline

Kangaroo

Perth

Fremantle

Esperance

Albany

Great Australian Bight

Great white shark

N

W   E

S

52

What is a coral reef made from?

Coral reef
The Great Barrier Reef stretches for 2,000 km (1,200 miles) along Queensland's coast. Many brightly coloured fish live on the reef.

Gulf of Carpentaria

Aboriginal paintings

Cape York Peninsula

Cairns

Cattle farming

Townsville

nnant Creek

The Devils Marbles

Mount Isa

Mackay

Rainbow lorikeet

Great Barrier Reef

Flying doctor

Queensland

Great Dividing Range

Rockhampton

lice Springs

Simpson Desert

Ranges

Sheep industry

Koala

Opals

Lake Eyre

Brisbane

Coober Pedy

Banana plantations

Pineapple farming

Broken Hill

Funnel-web spider

Sydney Opera House

Port Augusta

New South Wales

Sydney

Wollongong

Whyalla

Kookaburra

Wagga Wagga

CANBERRA
Australian Capital Territory

Port Lincoln

Adelaide

Murray River

Kangaroo Island

Victoria

Mount Gambier

Melbourne

Tram

Bass Strait

Tasmanian devil

Tasmania

Sailing

Hobart

The stony skeletons of sea creatures.

New Zealand and the Pacific

Hundreds of islands are scattered across the Pacific Ocean. Two of the biggest form the mountainous country of New Zealand.

Extreme sports

New Zealand is the world capital for extreme sports. Bungee jumping, sky diving, and white-water rafting are all popular.

Maori war dance

Most people in New Zealand are European, but about one in ten are Maoris – New Zealand's native people. On special occasions, Maoris paint their faces and perform a war dance called a haka.

Moving house

Earthquakes are common in New Zealand, so people live in wooden houses for safety. When people move home, they can carry their house away on lorries.

Sheep sheari

Kiwi

South Island

Mount Cook ▲
3,724 m (12,218 ft)

Christchurch

Southern Alps

Takahe

Rugby

New

● Queenstown

Bungee jumping

Sheep

Dunedin

Royal albatross

Oysters

54

What's unusual about New Zealand's kiwi birds?

Red snapper

N
W   E
S

Auckland

Pacific Ocean

Pohuto geyser

Maori carving

Kiwi fruit

North Island

Parliament building
(Wellington)

WELLINGTON

Cook Strait

perm
whale

New Zealand

Coconut palms
Forests of coconut palms
grow along the beaches
of the Pacific islands.
Islanders climb these tall
trees to gather the coconuts.

Pacific islands
About five million people live
among the tropical islands of
the central Pacific.

Northern Mariana
Islands (USA)

Marshall
Islands

Guam (USA)

Palau

Micronesia

Papua New
Guinea

Nauru

Kiribati

Solomon
Islands

Tuvalu

Tokelau (NZ)

Wallis
and
Futuna
(France)

Samoa

American
Samoa
(USA)

Pacific
islanders fish from
small wooden
canoes.

Vanuatu

Tonga

Niue
(NZ)

Cook Islands
(NZ)

New
Caledonia
(France)

Fiji

French
Polynesia
(France)

55

They can't fly.

Antarctica

The world's coldest continent is Antarctica, which is covered in ice. In winter, it doubles in size as the sea freezes around it.

Adélie penguins

Penguins

Lots of sea animals live around Antarctica's coast. Penguins are clumsy on land but superb swimmers underwater.

A signpost in Antarctica shows how far away the rest of the world is.

NORTH POLE 11708 MI.

CHRISTCHURCH 2,457 MI.

SEATTLE, WASH. 9,942 MI.

QUONSET PT. 10,598 MI.

ST. PAUL, MINN. 10,002 MI.

SOUTH POLE 831 MI.

SALINAS, CAL. 8,777 MI.

HOUSTON, TEXAS 9,141 MI.

MOBILE, ALA. 9,641 MI.

PONTIAC, MICH. 10,249 MI.

ERECTED BY VX-6 OF 3° WINTERING PARTY 1958 THEY WENT THAT-A-WAY →

Scott and the Antarctic

The British explorer Robert Scott was one of the first people to reach the South Pole, in 1912. He died from cold and hunger on the way home.

Southern Ocean

Weddell Sea

South polar skua

Halley Research Station (UK)

Antarctic Peninsula

Ronne Ice Shelf

Ellsworth Land

Emperor penguins

Krill

Blue whale

Ice-breaker ship

Southern Ocean

Antarctic Circle

Who was the first person to reach the South Pole?

Right whale

Southern Ocean

Dronning Maud Land

Molodezhnaya Station (Russian Federation)

Survey plane

Adélie penguins

Antarctica

Princess Elizabeth Land

Amundsen-Scott Station (USA), South Pole

SOUTH POLE

Transantarctic Mountains

Snow mobile

Elephant seal

Vostok Station (Russian Federation)

Casey Base (Australia)

Ross Ice Shelf

Ross Sea

McMurdo Air Station (USA)

Sno-cat

Dumont d'Urville (France)

Snow petrel

Killer whale

Antarctic science
The only people who live in Antarctica are scientists. They use huge balloons to study the climate on Antarctica.

Weather balloon

Life in the freezer
Antarctica is so cold that it freezes your breath into icicles around your mouth. People have to cover up in lots of very warm clothes.

Icicles from breath

The Norwegian explorer Roald Amundsen, in 1911.

Flags of the world

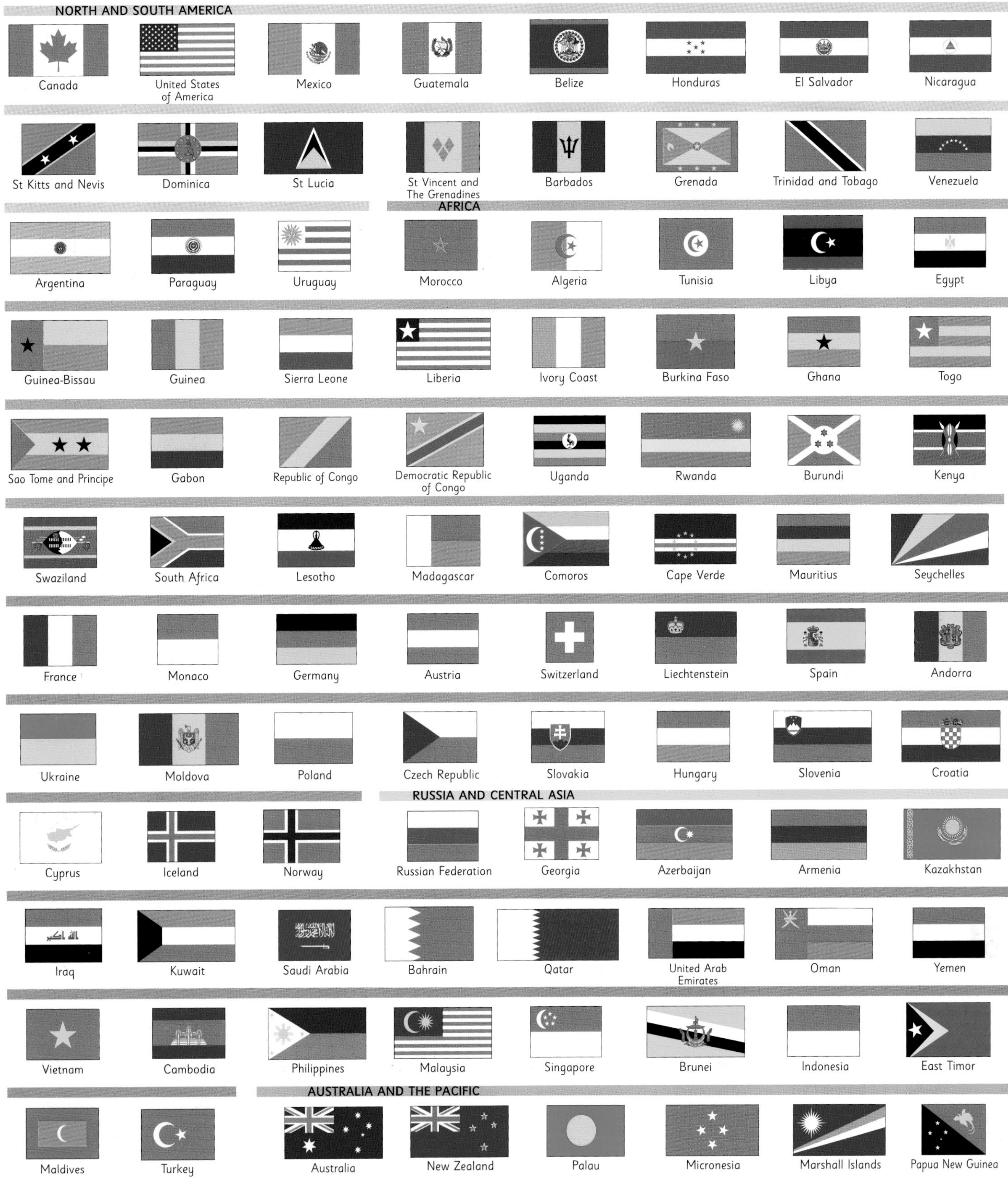
NORTH AND SOUTH AMERICA
Canada
United States of America
Mexico
Guatemala
Belize
Honduras
El Salvador
Nicaragua
St Kitts and Nevis
Dominica
St Lucia
St Vincent and The Grenadines
Barbados
Grenada
Trinidad and Tobago
Venezuela
Argentina
Paraguay
Uruguay
AFRICA
Morocco
Algeria
Tunisia
Libya
Egypt
Guinea-Bissau
Guinea
Sierra Leone
Liberia
Ivory Coast
Burkina Faso
Ghana
Togo
Sao Tome and Principe
Gabon
Republic of Congo
Democratic Republic of Congo
Uganda
Rwanda
Burundi
Kenya
Swaziland
South Africa
Lesotho
Madagascar
Comoros
Cape Verde
Mauritius
Seychelles
France
Monaco
Germany
Austria
Switzerland
Liechtenstein
Spain
Andorra
Ukraine
Moldova
Poland
Czech Republic
Slovakia
Hungary
Slovenia
Croatia
Cyprus
Iceland
Norway
RUSSIA AND CENTRAL ASIA
Russian Federation
Georgia
Azerbaijan
Armenia
Kazakhstan
Iraq
Kuwait
Saudi Arabia
Bahrain
Qatar
United Arab Emirates
Oman
Yemen
Vietnam
Cambodia
Philippines
Malaysia
Singapore
Brunei
Indonesia
East Timor
AUSTRALIA AND THE PACIFIC
Maldives
Turkey
Australia
New Zealand
Palau
Micronesia
Marshall Islands
Papua New Guinea

Which is the only country that doesn't have a rectangular flag?

Each of the 196 countries in the world has its own flag.

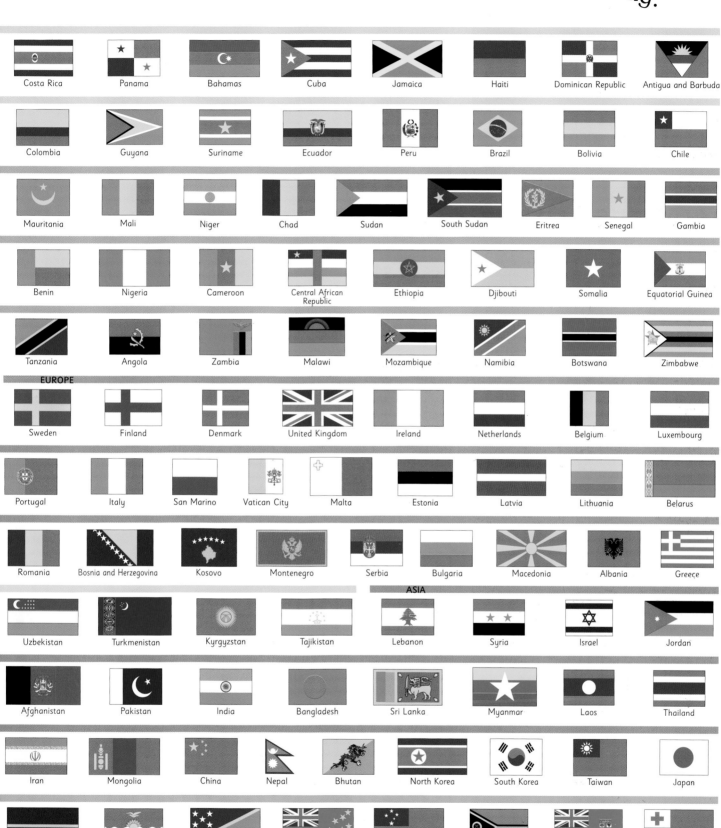

Costa Rica   Panama   Bahamas   Cuba   Jamaica   Haiti   Dominican Republic   Antigua and Barbuda

Colombia   Guyana   Suriname   Ecuador   Peru   Brazil   Bolivia   Chile

Mauritania   Mali   Niger   Chad   Sudan   South Sudan   Eritrea   Senegal   Gambia

Benin   Nigeria   Cameroon   Central African Republic   Ethiopia   Djibouti   Somalia   Equatorial Guinea

Tanzania   Angola   Zambia   Malawi   Mozambique   Namibia   Botswana   Zimbabwe

EUROPE

Sweden   Finland   Denmark   United Kingdom   Ireland   Netherlands   Belgium   Luxembourg

Portugal   Italy   San Marino   Vatican City   Malta   Estonia   Latvia   Lithuania   Belarus

Romania   Bosnia and Herzegovina   Kosovo   Montenegro   Serbia   Bulgaria   Macedonia   Albania   Greece

ASIA

Uzbekistan   Turkmenistan   Kyrgyzstan   Tajikistan   Lebanon   Syria   Israel   Jordan

Afghanistan   Pakistan   India   Bangladesh   Sri Lanka   Myanmar   Laos   Thailand

Iran   Mongolia   China   Nepal   Bhutan   North Korea   South Korea   Taiwan   Japan

Nauru   Kiribati   Solomon Islands   Tuvalu   Samoa   Vanuatu   Fiji   Tonga

World of people

More than seven billion people live in the world. These people have different customs, languages, beliefs, and lifestyles.

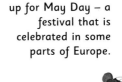

This girl is dressed up for May Day – a festival that is celebrated in some parts of Europe.

Language and people

One in every five people in the world lives in China. The most widely spoken language is Mandarin Chinese, which has almost one billion speakers.

Culture

People enjoy many different kinds of art and culture.

Writing is used to record information, news, views, stories, and history.

Theatre entertains audiences with acting, dance, and costume.

Painting is a way of expressing feelings and ideas through pictures.

Fashion is different all over the world, and is changing all the time.

Music styles can be classical or popular, traditional or modern.

May Day marks the first day of spring, after the long, cold months of winter.

Which is the second-most spoken language?

At work

All over the world, people work to earn a living. What job would you like to do? You could be an astronaut or a teacher, a farmer or a computer programmer.

At play

Having time for leisure and play is very important. Some people like watching or playing sport. Like these children, you might enjoy playing games with friends.

Celebrations

Important times in people's lives are celebrated with special feasts and festivals. These are times for people to enjoy themselves and to share their religious and cultural beliefs.

At some festivals in India, people exchange gifts of sweets, like these.

Picture detective

Look through the People and Society pages and see if you can identify the picture clues below.

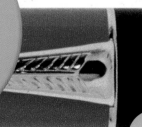

Turn and learn

Our world:
pp. 6-7
World of history:
pp. 80-81

Spanish.

Religious lands

Many people follow a religion. A religion is a set of beliefs and a way of worship. The main religions today are Hinduism, Judaism, Buddhism, Christianity, Islam, and Sikhism.

Hinduism

Hinduism began in India about 4,000 years ago. Hindus believe in a supreme being called Brahman. They worship many gods and goddesses, who represent different parts of Brahman.

Hindus bathing in the holy River Ganges, in India

Rosary

The Church of the Holy Sepulchre, in Jerusalem

Sacred symbols

Each of these symbols has a special meaning.

 In **Hinduism**, the "Aum" symbol represents the first sound of creation.

 In **Judaism**, the Star of David reminds Jews of a great Jewish king.

 In **Buddhism**, the spokes of the wheel represent the eight points of the Buddha's teaching.

 In **Christianity**, the cross reminds Christians of Jesus' death on a cross.

 In **Islam**, the star and crescent moon appear on many Islamic flags.

 In **Sikhism**, the khanda symbol reminds Sikhs of God and of God's power.

Christianity

Christians follow the teachings of a man called Jesus Christ who lived about 2,000 years ago. They believe that Jesus was the son of God, who died to save them from sin.

What is the Christian holy book called?

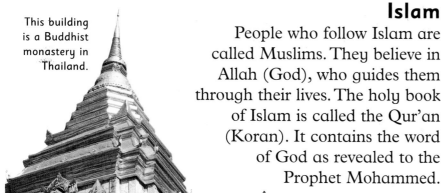

This building is a Buddhist monastery in Thailand.

Islam

People who follow Islam are called Muslims. They believe in Allah (God), who guides them through their lives. The holy book of Islam is called the Qur'an (Koran). It contains the word of God as revealed to the Prophet Mohammed.

Mecca (Makkah) is a holy city for Muslims.

The Western Wall (Wailing Wall), in Jerusalem, is a holy place for Jews.

Western Wall

Buddhism

Buddhists follow the teachings of the Buddha. He was an Indian prince who lived about 2,500 years ago. He showed people how to live good, happy lives, full of peace.

Statues of the Buddha often show him meditating (focusing the mind).

Judaism

Judaism is the religion of the Jews. Their holy book is called the Torah. It tells the story of the Jewish people and their special relationship with God.

Menorah (Jewish candlestick)

Turn and learn
Art and architecture:
pp. 68-69
Ancient Egypt:
pp. 84-85

The Golden Temple in Amritsar, India, is the holiest of all Sikh shrines.

Sikhism

The Sikh religion was started by a teacher called Guru Nanak. Sikhs worship in a building called a gurdwara. Their holy book is the Guru Granth Sahib.

The Bible.

Religious life

In their religious lives, people honour their God or gods. They may come together for worship and celebrate special events with feasts and festivals.

Statue of the Buddha

Islam

Muslims (followers of Islam) must pray five times a day: at dawn, midday, mid-afternoon, sunset, and night-time. Muslims follow a set of special prayer positions.

Buddhism

Buddhists do not worship a god, but honour the life and teachings of the Buddha. In the temple, they offer flowers, candles, and incense to the Buddha to show their respect.

In some Buddhist countries, boys spend time as monks.

What is a mosque?

In a synagogue, Jews listen to readings from the Torah, their holy book.

Torah scroll

Silver pointer

Judaism

Jewish people meet to worship and pray in a special building called a synagogue. A man or woman called a rabbi leads the worship.

This is Ganesha, the elephant-headed god.

Hinduism

Hindus worship the gods and goddesses in their homes and in mandirs (temples). The god Ganesha is said to bring good luck and success.

Turban

Small sword

Steel bangle

Sikhism

Many Sikh men wear five things to show their faith. These are uncut hair (often kept tidy in a turban), a wooden comb, a small sword, a steel bangle, and white undershorts.

Christianity

Christmas is a joyful festival when Christians remember how Jesus was born. There are services in church, and people celebrate by exchanging cards and gifts.

Jesus was born in a stable in Bethlehem. Three kings brought presents for him.

Joseph

These children are acting out the story of the first Christmas.

Three kings

Jesus

Mary

65

A building where Muslims worship Allah (God).

Writing and printing

People began to write things down about 5,500 years ago. Before this, they told stories and passed news on by word of mouth. Today, writing is all around you.

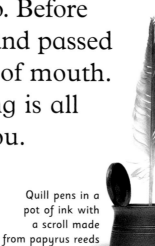

The alphabet

Fountain pens are filled with ink.

Quill pens in a pot of ink with a scroll made from papyrus reeds

Paper and pens
The paper you use today comes from trees. Long ago, people made paper from reeds or animal skins. The first pens were pieces of reeds, dipped in soot or ink.

Signs and symbols
Sometimes, signs and symbols are used to write letters and words, or even secret codes.

Pictograms are pictures used for writing. This old, Chinese word means "to sell".

Hieroglyphs were used by the ancient Egyptians. This one stands for "chick".

Runes were Viking symbols that were carved on stone or wood. This is the "M" sound.

Music symbols like these are used to write down musical sounds (notes).

Morse code changes the alphabet into dot and dash signals for sending messages.

Writing machines
The first typewriters were invented about 200 years ago. They made writing much quicker. Today, modern word processors, like this laptop computer, are used instead.

Early typewriter

Laptop computer

How long did it take to create this book?

Printing books

At first, books were written out by hand. This took a long time and was very costly. Printing presses, like the one shown here, were first used nearly 600 years ago. Printing books by machine was much quicker and cheaper.

An old wooden printing press

The different parts of the machine were worked by hand.

Turn and learn
Ancient Egypt:
pp. 84-85
The Vikings
pp. 90-91

This machine sorts printed sheets into newspapers.

Printing the news

The first, handwritten newspapers date from Roman times. They told people about battles and gladiator contests. Today, giant rotary presses are used to print millions of books, newspapers, and magazines every day.

Magazines are a great way to get information and entertainment.

One rotary press can print more than 75,000 newspapers in one hour.

67

Art and architecture

Since ancient times, artists have painted pictures and used stone and wood to make sculptures. Architects plan the world's buildings.

Cave painting
Prehistoric artists painted pictures of figures and animals on cave walls. This cave painting is from Africa.

Church art
The Italian artist Michelangelo painted scenes from the Bible on the ceiling and walls of the Sistine Chapel in Rome, Italy.

Modern sculpture
Modern British artist Henry Moore used bold shapes to create this interesting – and "touchable" – giant stone sculpture.

Skyscraper

Singapore skyline

Which is the world's tallest building?

Architecture

Every building you see has been planned by an architect. Styles of architecture have changed over thousands of years. Buildings are designed for living, working, worship, or simply for fun.

Castles were built to defend people from attack. This castle is in Spain.

Making art

People use different types of art to capture a scene or express their ideas. Here are a few of them.

Drawing a quick "sketch" in pencil is a way for artists to plan a colour painting.

Painting can be done on paper using watercolours, or on canvas with oil paints.

Sculpting is the skill of making works of art out of stone, wood, metal, or clay.

Photography uses a film or digital camera to make images of people and places.

Graphic design combines words and images on a computer in colourful ways.

The Taj Mahal

The beautiful Taj Mahal in India was built by Emperor Shah Jahan as a tomb for his wife, Mumtaz Mahal. It is made from white marble, set with coloured stones.

Modern skyscrapers make up the Singapore skyline.

An opera house

The Opera House in Sydney, Australia, is a modern building. Its wing-like roof makes it easy to identify. It was designed to look like the sails of boats in the nearby harbour.

Turn and learn

Ancient Greece **pp. 86-87**
The Romans: **pp.88-89**

The Burj Khalifa in Dubai. It is 828 m (2,717 ft) tall.

Music

What is your favourite song or tune? Do you like classical, jazz, folk, rock, or pop music? If you play a musical instrument, you can make music of your own.

Conductor

An orchestra
Some musicians perform together in a group called an orchestra. There are about 90 musicians in a symphony orchestra. The conductor keeps them in time. Orchestras usually play classical music.

Drums and cymbals are percussion instruments.

Cymbal

Musical instruments
In an orchestra, there are four kinds of instruments – brass, woodwind, percussion, and strings. Each instrument makes its own individual sound. The different sounds blend together.

Drum

Flute

What sort of instrument is a xylophone?

Recording music

In a recording studio, each voice or instrument can be recorded on its own. These are called tracks. Engineers mix the tracks together.

Mixing desk

The knobs on the mixing desk control the volume and tone of each track.

Types of music

Many different kinds of music are played all over the world.

Early music was probably played on instruments made from animal bones.

Opera is a play set to music in which the performers sing their lines.

Jazz musicians make up some or all of the music as they play it.

Rock music, or rock and roll, has punchy lyrics (words) and a strong beat.

Pop is short for popular music. It has catchy tunes and is good for dancing to.

Madonna is one of the most successful pop singers of all time.

Madonna

Vinyl record

CDs

Minidisc   Mp3 Player

You can listen to music on records, CDs, and Mp3 players, as well as handheld devices and computers.

Many rock and pop musicians play music on electric guitars.

Pop concerts

Watching your favourite pop star perform live on stage can be thrilling. Many people work behind the scenes to make the show run smoothly.

Cello

French horn

Piano keyboard

hands on

Would you like to be a pop star? Try writing your own pop song. Start by writing a poem, then make up a tune to go with it.

A percussion instrument.

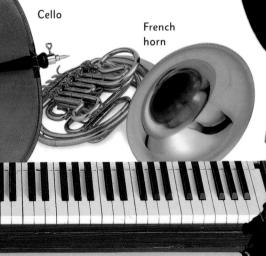

Theatre and dance

Theatre began thousands of years ago in ancient Greece. Actors and dancers put on shows to entertain and inform people.

Actors and acting

Putting on a play is a long task. First, the playwright writes the play. Then actors bring the story and the characters in the play to life. They also have to remember their words!

Actors use their body, as well as the words, to create a character and perform the scenes.

These actors are playing two characters called Romeo and Juliet.

Costumes help to show when and where the play's action is happening.

Musical theatre

Going to the theatre to see a musical is a special treat. Musicals are an exciting mixture of acting, dancing, and song. This is a scene from the musical *Oliver!*.

72

Who wrote the play *Romeo and Juliet*?

Japanese theatre

These actors are performing an ancient type of Japanese play, called Kabuki. They wear beautiful costumes and mix acting, singing, dancing, and music to put on a dazzling show.

Indian dance

Dancing is a way of telling a story or showing a feeling using movement and music. This type of dancing, from India, is made up of special movements and expressions.

Forms of dance

There are many different types and styles of dance from all over the world.

Tap dancers wear metal-capped shoes to make "tap" sounds.

Ballet is a graceful type of dance, set to music, that tells a tale.

Country and **folk** dances from around the world are lively and fun.

Flamenco is a dramatic Spanish dance set to the sound of clicking castanets.

Jazz dance uses the rhythm and beat of jazz music to create an exciting dance.

Punch and Judy are famous puppets from Britain.

Puppet shows

Puppet shows are a very old type of theatre. These glove puppets are simple to work. A hand inside makes the puppet move. One finger works the puppet's head, while two other fingers work the arms.

Punch

Judy

Turn and learn
Music
pp. 70–71
Ancient Greece
pp. 86–87

William Shakespeare.

Clothes and fashion

What are you wearing today? A T-shirt? Trousers? Trainers? Clothes can make you look good. They may also have a special job to do.

Types of fabric
Clothes are made from a variety of materials.

Cotton is made of fibres from the cotton plant. The fabric is usually woven.

Silk is a thin, soft fabric made from threads spun by silkworms.

Leather is made from the skins of animals, such as cows.

Wool is made from the hair of sheep. It is often knitted to make clothes.

Nylon and other **artificial fabrics** are made from chemicals.

This Vietnamese boy is wearing casual clothes.

This Indian girl is wearing a sari.

A raincoat, wellington boots, and umbrella are useful when it rains.

This French girl wears a top and skirt for school.

What do you wear?
What you wear depends on where you live and what you are doing. People wear different clothes for keeping warm, staying cool, for playing sport, and for going to school.

What is a beret ("berr-eh")?

Fashion shows

Some people design clothes to look stylish or unusual. They are called fashion designers. They put on fashion shows where models show off their clothes.

Clothes for the cold

In cold climates, clothes were traditionally made from animal fur and skins. Today, synthetic (artificial) fabrics are often used instead.

Uniforms

Some people have to wear special clothes for work. These are called uniforms. This firefighter's uniform protects against heat and flames. Do you wear a uniform at school?

This Masai girl from Tanzania is wearing her colourful national dress.

Children from the Arctic need thick, fur-lined clothes for warmth.

This outfit is the national dress of a hill tribe from Vietnam.

This girl is wearing a kimono, the national dress of Japan.

National dress

A country's traditional clothes are called its national dress. In many countries, people only wear their national dress for festivals or other special occasions.

A round, flat type of hat.

Sport and leisure

What do you do in your spare time? Do you enjoy a favourite sport? Or do you have fun with toys or play computer games?

Soccer is the most popular sport in the world.

Spectator sports

A spectator sport is a sport that people like to watch. Soccer, rugby, American football, baseball, and golf are all spectator sports.

Snowboarders wear warm, baggy clothes.

Snowboarders do amazing spins and jumps.

Plastic clips attach the boot to the snowboard.

Outdoor sports

Snowboarding, rock climbing, canoeing, skiing, and sailing are outdoor sports. You need special equipment and clothes to do outdoor sports safely.

Team sports

All of these spectator sports are played by two teams of players.

In **baseball**, teams score runs by batting. Fielders wear a catching glove.

In **basketball**, points are scored by throwing the ball into a raised hoop (basket).

In **soccer**, each team tries to kick or head the ball into the other team's net.

In **ice hockey**, teams score goals by hitting a puck with flat sticks.

In **rugby**, teams score "tries" by putting the oval ball over the opposing line.

Which games are played with cues on a table?

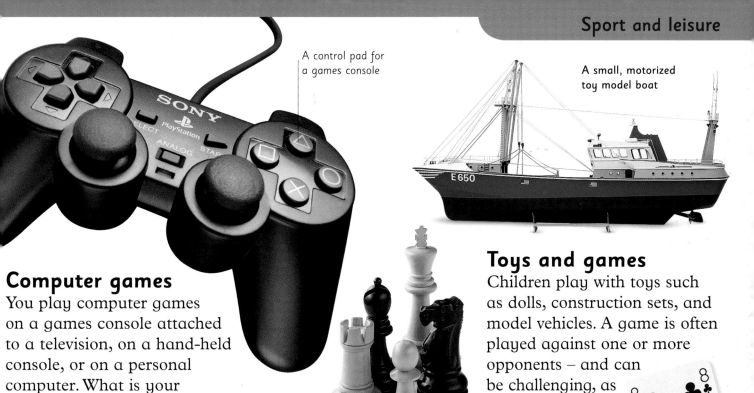

A control pad for
a games console

A small, motorized
toy model boat

E 650

Computer games

You play computer games
on a games console attached
to a television, on a hand-held
console, or on a personal
computer. What is your
favourite computer game?

You play chess
with pieces on
a board.

Toys and games

Children play with toys such
as dolls, construction sets, and
model vehicles. A game is often
played against one or more
opponents – and can
be challenging, as
well as fun.

Playing
cards

Individual sports

In these, people play
on their own, against
one or more opponents.

In **tennis**, players hit a
ball with rackets. They must
keep the ball in the court.

While **swimming**,
swimmers race each
other up and down a pool.

In **golf**, players hit a ball
around a course, using
as few shots as they can.

While **running**, runners
race against each other
on a track or on roads.

In **table tennis**, players hit
a ball with small bats. The
game is played on a table.

Doll

Going to the movies

When new films are made, they are first
shown on large screens at cinemas. Today,
many films are made using animation
and special effects.

77

Working people

What do you want to be when you grow up? All over the world, people do different kinds of work to earn the money to buy their food, clothes, and homes.

Astronauts

Astronauts are people who fly spacecraft and work in space. They carry out experiments in orbiting laboratories called space stations, and often spend months in space.

Market sellers

There are markets selling food and other goods in almost every town and city. This man is selling fruit and vegetables from his market stall in Cairo, Egypt.

What do you call someone who writes books to earn a living?

This vet is giving a dog a health check.

The farmer's plough is being pulled by an ox.

Vets

If your pet is ill, you take it to the vet. Vets look after sick and injured animals. Some vets treat small animals, such as cats and dogs. Others work with farm or zoo animals.

Farmers

All over the world, farmers grow crops and raise animals. They grow food for themselves and to sell at market. This farmer is ploughing his rice field in Thailand.

Teachers

At school, teachers help you to learn science, languages, and other subjects. Teachers have to go to college to learn how to teach you! Who is your favourite teacher?

This teacher is helping some children to learn to read.

Teacher

Pupils

These engineers are making a part for a power station.

Engineers

Engineers are people who design or make cars, aeroplanes, machines, and buildings. To be an engineer, you need to be good at science and mathematics.

79

An author.

World of history

History tells us the story of how people lived in the past. From the things they left behind, we can find out about their homes, food, clothes, work, and beliefs.

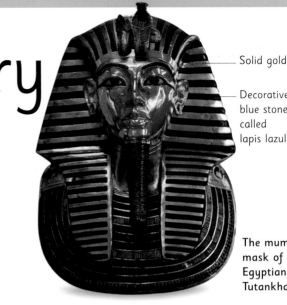

Solid gold

Decorative blue stones called lapis lazuli

The mummy mask of the Egyptian king Tutankhamun

Early people
About 10,000 years ago, groups of people began to settle down in certain places. They started to farm the land and to raise animals for food.

Powerful kings
Many great civilizations were ruled by powerful kings. In ancient Egypt, the kings were called pharaohs. They were so important that people worshipped them as gods.

Early farmers cut down the ripe wheat stalks with a sickle made from a sharp flint stone set in a wooden handle.

People learnt how to grow crops for food.

Spanish galleon

80

Greeks and Romans

About 2,500 years ago, ancient Greek culture flourished. Then, around 27 BCE, the Romans grew in strength and ruled over a great empire from Rome in Italy.

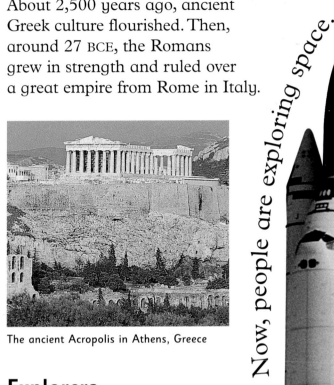

The ancient Acropolis in Athens, Greece

Explorers

For centuries, people have travelled far and wide across the world. They went in search of new lands, goods to trade, and adventures.

These coins were made by European explorers using the gold they discovered on their travels.

Now, people are exploring space.

The first Space Shuttle flight was made in 1981 with a shuttle called *Columbia*.

20th century

The 20th century saw many new inventions and discoveries being made. People flew in space for the first time, and even walked on the Moon.

Picture detective

Look through the History of People pages and see if you can identify the picture clues below.

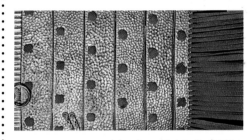

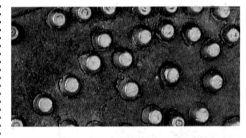

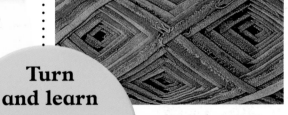

Turn and learn

Writing and printing: **pp. 66-67**
Men on the Moon: **pp. 280-281**

81

Homo habilis skull

Neanderthal skull

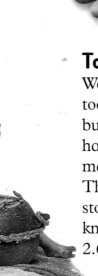
Modern human skull

From apes to human beings

Our oldest ancestors looked like apes. Slowly, they became more human-like and began to walk upright on two legs.

Early people

The first human ancestors lived about four million years ago. We do not know exactly what they looked like, but we do know how they lived.

Cave shelters

Early people used caves like these as shelters. Inside, the caves were safe and warm. Sometimes, people painted the walls with pictures of the animals they hunted.

The first farmers

About 10,000 years ago, people learnt how to grow food out of the ground. They were the first farmers. They also made pots to store grains, which they ground in stone grinders.

Fire

A flint hand axe from Egypt

Flint blade

Tools and fire

We take fire and tools for granted, but early people had to learn how to make and use them. The first tools were stone choppers and knives, made about 2.6 million years ago.

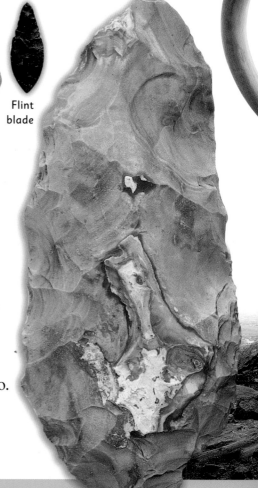

This woman is grinding grain between two stones to make flour for bread.

How did early people start fires?

The first cities

When people started growing their food, they were able to settle in one place. They began to build houses, villages, and cities. One of the first cities was Jericho in Jordan.

Hunters and gatherers

Early people hunted woolly mammoths, cave bears, reindeer, and other animals for food. They also collected fruit, nuts, and roots, and caught fish.

Early achievements

Here are some of the everyday things that early people used.

Dogs, one of the first animals to be **domesticated**, were used for hunting about 14,000 years ago.

The first **metal tools** were made from copper about 10,000 years ago.

The earliest **clay pots**, used for cooking, were made in Japan about 10,000 years ago.

Mammoth hunting was dangerous work!

Turn and learn

Aztecs, Incas, and Mayas: **pp. 92-93**

The meat from a mammoth was enough to feed a family for a whole year.

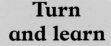

Hunters used wooden spears.

By rubbing two sticks or striking two stones together.

Ancient Egypt

The ancient Egyptians lived by the banks of the River Nile about 3,500 years ago. Their powerful rulers were called pharaohs.

Beautifully decorated mummy

The pyramids

The ancient Egyptians believed in life after death. The pharaohs built magnificent tombs, called pyramids, for themselves.

Mummy of a cat

Building skills

Egyptian builders did not have modern tools and machines to help them. The workers carried huge stone blocks into place, or sent them on barges along the river.

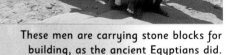

These men are carrying stone blocks for building, as the ancient Egyptians did.

Mummification

When an important person died, the body was "mummified". Some of the inside parts were removed. Then the body was treated with chemicals and wrapped in bandages.

hands on

Try writing out a message using only Egyptian hieroglyphics. You could also make up your own set of hieroglyphic symbols.

84

Why did the Egyptians mummify their dead?

The Nile floods

Each year, the River Nile flooded and spread rich, black soil on its banks. Farmers grew crops in the soil and used the river water to water their fields.

The River Nile in Egypt

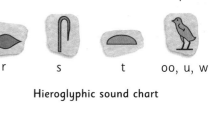

A funeral barge

Nile barges were important for transport.

Hieroglyphics

The Egyptians used picture writing called hieroglyphics. Symbols, such as those below, stood for letters and sounds.

Hieroglyphs

ah	b	c, k	d
ee, y	f	g	h
kh	m	n	p
r	s	t	oo, u, w

Hieroglyphic sound chart

The Sphinx is carved out of one massive stone.

The Sphinx

A huge stone statue, called the Sphinx, guards the pyramids at Giza. It has the body of a lion and a human head, which was modelled on the pharaoh's own features.

The great Sphinx guards the pyramid of a pharaoh called Khafra.

To keep the body whole for the next life.

Ancient Greece

About 2,500 years ago, Greece was made up of powerful "city-states", such as Athens and Sparta, which fought wars against each other.

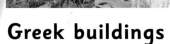

Greek buildings

The ancient Greeks built beautiful temples where they worshipped their gods. This temple in Athens was built to honour the goddess Athena.

Greek theatre

Going to the theatre was very popular in ancient Greece. The Greeks wrote many plays, both tragedies and comedies. People watched their favourite plays in large outdoor theatres, like the one above.

Where were the first Olympic Games held?

The Trojan War

Legend says that during a long war with the city of Troy, the Greeks gave the Trojans a huge wooden horse as a gift. But the horse was full of soldiers, who attacked the Trojans as they slept.

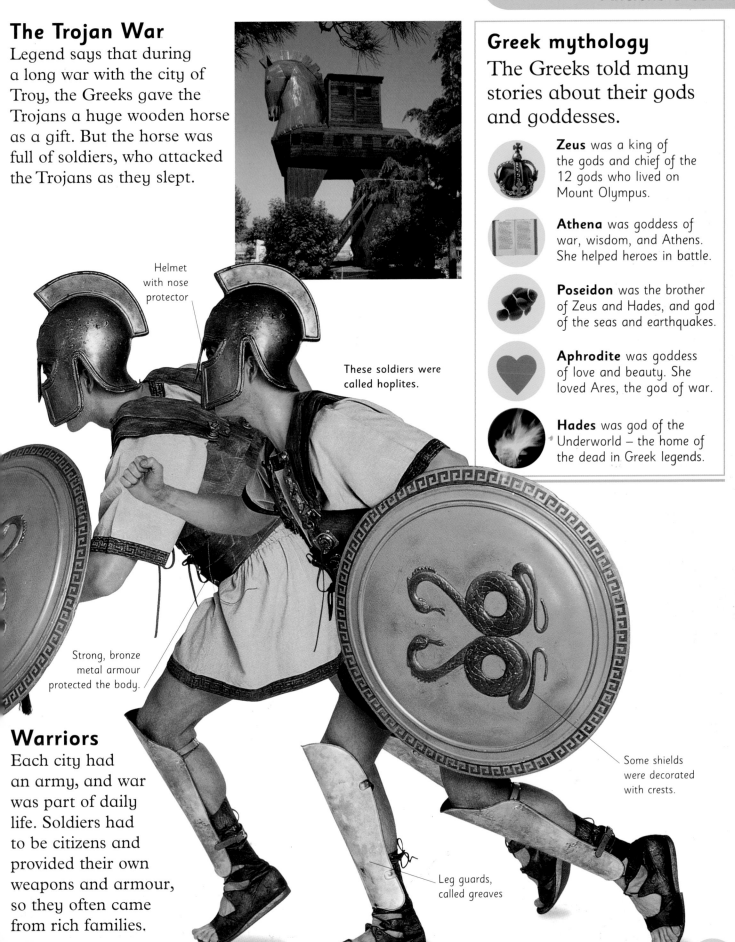

Greek mythology

The Greeks told many stories about their gods and goddesses.

Zeus was a king of the gods and chief of the 12 gods who lived on Mount Olympus.

Athena was goddess of war, wisdom, and Athens. She helped heroes in battle.

Poseidon was the brother of Zeus and Hades, and god of the seas and earthquakes.

Aphrodite was goddess of love and beauty. She loved Ares, the god of war.

Hades was god of the Underworld – the home of the dead in Greek legends.

Helmet with nose protector

These soldiers were called hoplites.

Strong, bronze metal armour protected the body.

Some shields were decorated with crests.

Leg guards, called greaves

Warriors

Each city had an army, and war was part of daily life. Soldiers had to be citizens and provided their own weapons and armour, so they often came from rich families.

The Romans

Ancient Rome began as a group of small villages along the River Tiber in Italy. It grew into a great and powerful city that ruled a mighty empire.

A Roman forum

The city of Rome

The city of Rome is still a busy place, just as it was in ancient times. If you visit Rome today, you can see the ruined Forum (ancient city centre), the Colosseum, and many other buildings.

Gladiators

The Colosseum was a huge building in Rome where people went to watch wild beast shows and gladiator fights. Gladiators often fought to the death.

Lions and other wild animals were killed during the shows.

Gladiators were armed with nets and spears, or small shields and swords.

50,000 people could sit and watch the fights in the arena.

What was a Roman villa?

Latin language

The Romans spoke a language called Latin. Roman children learnt to write Latin by scratching letters on wooden boards that were covered in wax.

This inscription is written in Latin.

The Roman Empire

The Romans conquered a vast empire. They built this wall between Scotland and England to protect the boundary of their empire.

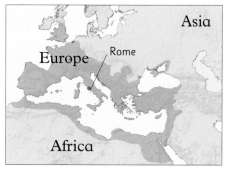

The purple area on this map shows the size of the Roman Empire in around 100 CE.

Hadrian's Wall

Famous Romans

Below, you can read about some of the most famous Romans.

Spartacus was a slave who led an army of slaves against the Romans.

Julius Caesar was a great general who ruled Rome. He was murdered.

Augustus was the first Roman emperor. After his death, he was made a god.

Ovid was a Roman poet. He wrote many poems about myths and legends.

Emperor Hadrian toured the empire, and built walls and forts to guard it.

The Roman army

The Romans had the best army in the world. Their soldiers conquered many countries and guarded the empire. The soldiers often had to march long distances.

A standard (army flag)

A soldier's sandals

Roman roads

In peacetime, Roman soldiers were kept busy building roads. Roads were important for moving the army around the empire. Roman roads were usually very straight. Some are still used today.

A large house in the countryside.

The Vikings

The Vikings lived more than 1,000 years ago. Their home was in Scandinavia, in northern Europe, but they are famous for their long sea journeys to distant lands.

Mast

The sail was made from wool or linen.

Ropes

Longships
Viking boats were called longships. They were built from wood, and were fast and strong enough to cover vast distances. A longship carried about 80 Vikings, who rowed and sailed the ship.

Important Vikings were buried in their longships.

Viking travellers
The Vikings were daring sailors and explorers. They made fierce raids on the countries of western Europe. They went in search of trade and new lands to live in – even as far away as North America.

Scandinavia

Atlantic Ocean

Europe

North America

The Vikings reached North America in about the year 1000 CE.

What is the Viking alphabet called?

Warrior duty

Most Vikings were farmers, but they had to be ready to fight at a moment's notice. They always kept their weapons and armour close by.

Viking houses were usually built of stone or wood.

Viking homes

Viking families lived in houses made from wood, stone, or turf. An opening was made in the roof to let out smoke from the cooking fire. People sat on stools or benches around the fire and slept on raised beds.

Spear made of iron and wood

Viking warriors carried wooden shields and wore armour made from leather or chain mail.

Padded leather tunic

Helmet with noseguard

Chain-mail shirt

A small statue of a Viking god called Freyr

Story-telling

To entertain each other, the Vikings told long stories about their heroes, gods, and great warriors. The stories were called sagas.

Runes

The Vikings carved poems and inscriptions using symbols called runes. Runes were mostly made of straight lines, so it was easy to carve them on wood or stone.

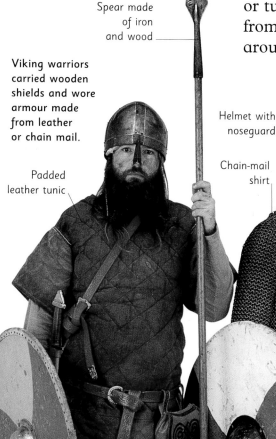

Round wooden shield

Iron sword

Long woollen socks

Goat-skin shoes

Swords and spears were used for fighting.

Runes

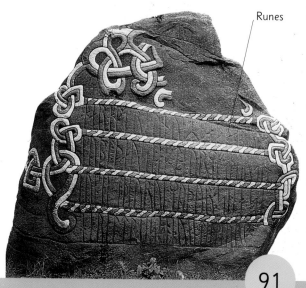

91

Aztecs, Incas, and Mayas

Three great civilizations grew up in the ancient Americas. They were called the Aztecs, Mayas, and Incas. These people built great cities and temples to their gods.

Aztec warrior's headdress

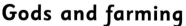

Where did they live?

The Mayas lived in Central America, while the Aztecs ruled most of Mexico. The Inca Empire was on the west coast of South America.

Pyramid of the Moon at Teotihuacan

Pyramid temple

Both the Aztecs and the Mayas had pyramid-shaped temples, with long flights of steps leading to a shrine on top. Here their priests sacrificed captives as offerings to the gods.

Chicomecoatl, the Aztec goddess of maize

Gods and farming

The Aztecs prayed to the gods to make their crops grow. Most important crop was maize (corn). It was ground into flour for making flat breads called tortillas.

How were the Incas like the ancient Egyptians?

Spanish galleon

Spanish invasion

In the 16th century, Spanish explorers came to the Americas. Their arrival meant the end of the Aztec, Maya, and Inca civilizations. Many people were killed and their cities destroyed.

Inca gold

The Incas made objects from gold. The Spanish greed for gold led to the end of the Inca Empire.

Llamas were important to the Incas. They were used for wool and for transport.

Gold armbands may have been worn by the bravest Inca warriors.

Statues of Inca gods were made from gold to show honour towards them.

Mayan cities

The Maya built great cities, filled with magnificent stone temples, palaces, and squares. This is the Temple of the Great Jaguar in the Mayan city of Tikal.

Tikal in Guatemala, Central America

get mucky
Make an Aztec headdress from card. Cut a circle of card to fit your head and stick on card feathers. Paint it and tape the ends together.

Inca farmers

This is the Inca city of Machu Picchu, located high in the Andes mountains in Peru. Farmers grew crops in level fields cut into the mountainside. Maize, legumes (beans), and squash were their main crops.

Ruins of Machu Picchu's buildings can still be seen in Peru today.

They made mummies.

Knights and castles

Types of castle

The first castles were made from wood, but stone was stronger.

Early castles were strong square keeps (towers) built of stone.

French castles (châteaux) were defended by lofty towers and moats.

Japanese castles were built by warrior lords and had decorative roofs.

The **Red Fort** in India was a palace with stone walls 30 m (100 ft) tall.

Even for brave knights, attacking a castle was dangerous. Thick walls kept them out, and the castle archers had their bows and arrows at the ready.

Castle design

Massive walls and towers made castles almost impossible for enemy soldiers to attack. Many castles were built on hills, so they were difficult to reach.

hands on

Make a knight's shield from a big piece of coloured card. Decorate the shield with your own coat of arms, cut out of silver paper.

Jousting

In peacetime, knights fought practice battles, called jousts, to train for war. They used poles (lances) to knock each other off their horses.

Battlements

Tower

Thick walls

94

Helmet

Knights

Knights were soldiers who fought on horseback. They wore heavy armour made from iron and were armed with axes, swords, and maces (clubs).

Mace

A knight used his sword to stab between the gaps in an enemy's armour.

Samurai warriors

In Japan, knights were called samurai. They were warriors who fought for a powerful lord and followed a strict code of honour.

Leg guard (greave)

Spur

Buffalo horns

Samurai warriors wore armour made from coated wood or plates of metal laced together.

Leather leg protector

Samurai sword

Archers aimed arrows from the walls at their attackers.

Lance

Each knight had his own pattern, called his coat of arms.

Shield

Moat

95

Armour made from small loops of metal.

20th century

The 20th century was the time from 1901 to 2000. In the 20th century, there were many events, inventions, and discoveries that changed people's lives for ever.

British air force symbol

A British fighter aircraft from World War II

World wars

There were two world wars during the 20th century. World War I lasted from 1914 to 1918. World War II lasted from 1939 to 1945. Millions of soldiers and civilians died in these wars.

Nearly three quarters of France's electricity is made at nuclear power stations. This one is on the River Seine.

Nuclear power

The first nuclear power station was opened in 1954. Today, there are about 400 of them in the world. While they provide energy, these power stations also produce dangerous waste.

This is *Sirius*, a ship owned and used by the Greenpeace organization.

The tracks stop the heavy tank from sinking into mud.

Tank

Thick armour protects the crew of the tank.

Who was the first person to go into space? And when?

Pop music

The Beatles was one of the most successful pop groups of all time. In the 1960s, millions of people bought their records. Performances on television also helped to boost their fame. The Beatles split up in 1970.

Live telecast of a Beatles performance in New York, USA

Man on the Moon

In 1969, astronauts visited the Moon for the first time. People all around the world watched on television as the US astronauts stepped onto the Moon's grey, dusty surface.

Buzz Aldrin

Buzz Aldrin was the second man on the Moon; Neil Armstrong was the first.

Space suit

Advances

Advances made in the 20th century made many people's lives easier.

Mobile telephones and the **Internet** make it easy to keep in touch.

Medical advances help us to fight diseases and recover from injuries.

Inventions such as the jet engine have made travel fast and cheap.

Sport became extremely popular, and many sports people became very famous.

Scientific discoveries, such as DNA, helped medicine and technology.

A microchip is a set of circuits, through which electricity flows, on a small plate.

The environment

Some people began to worry about the damage that humans are doing to the environment. They formed organizations such as Greenpeace and Friends of the Earth.

Nelson Mandela

There were many important political changes during the 20th century. Nelson Mandela fought against an unfair political system in South Africa. He became president of South Africa in 1994.

Technology

Many new types of technology were developed in the 20th century. Microchips were invented in the 1950s. They are used in computers, televisions, stereos, and many other machines.

A Russian cosmonaut (astronaut) called Yuri Gagarin. In 1961.

Your amazing body

The greatest machine you'll ever own is your body. It's more complicated than any computer, it lasts for a lifetime, and it's yours for free.

Turn and learn
Bones and muscles: **pp. 106-107**

Body parts
Your body is made up of hundreds of different parts. You probably know the names of the bits you can see, but there are many more hidden deep inside you.

Hair

Forehead

Ears

Eyebrows

Cheeks

Nose

Eyes

Lips

Teeth

Inside your body
Doctors can see inside your body with special cameras. X-ray cameras take pictures of hard body parts like bones. Other cameras, called scanners, can see soft body parts.

Hands

Fingers

Wrists

Two of everything
Body parts often come in pairs. You have two feet, two eyes, two ears, two lungs, and so on. This means you have a handy spare in case one of them gets damaged.

A chest X-ray shows the bones in your chest. The white shape in the middle is the heart.

98

What do we call the study of the human body?

Water, water

Water is the most important chemical in your body. About two-thirds of your weight is water.

Robot

No substitute

The human body is too complicated for robots to copy. Robots can copy the way we walk, but they can't think or feel like we do.

The ingredients

Your body is made of just a few simple chemicals, apart from water.

Carbon is the chemical in diamonds and coal. A fifth of you is carbon.

Iron makes your blood red. You have enough to make one small iron nail.

Phosphorus is in the tips of matches, as well as your bones and teeth.

Sodium and **chlorine** make salt. Blood is one-third as salty as sea water.

Potassium is used in some types of soap. It's also in your body fluids.

Nitrogen is important in muscles. It's also the main ingredient in air.

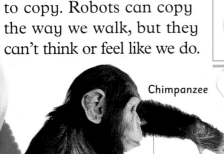

Chimpanzee

Chimps have hands like ours.

Compared to chimps, our bodies look almost hairless.

Picture detective

Take a look at the first few pages and see if you can find these pictures.

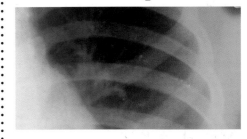

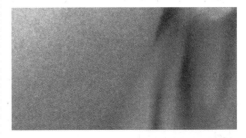

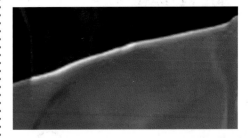

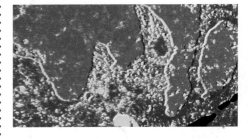

Being human

Although we look different to animals, our bodies are similar on the inside. Our closest animal relatives are chimpanzees.

99

What makes you you?

All human bodies work the same way, but everyone is different. Nobody looks, sounds, or thinks exactly like you. You're different because of the way your genes and experience shape you as you grow up.

Unique
The shape of your face, the colour of your hair, and many other things make you unique – different from everyone else.

Light brown eyes

Fair skin

Curly hair

Black hair

Freckles

How many genes are there in the human body?

In the genes

Genes are instructions that build your body and tell it how to work. Your genes control many of the things that make you unique, like the colour of your eyes or how tall you'll be.

This girl has genes that allow her to roll up her tongue. The boy doesn't have those genes, so he can't roll his tongue.

There's enough DNA inside you to stretch to the Sun and back 400 times.

DNA

Your genes are stored in a chemical called DNA, which looks like a twisted ladder with four different types of rung. The rungs make up a four-letter alphabet that spells out your genes, like letters in a book.

DNA can split and copy itself.

hands on

Look in a mirror and see if you can roll your tongue. Don't cheat by squeezing it with your lips. Test your family to see who has the gene.

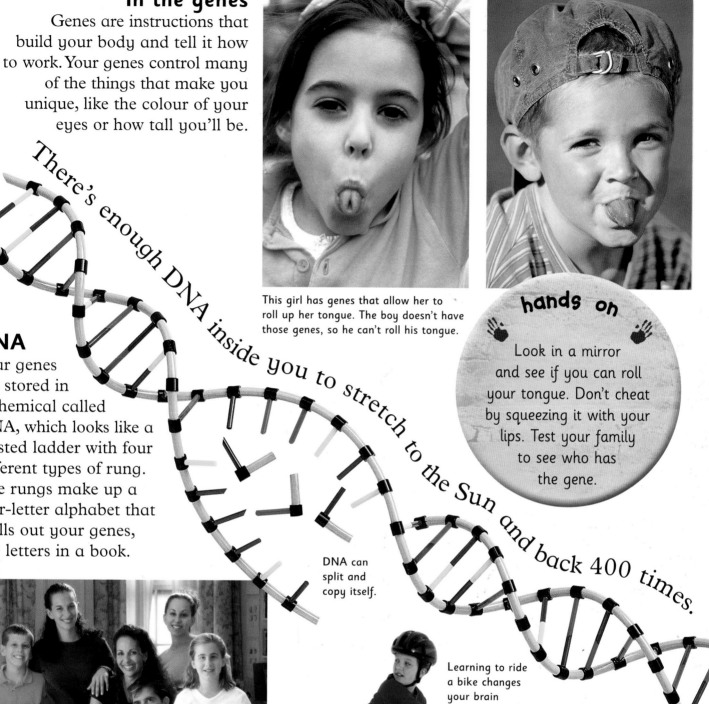

Learning to ride a bike changes your brain and your body.

In the family

Your genes came from your parents. Half come from your mother and half come from your father. If you look like your parents, it's because you share the same genes.

Changing body

Genes don't control everything – experience also shapes you. If you exercise a lot, for instance, your body gets stronger.

About 20,000.

Building blocks

Every part of your body is made of tiny building blocks called cells, which fit together like bricks in a wall. Cells are so small that hundreds could fit on the point of a pin.

The nucleus controls the rest of the cell.

DNA is stored in the cell nucleus.

DNA

The inside of a cell is packed with a kind of living jelly called cytoplasm.

The skin on your fingertips is made of lots of small ridges.

Inside a cell

In the middle of a cell is its control centre – the nucleus. The nucleus sends instructions to the rest of the cell, telling the cell what chemicals to make.

The outer skin, or membrane, stops things from leaking out.

Tiny generators provide cells with power.

Before a cell divides, the nucleus splits to make two nuclei.

Making new cells

A cell makes new cells by dividing. The two new cells are half the size, but they soon grow back. Millions of your cells die every second, but millions of others divide to replace them.

The new cells pull apart and separate, but they usually stay close neighbours.

How many cells are there in the human body?

How big are cells?

Cells are too small to see with the naked eye, but scientists can photograph them through powerful microscopes. The cells on your skin are about a hundredth of a millimetre wide.

More than 2,000 dead skin cells fell off you while you read this sentence.

The cells on the surface of your skin are tough and flat. They overlap to form a layer – like an armour – that protects the softer cells below.

A microscope can zoom in to see the tiny, flaky cells on the ridges of a person's fingertips.

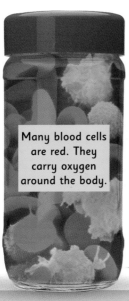
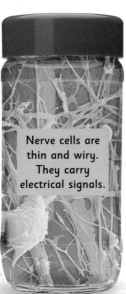
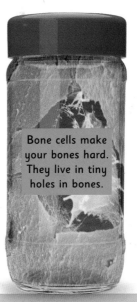

Fat cells are bubble-shaped. They store fat under your skin.

Many blood cells are red. They carry oxygen around the body.

Nerve cells are thin and wiry. They carry electrical signals.

Bone cells make your bones hard. They live in tiny holes in bones.

Cells make tissue

Your body contains about 200 different types of cells that do different jobs. Cells of the same type usually group together to form tissue. Fat, muscle, bone, and nerves are types of tissue. Blood is a liquid tissue.

About 100 trillion.

Organizing the body

Your cells and tissues are organized into larger body parts called organs. In turn, your organs work together to form body systems.

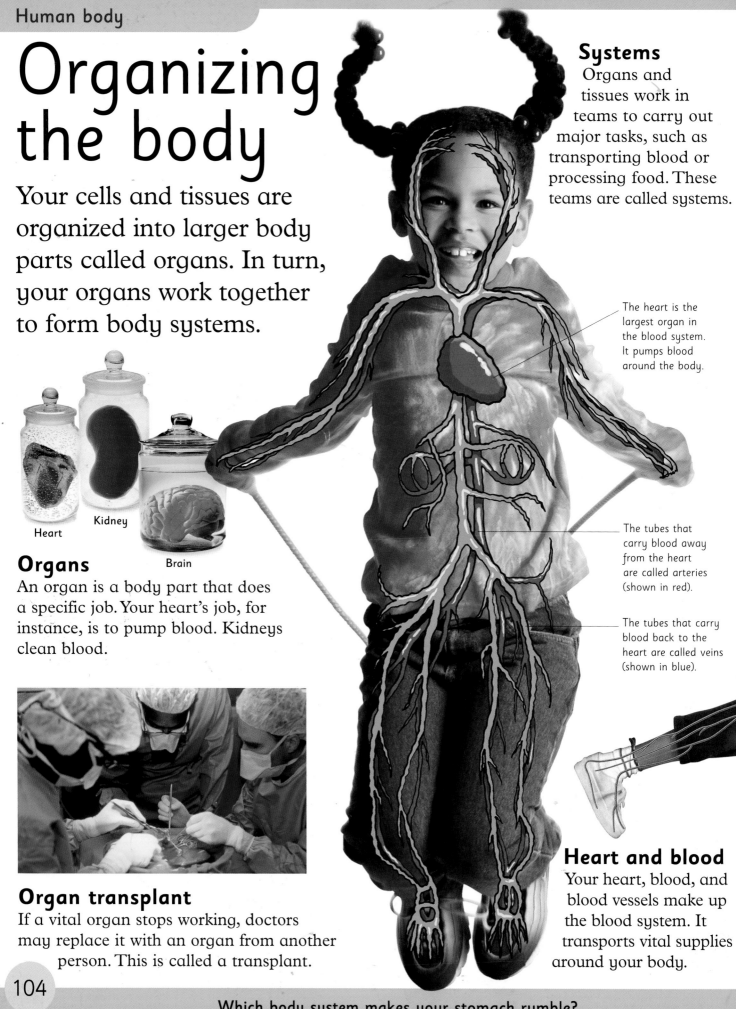

Systems
Organs and tissues work in teams to carry out major tasks, such as transporting blood or processing food. These teams are called systems.

The heart is the largest organ in the blood system. It pumps blood around the body.

Heart

Kidney

Brain

Organs
An organ is a body part that does a specific job. Your heart's job, for instance, is to pump blood. Kidneys clean blood.

The tubes that carry blood away from the heart are called arteries (shown in red).

The tubes that carry blood back to the heart are called veins (shown in blue).

Organ transplant
If a vital organ stops working, doctors may replace it with an organ from another person. This is called a transplant.

Heart and blood
Your heart, blood, and blood vessels make up the blood system. It transports vital supplies around your body.

Which body system makes your stomach rumble?

Muscles

Your muscle system is made of tissues that move parts of your body by pulling on them or squeezing them. Your biggest muscles all pull on bones.

Your fingers are moved by muscles in your arm.

Muscles change the position of your skeleton by pulling different bones.

The most powerful muscles are in your legs.

Other systems

Some of your other important systems are shown in this list.

In the **breathing system**, the main organs are your lungs, which take in air.

The **hormone system** uses powerful chemicals to control your body and mood.

Skin, hair, and nails, form your body's protective covering.

The **immune system** seeks and destroys germs that get into your body.

The **urinary system** cleans blood and gets rid of waste chemicals.

The **reproductive system** are the organs that make babies.

Skeleton

Bones and joints make up the skeletal system, an inner frame that supports the body.

A quarter of your bones are in your feet.

Nerves

Your nervous system carries electrical signals around your body. You need this system to see, hear, think, and react.

Signals shoot along nerves to muscles, telling them when to pull.

enses, such as touch, rely on erve cells that end signals to your brain.

Your brain is the nervous system's control centre.

Digestive system

Your digestive organs break down food to provide your body with energy and raw materials.

Your mouth is the first part of the digestive system.

A long, twisting tube makes up your intestines, where digested food is absorbed.

The digestive system.

105

Bones and muscles

You would be like a lump of jelly without your skeleton – a frame of bones that holds you up and protects your internal organs.

Skull

Ribcage

Backbone

Bending backbone

Your backbone contains 24 small bones called vertebrae. They move almost every time you do.

The vertebrae in your back allow you to twist and bend.

The wrist is made up of eight small bones.

Cranium

Head case

The bones that make up your skull join after you are born. The skull has two parts – the lower jaw and cranium. Only your jaw can move.

Lower jaw

The hip is a ball and socket joint, allowing the legs to move around.

Bone marrow supplies your body with red blood cells.

The honeycomb structure of some bones make them weigh less than if they were solid.

Both the knee and elbow are hinged joints that only move in one direction.

Brilliant bone

Bones have a clever structure that makes them light but strong. They can heal themselves if broken.

Snake ribcages can run almost the entire length of their bodies.

Ribcage

A ribcage has long, curved bones that protect vital organs such as the heart and lungs.

How many bones does an adult human have?

Bending bits

Different kinds of joints all over your body keep you moving.

 Fingers and **thumbs** have joints that allow them to move in many ways.

 Ankles contain different joints for up-and-down and side-to-side movement.

 Wrists have a joint that allows them to turn but not go all the way round.

 Neck bones feature a pivot joint that allows your head to turn.

Muscle magic

Muscles are rubbery, stretchy straps. You can control some of your muscles, like the muscles in your arms and legs. Others, such as your heart and bladder, operate without you having to think about it.

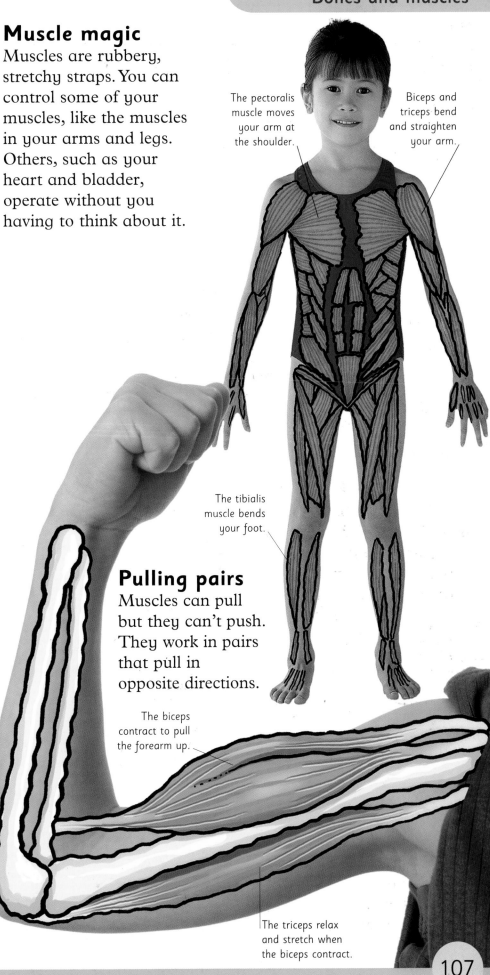

The pectoralis muscle moves your arm at the shoulder.

Biceps and triceps bend and straighten your arm.

The tibialis muscle bends your foot.

Making faces

Muscles in your face are attached to skin as well as bone. They allow you to make all kinds of expressions to show how you are feeling.

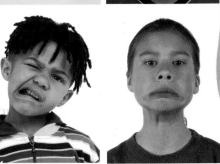

Pulling pairs

Muscles can pull but they can't push. They work in pairs that pull in opposite directions.

The biceps contract to pull the forearm up.

The triceps relax and stretch when the biceps contract.

107

There are 206 bones in an adult skeleton.

You use your brain to think.

Brain and senses

Your brain is the part of your body that makes you think, feel, and remember. It makes sure that the rest of you works properly.

Your brain
Your brain is hidden inside your head. It looks a little bit like a soft, wrinkly lump of greyish-pink blancmange, or jelly.

Your hard, bony skull protects your brain from damage.

Nerves
Your brain is linked to your body by fibres called nerves. Nerves carry messages from your body to your brain, and back again.

A bundle of nerves runs down your back, inside your backbone.

Your brain weighs about the same as 12 apples.

If you prick your finger, your brain makes you feel pain.

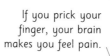

Reflex actions
If you accidentally prick your finger on a rose thorn, your brain quickly makes you pull your hand away. This fast reaction is called a reflex action.

Do clever people have bigger brains?

Your senses

You know what is happening around you by seeing, hearing, smelling, tasting, and touching things. These are called your senses.

Your eyes see the pictures, then your brain tells you what they are.

Eyes and seeing

Your eyes have special nerves that pick up light. They send messages to your brain, telling you what you are looking at.

Your ears pick up loud and soft sounds.

Different parts do different jobs.

Ears and hearing

Your ears catch sounds and send them deep inside your head. Nerves send messages about the sounds to your brain.

Nose and smelling

Nerves inside your nose tell you what you are smelling. Some things, such as this shoe, smell terrible. Other things smell nice!

Tongue and tasting

You taste with your tongue. It is covered with tiny bumps, called taste buds, which pick up tastes from your food.

Skin and touch

Nerves in your skin tell you if things feel hard, soft, hot, or cold. They also warn you of danger by making you feel pain.

Brown sugar   Grapes   Spaghetti

Can you tell what you are touching, without looking?

No. Everyone's brain is about the same size.

Breathing

We have to breathe all the time in order to supply our bodies with oxygen and to get rid of carbon dioxide. We use our lungs to do this.

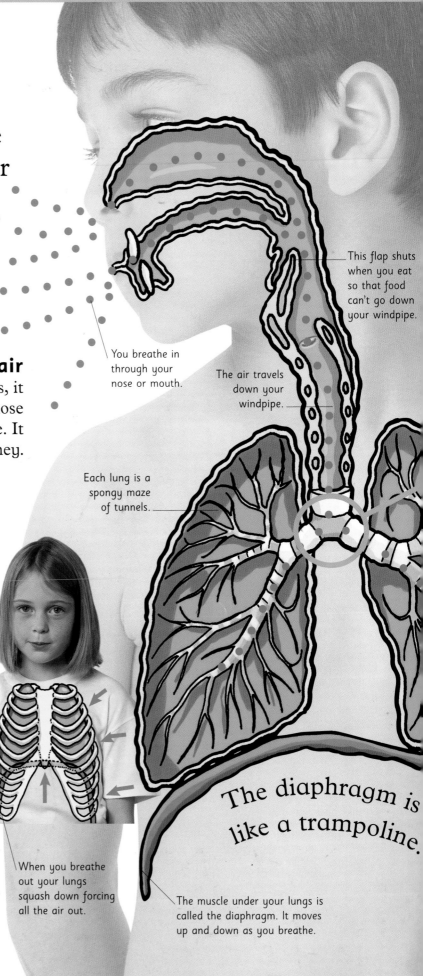

This flap shuts when you eat so that food can't go down your windpipe.

You breathe in through your nose or mouth.

The air travels down your windpipe.

Each lung is a spongy maze of tunnels.

Prepare the air

Before the air reaches your lungs, it travels through your mouth and nose and then goes down your windpipe. It gets warm and damp on its journey.

When you breathe in, your lungs stretch out and take in lots of air.

When you breathe out your lungs squash down forcing all the air out.

The diaphragm is like a trampoline.

The muscle under your lungs is called the diaphragm. It moves up and down as you breathe.

In and out

Your ribs and diaphragm help you to breathe. Your lungs fill with air when you raise your ribcage, then empty out when you lower it. A muscle called the diaphragm helps you do this.

How many breaths do you take in a day?

A helping hand
Some newborn babies have trouble breathing. They are put into an enclosed cradle called an incubator. Extra oxygen is pumped into the incubator for them.

No lungs
Not every animal has lungs. There are other ways animals breathe.

The view from the bottom of your windpipe.

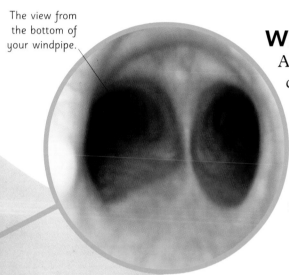

Windpipe
Air from your mouth and nose enters your windpipe, which goes down your throat into your chest. Then it splits into two passages – one for each lung.

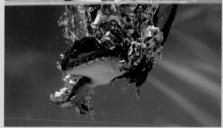

Frogs can absorb oxygen through their skin – even underwater.

The alveoli are surrounded by tiny blood capillaries to take the oxygen round the body.

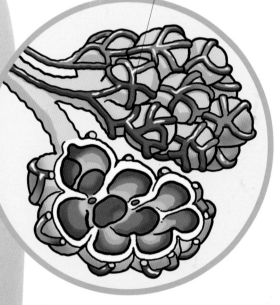

Insects such as caterpillars breathe through body openings called spiracles.

Air sacs
Your lungs are full of tunnels ending in tiny air sacs called alveoli. Here, oxygen from the air passes into your blood. Your blood carries oxygen around every part of your body.

Many sea creatures such as sharks breathe through gills.

About 23,000.

All about skin

Skin covers your whole body. It protects you from germs, water, and sunshine, and helps keep your body at the right temperature.

The skin on your eyelids is the thinnest on your body.

Two layers

Your skin has two main layers. The top one – the one you can see – is called the epidermis. Underneath is the dermis, where there are nerves and blood vessels.

There are flat cells on the surface of your skin. These are made from a tough material called keratin. When the cells die, they dry out and flake off.

Skin cells lower down replace the dead ones that flake off.

Waterproof seal

Skin stops water getting into your body when you have a shower or go for a swim. It also stops fluids escaping from inside you.

Magnified skin flakes

Heavy load

Skin is the heaviest single part of your body. It can weigh as much as a bag of shopping.

Skin is a sort of stretchy overcoat.

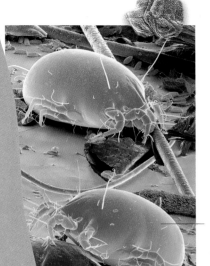

House dust

Dust is mostly made of dead skin. Dust mites feed on this skin. They live in beds, pillows, and carpets.

Dust mites aren't really this big! They're so small, you can't see them without a magnifying glass.

The thickest skin on...

How many dead skin flakes fall off every day?

Sweat

Sweat pore

Sweat gland

If you uncurled a sweat gland, it could be over 1 m (3 ft) long.

Skin colour

The colour of your skin is affected by a substance called melanin. The more melanin you have, the darker you will be. When you are outside in the sun, your body produces extra melanin to protect your skin. This melanin makes your skin darker and you get a suntan.

... your body is on the soles of your feet.

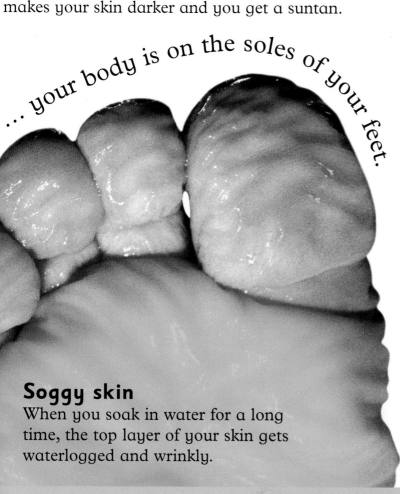

Soggy skin

When you soak in water for a long time, the top layer of your skin gets waterlogged and wrinkly.

Cooling down

When sweat dries on your skin, it helps to cool you down. Sweat comes from coiled tubes under the surface. It gets out through tiny holes called pores.

Body defences

Although you can't see them, germs are always landing on your body and trying to get inside it. Your body has lots of clever ways of keeping them out.

Poison tears

Germs that land on your eyes are washed away by tears, which come from glands above your eyes. Tears contain the chemical lysozyme, which kills bacteria by making them burst open.

You make about 1 litre (2 pints) of saliva a day.

Saved by spit

The liquid in your mouth is called saliva. As well as helping you digest food, saliva protects your mouth, tongue, and teeth from attack by bacteria.

Earwax flows slowly out of your ears all the time, flushing out dirt and germs.

Sticky business

Germs get into your lungs when you breathe in. They get trapped in a sticky liquid called mucus, which lines your airways. Tiny beating hairs continually push the mucus up to your throat to be swallowed.

114

Which is your largest defensive organ?

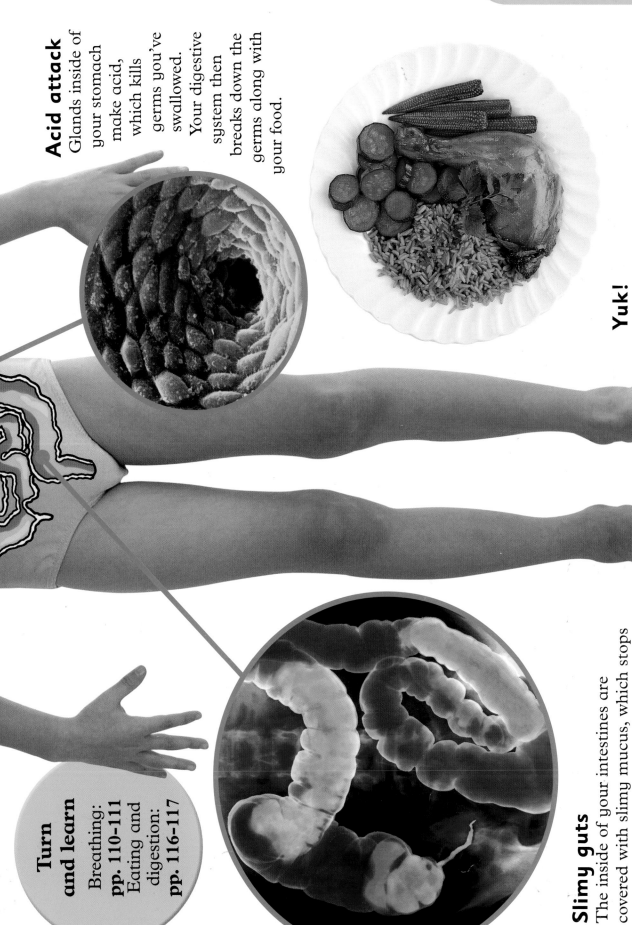

Acid attack

Glands inside of your stomach make acid, which kills germs you've swallowed. Your digestive system then breaks down the germs along with your food.

Yuk!

The feeling of disgust protects you from germs. Anything that smells revolting or looks horrible is probably full of germs. Disgust stops you from touching it.

Turn and learn

Breathing: **pp. 110–111**
Eating and digestion: **pp. 116–117**

Slimy guts

The inside of your intestines are covered with slimy mucus, which stops germs from getting into your blood. Your large intestine also contains millions of "friendly" bacteria, which prevent other germs from growing.

Eating and digestion

Your body needs food to keep it working. But before it can use the food, it breaks it into tiny pieces, which seep into your blood. This is called digestion.

Teeth

Tongue

Mouth

In your mouth, your teeth chop up and chew your food. Your spit helps to break food down and makes it easy to swallow. When you swallow, your food goes down a tube in your throat and into your stomach.

Turn and learn
Carbon cycle: **pp. 222–223**
What is energy?: **pp. 234–235**

Your food travels through your body...

This tube diagram is not the same shape as the tubes inside your body.

This photograph of part of the stomach lining was taken through a microscope.

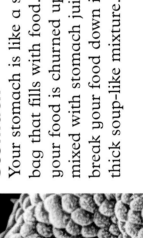

Stomach

Your stomach is like a stretchy bag that fills with food. Inside, your food is churned up and mixed with stomach juices. They break your food down into a thick soup-like mixture.

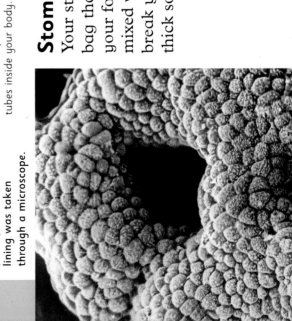

116

Intestines

Next, your food goes into long tubes called your intestines. It seeps through the walls of the intestines into your blood. Your blood takes the nutrients (goodness) in the food around your body.

Small intestine

This intestine is called your "small" intestine because it is narrow. In fact, it is as long as a bus!

Stomach

Small intestine

Large intestine

You get rid of waste water and solid waste when you go to the toilet.

Getting rid of waste

Any waste food travels from your small intestine into your large intestine. It is stored there until you go to the toilet and push it out as solid waste.

Your small and large intestines are coiled up inside your abdomen.

A meal takes about three days to pass all the way through your digestive system.

... along a series of pipes and tubes.

Your mouth, stomach, and intestines are called your digestive system.

A balanced diet

You need to eat a mixture of foods to keep you strong and healthy. This is called a balanced diet.

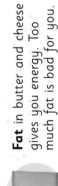

Carbohydrates, such as pasta, rice, and bread, give you lots of energy.

Protein in foods such as milk, meat, and nuts helps you to grow.

Vitamins in fruit and vegetables keep your body working properly.

Fibre in brown bread and vegetables keeps your digestive system working.

Fat in butter and cheese gives you energy. Too much fat is bad for you.

Because of air mixed up with your food.

Making a baby

You need a mother and a father to make a baby. The mother's body does most of the work, but the father also has an important job – his sperm joins with the mother's egg and a new life begins...

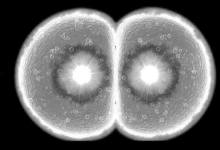

The first cells
After 36 hours, the cell has divided and made an exact copy of itself. These are the first two cells of a baby.

Eggs are the biggest cells in the human body. But they are still very small – 10 would fit across a pinhead.

Sperm look like tiny tadpoles. Under a microscope, you can see their tails wriggling as they swim.

By the time the baby is born, the fertilized cell will have become 100 trillion cells.

Sperm race
Millions of sperm swim towards the egg cell. Only one sperm can join with the egg to make a new cell.

What is another name for the uterus?

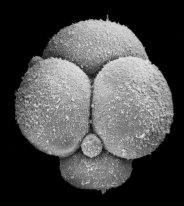

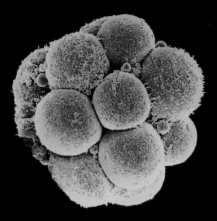

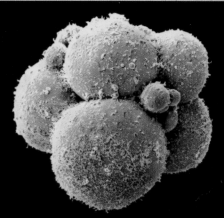

Divide again
You don't grow much in the first few days. The two cells divide to make four, then eight, and so on.

At three days
The cells have carried on dividing. There are now 16 cells and they are almost ready to plant themselves in the uterus.

The future you
Each cell is unique to you. Cells are full of instructions about what you will look like.

Where it all happens
The sperm fertilizes the egg in a tunnel, called a Fallopian tube. The fertilized egg moves down the tunnel towards the mother's uterus. The journey takes about five days.

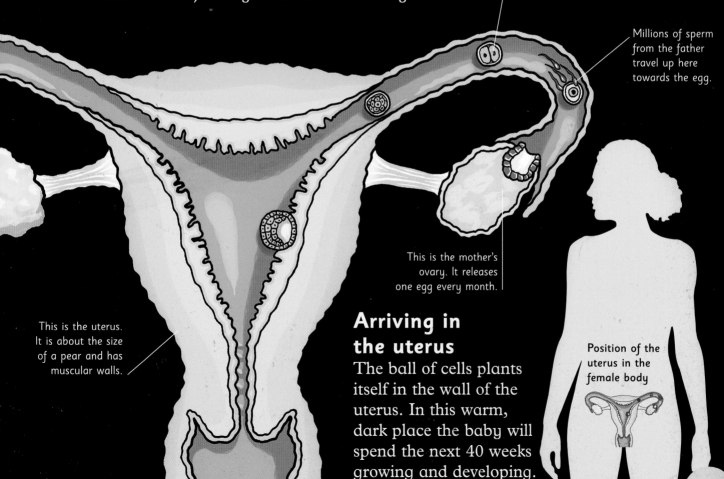

The cells start dividing as they move down the Fallopian tube towards the uterus.

Millions of sperm from the father travel up here towards the egg.

This is the mother's ovary. It releases one egg every month.

This is the uterus. It is about the size of a pear and has muscular walls.

Arriving in the uterus
The ball of cells plants itself in the wall of the uterus. In this warm, dark place the baby will spend the next 40 weeks growing and developing.

Position of the uterus in the female body

119

Amazing facts about YOU!

Skeleton and bones

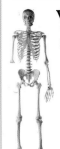

Without a skeleton to hold you up, you'd collapse on the ground like a heap of jelly.

Your smallest bone is the stapes in your ear, which is smaller than a rice grain.

Weight for weight, bones are stronger than steel or concrete.

A baby has more than 300 bones but adults have only 206.

Muscles and movement

Muscles move your body by pulling bones. You use hundreds of them when you walk.

Every hair in your body has a tiny muscle that can pull it upright.

Your strongest muscle is the masseter (jaw muscle), which closes your mouth.

You use more muscles when you frown than when you smile.

Brain and nerves

Your brain is the body's control centre. Signals zoom to and from the brain along your nerves.

Nerves carry signals at up to 400 kph (250 mph).

Your brain is made of about 100 billion tiny cells called neurons.

The left side of your brain controls the right side of your body and vice versa.

The human eye can see a candle flame at night from 1.6 km (1 mile) away.

When you're bored, the pupils in your eyes get smaller.

Heart and blood

Your heart pumps blood around your body. It works nonstop without getting tired.

Your smallest blood vessels are ten times thinner than a hair.

Your body contains enough blood vessels to circle the world twice.

Breathing

Lungs take air into your body so that life-giving oxygen can enter your blood.

Laid out, the inside of your lungs is a third as big as a tennis court.

The fastest recorded sneeze reached 167 kph (104 mph).

In one day, you breathe in enough air to fill 33,000 drink cans.

Skin, nails and hair

The tough, protective surface of your body is almost entirely dead.

Every four years, you shed your own body weight in dead skin.

You have about 5 million hairs, but only 100,000 are on your head.

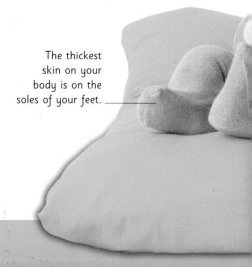
The thickest skin on your body is on the soles of your feet.

Fighting disease

Germs are always trying to get inside you, but your body fights back.

The dangerous lassa fever kills about a fifth of its victims.

Bacteria are so small that 1,000 could fit on the head of a pin.

The world's most common disease is the common cold.

Cancer happens when your own cells multiply out of control.

When you recover from an infectious disease, your body usually becomes immune to it.

Digestive system

Digestion turns food into simple chemicals that your body can make into new cells or use for fuel.

The food you eat in a year weighs as much as a car.

You make enough spit in your lifetime to fill two swimming pools.

Your digestive glands start working as soon as you smell or see food.

Your tongue senses five tastes: salty, sweet, sour, bitter, and umami.

The smell of poo comes from a chemical called skatole.

Urinary system

Urine gets rid of chemicals that your body doesn't need.

You will make enough urine in your lifetime to fill 500 baths.

Asparagus can turn your urine green. Blackberries can turn it red.

Reproduction

The reproductive organs create new people from tiny specks of matter.

The most babies born to one mother is 69. Most were twins, triplets, or quads.

The first quintuplets known to have survived infancy were born in 1934.

Growth

As you grow, you slowly change into an adult, but it takes a long time!

The fastest-growing part of a baby's body is its head.

A girl is about three-quarters of her adult height at 7 years old.

A boy is about three-quarters of his adult height at 9 years old.

Each hair on your head grows for about seven years and then falls out. A new one grows in its place.

The living world

Our amazing world is filled with millions of species, or types, of living thing. They can be as big as elephants or so small that you have to look through a microscope to see them.

Spider

Dragonfly

Animals
The animal kingdom is made up of vertebrates (animals with a backbone) and invertebrates (animals without a backbone).

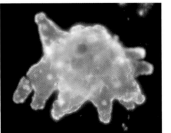

Micro-organisms
Micro-organisms are very tiny – each of them is made up of a single cell. This amoeba has been magnified more than 100 times.

Coral reef, home to a variety of living organisms

Mammals, birds, reptiles, amphibians, and fish are vertebrates.

Sunflower

Deer

122

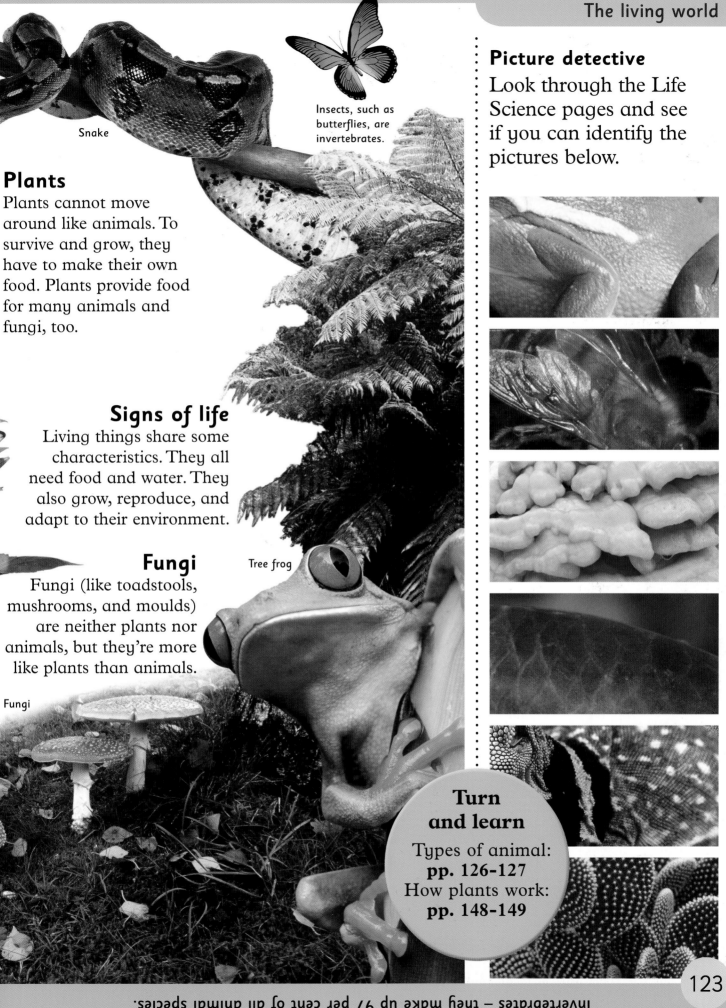

Snake

Insects, such as butterflies, are invertebrates.

Plants

Plants cannot move around like animals. To survive and grow, they have to make their own food. Plants provide food for many animals and fungi, too.

Signs of life

Living things share some characteristics. They all need food and water. They also grow, reproduce, and adapt to their environment.

Fungi

Fungi (like toadstools, mushrooms, and moulds) are neither plants nor animals, but they're more like plants than animals.

Fungi

Tree frog

Picture detective

Look through the Life Science pages and see if you can identify the pictures below.

Turn and learn

Types of animal: **pp. 126-127**
How plants work: **pp. 148-149**

Invertebrates – they make up 97 per cent of all animal species.

What is an animal?

A key definition of an animal, as opposed to a plant, is that most animals can move voluntarily. Animals must also eat other living things to survive. Let's take a look at some of the things animals do.

Bald eagle

Food is fuel

All animals have to find and eat food to survive. Carnivores are animals that eat meat. Herbivores eat mainly plants. Omnivores are creatures that eat both plants and meat.

Squirrels eat seeds, nuts, fruits, and fungi.

Getting around

Many animals have muscles, which allow them to move in a variety of ways.

Birds **fly** by flapping wings or gliding on currents of hot air.

Animals like fish **swim** by moving their bodies and fins.

Some snakes **wriggle**, others raise and flatten their bodies.

Many animals **walk** and **run** using their legs.

Sea anemones **reach out** their tentacles to sting prey.

What a nerve!

Animals have nerves, which carry information from their sense organs. Most animals have brains to monitor this information. The nerves also carry orders from the brain to the organs and muscles – such as instructions to stay still, attack, or run away!

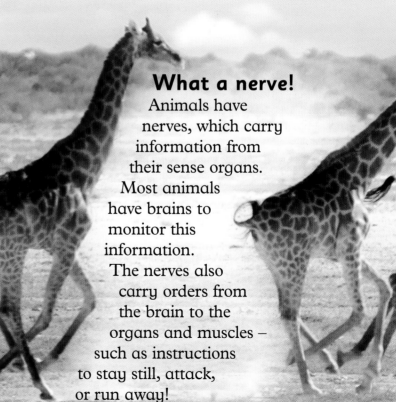

How many species of animal are there on the Earth?

Pythons can go without food for months after one big meal!

Do animals talk?

Many animals are able to communicate with each other using either sounds or signals.

Most beetles will send "messages" to other beetles using special chemicals.

Making babies

Most animals reproduce when a female egg is fertilized by a male sperm. Some animals give birth to babies, while others lay eggs.

Birds lay hard-shelled eggs, which hatch into chicks or ducklings.

Baby birds have to break out of the egg on their own.

Honey bees constantly communicate. They give directions with a special dance.

Giraffes have seven vertebrae in their necks – the same as most other mammals. They are just much longer.

Monkeys scream at each other to sound an alarm.

Types of animal

There are many different types, or species, of animals. Scientists put them in groups based on their similar characteristics. Mammals, birds, reptiles, amphibians, and fish are vertebrates. Creepy-crawlies are invertebrates.

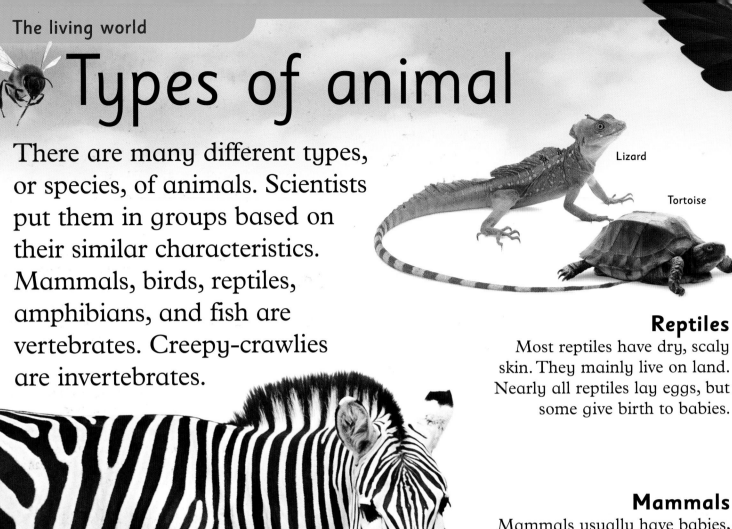

Lizard

Tortoise

Reptiles

Most reptiles have dry, scaly skin. They mainly live on land. Nearly all reptiles lay eggs, but some give birth to babies.

Mammals

Mammals usually have babies, which feed on their mother's milk when they're born. Mammals often have fur on their bodies. Humans are mammals.

Zebra

Wolf

Mouse

Lion cub

Deer fawn

Which is the only mammal that can fly?

Parrot

Birds
All birds have wings, and most (but not all) can fly. They have feathers and a beak. Baby birds hatch from eggs.

Ostriches can run fast but can't fly.

Amphibians
Amphibians live both in water and on land. They usually have slimy skin. Baby amphibians hatch from jelly-like eggs.

Salamander

Frog

Spineless creatures
Animals without backbones are called invertebrates. There are several types of invertebrate.

 Insects, spiders, and **crustaceans** are part of the largest animal group.

 Snails and **slugs** are part of an invertebrate group called gastropods.

 Worms have long, soft bodies and no legs. They like damp areas.

 Jellyfish, starfish, and **sponges** are invertebrates that live in water.

 Octopus and **squid** live in the sea. They have eight arms.

Butterfly

Ladybird

Fish
Fish need to live in water. They breathe through gills, and most are covered in scales. Fish use their fins to move through water.

Insects
There are more types of insect on the Earth than any other animal. There are species of insects living almost everywhere. They have six legs and bodies with three sections.

127

The world of mammals

Mammals include animals such as the whale, the kangaroo, and you and me! We all have fur, we are warm-blooded, and we feed new babies our milk.

Gorilla skeleton

The skeleton

Mammals may look very different, but stripped back to the bone, we all have the basic bony skeleton. Scientists call us vertebrates – animals with a backbone.

Mammal babies

Most mammal females give birth to live babies, rather than laying eggs. The baby grows inside the mother's body until it is born.

Feeding babies

All female mammals produce milk from their bodies that they feed to their babies; this feeding is called suckling. The milk helps babies to grow.

Turn and learn

Marsupials: **pp. 130–131**
Water mammals: **pp. 132–133**

Gorillas are members of the primate family.

Baby gorilla

Within the mammal group, there are many different families.

How many mammal families are there?

Polar bears can live in chilly Arctic regions because they are warm-blooded and have thick fur.

Hairy beasts

All mammals have hairy bodies, though some are much hairier than others. This hair, or fur, keeps them warm.

Elephant trunk

This elephant may not look hairy but it does have hair on its body.

Warm blood

Mammals are warm-blooded, which means they can warm up and cool down their bodies to keep their temperature level. An elephant in the hot jungle has the same temperature as a polar bear in the snow.

Polar bears have thick fur all over their bodies.

Getting around

Mammals have developed different ways of moving about.

Some mammals, such as **cats**, have long legs to run with.

Bats are the only mammals that can fly – they have wings.

Dolphins are sea mammals, and have flippers and strong tails to swim with.

Moles have feet like spades, which are useful for burrowing.

Polar bear

The odd one out

It is usually true that animals give birth to live babies, but there are a few species, including this duck-billed platypus, that lay eggs. Platypus eggs are soft and the size of marbles.

There are 153 different mammal families in the world.

Marsupials

A marsupial is a mammal with a pocket, called a pouch, for carrying its babies in.

Koala

Koalas look like little bears. They live in Australia and are the only animal that eats eucalyptus leaves. They are so hard to digest that koalas spend 19 hours of the day sleeping to let their tummies settle.

More marsupials

Apart from a few that live in South America, almost all marsupials come from Australasia. They vary a lot in looks.

Dorian's tree kangaroo: this small kangaroo can climb trees.

Numbat: this marsupial feeds almost entirely on ant-like termites.

Rabbit-eared bandicoot: These large-eared burrowers are most active at night.

Little devil

The Tasmanian devil is not much bigger than a small dog but it is very aggressive. It is the biggest meat-eating marsupial and has such powerful jaws that it can eat the entire animal – bones and all!

A kangaroo's front legs are...

Bouncing marsupials

Kangaroos cannot walk. Instead they have enormous back legs that they use to jump everywhere. They can move very fast just by leaping.

Turn and learn

Australia:
pp. 52-53
The world of mammals:
pp. 128-129

Which are bigger, wallabies or kangaroos?

Supermum!

Opossums live in the Americas. Unusually for marsupials, the mother has no pouch. Instead, her babies cling to her. Sometimes one mother can have up to 20 babies at one time!

Opossums are very good tree climbers.

The joey belonging to this mother is definitely big enough to climb out of its pouch.

In the pouch

Most marsupials have pouches. When the babies are born, they are as small as beans and wriggle straight into the pouch. They do most of their growing there, instead of in their mother's tummy.

Little joey

Kangaroo and wallaby babies are commonly known as joeys. They spend several months in the mother's pouch, and even when they are big enough to walk, they sometimes jump back in for safety.

... not used when it hops.

Their huge tails help to balance them when they hop.

131

Kangaroos look like wallabies, but they are bigger.

Water mammals

Not all mammals live on land – some live in water. Unlike fish, however, water mammals have to go to the surface to breathe.

Seals

Seals, which include sea lions and walruses, have flippers instead of arms and legs. These make them very good at swimming but not good at walking.

Sea lions can walk more easily than other seals because their flippers are able to move in several directions.

Underwater lives

Seals spend most of their lives in water, but return to land to have babies. They have a thick layer of fat, called blubber, which keeps them warm.

Seals are often very playful in the water.

132

What noise do seals make?

Otters

Otters are mammals that have webbed feet to help them swim. The river otter lives along river banks and spends its day swimming to catch food.

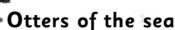

Otters of the sea

The sea otter is the smallest sea mammal. It has luxurious, thick fur that keeps it very warm. It rarely comes to land, and even sleeps in the water. When it nods off, it wraps itself up in kelp plants to stop it from drifting away!

Sea cows

Manatees are often called sea cows because they are so big and they "graze" on underwater plants. They spend all their lives in water, and even give birth there.

Walruses use their noses, like pigs, to root around the sea floor for food, such as crabs or sea urchins.

Walruses

Walruses are huge sea mammals. They have powerful, blubbery bodies and two large, front teeth, called tusks, which can grow up to 1 m (3 ft) long. Their tusks help them cut through ice sheets and keep enemies away.

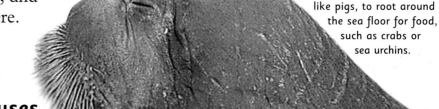

In the pink

Walruses are normally greyish brown in colour. But when they sunbathe, they turn blush-pink because their blood rushes to the surface of their skin to cool it down.

Seals bark like dogs!

The world of birds

Only a few animals in the world are able to fly – insects, bats, and birds. But none of them are more powerful or skilled than birds.

Feathers are made up of tiny hair-like barbs that all mesh together.

Feathered friends

Birds are the only creatures that have feathers. They use them to fly and to keep warm. Some birds use brightly coloured feathers for display.

A rigid "backbone", or quill, runs through the centre of the wing feathers, strengthening them for flying.

Feathers

Different feathers have different jobs on a bird.

Outer wing: strong feathers to provide power in flight.

Inner wing: has smooth and flat feathers to help in flight.

Tail feather: long and thin for steering and balancing during flight.

Body feather: soft and downy to keep a bird warm. Some have exotic colours.

Birds spend much of their time looking after, or preening, their feathers to keep them in good condition.

What is the world's smallest bird?

Flight

Birds that can fly have wings and a very light skeleton – many of the bones are hollow. Their short and compact bodies also help make them neat fliers.

By flapping its wings up and down, the bird remains in the air.

There are two methods of flying; flapping, like this red-tailed minla, and gliding.

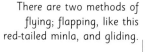

Red-tailed minla

Travelling birds

About one-third of birds spend summer in one place then when the winter sets in they fly thousands of miles to a warmer spot. Often they go to exactly the same places year after year.

Feet

The shapes of birds' feet vary in different habitats.

Eagle foot: birds of prey have sharp talons to kill and grip animals.

Perching foot: songbirds have three toes in front and one behind for perching.

Webbed foot: waterfowl have webbed feet to help them to paddle on water.

Ostrich foot: two thick toes help this flightless bird to run very fast.

Bills

The shape and size of a bird's bill, or beak, show what they eat.

Duck: wide and flat to tear plants and filter food underwater.

Woodpecker: long and hard to chisel into wood and pick out insects.

Chaffinch: short and cone-shaped, ideal for cracking seeds.

Heron: ideal for stabbing fish underwater.

Communication

All birds have good hearing so they can respond to songs from other members of their family. Birds are well known for their tunes, and some, like this parrot, even speak.

The world of reptiles

Reptiles are mainly egg-laying animals that have a tough skin covered in scales. They live on land and in water.

The reptile groups

There are four main groups of reptiles.

The tortoise family: these reptiles all have a shell over their bodies.

Snakes and lizards: the majority of reptiles fall into this group.

The crocodile family: this group are the giants of the reptile world.

Tuataras: these reptiles are very rare and look a bit like lizards.

Eating habits

Most reptiles are meat-eaters, apart from tortoises, which move too slowly to catch fast-moving prey. Lizards, such as this gecko, can eat half their own weight in insects in one night.

Reptiles can eat huge meals, then go without food for days.

All reptiles shed their skin from time to time.

Most reptiles, like this lizard, swing their bodies from side to side when walking.

Flying gecko

Hot and cold

Reptiles have scales, which can control how much water they lose through their skin. This means they can live in dry places. They are, however, cold-blooded, and so rely on the climate to keep their bodies warm.

European eyed lizard

Reptile babies

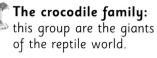

Nearly all reptiles lay eggs, which hatch into miniature versions of their parents. However, a few, such as this slow worm, give birth to live young.

This lizard, which lives in the desert, basks on rocks to warm up its body.

136

Tuataras live in burrows and hunt at night. They can live for 100 years.

Living fossils

Tuataras are the only survivors of a group of reptiles that lived with the dinosaurs millions of years ago. Today, they live on a group of islands off New Zealand.

Scaly skin

A reptile's skin is covered with scales made of keratin, like your nails.

Tortoise: the shell of a tortoise has lots of large, hard scales on it.

Lizard: lizards' scales have stretchy skin between them.

Crocodile: these scales are strengthened in between by bony plates.

Snake: the skin on snakes has overlapping scales for extra protection.

Reptile relatives

The reptiles of today are living relatives of dinosaurs and look very similar to their ancient ancestors. You can see similarities between the *Tyrannosaurus rex* and this lizard.

Tyrannosaurus rex

Collared lizard

Turn and learn

The world of amphibians:
pp. 138-139
The world of fish:
pp. 144-145

The reticulated python can reach lengths of 10 m (33 ft).

The world of amphibians

Amphibians are different from reptiles in that they have smooth skin with no scales. They are born in water, then live on land or in water when they grow up.

Fire salamander

Amphibians

There are three main types of amphibians.

Frogs and toads have big black legs and no tail.

Salamanders and newts are lizard-shaped animals that live on land or in water.

Caecilians are worm-like creatures that have no legs.

Amazing skin

Most adult amphibians, such as this salamander, can breathe through their skin as well as their lungs. In order for the skin to breathe it has to be kept moist, which is why most amphibians like to live near water.

Turn and learn

Other creepy-crawlies: pp. 142-143
The world of fish: pp. 144-145

Colourful creatures

Many amphibians are incredibly colourful creatures. Some are spotted, others are striped, and some are just very bright.

What is the world's most poisonous frog?

A choice of home

Frogs and toads can live both on land and in water. Some even live in trees.

Land frogs tend to be more rounded in shape than water frogs.

Some frogs live in the tops of tall trees.

Water living

Some salamanders spend the whole of their lives underwater. This cave salamander does not have any lungs; it breathes using gills, like a fish. It is almost blind.

Caecilians

Legless caecilians are rarely seen by humans because they live either underwater or underground. They have a pointed head, which they use as a shovel.

Tomato frogs

If an animal is poisonous it is often a very bright colour that warns predators.

Common newt

Travelling parents

Each spring salamanders, newts, frogs, and toads lay their eggs in ponds or streams. Some travel 5 km (3 miles) to get there.

The most poisonous frog is the golden poison dart frog.

The world of insects

A huge majority of creepy-crawlies are insects. In fact, there are more types of insect in the world than any other animal. They are absolutely everywhere. Some are almost too small to see while others are surprisingly large.

Most insects have two pairs of wings.

Beetle

When a pile of dung appears in Africa, dung beetles are on the scene in minutes.

What is an insect?
You can tell if a creepy-crawly is an insect because insects always have six legs. They also have three body parts – a head, a thorax, and an abdomen.

Nature's recycling service
Although many people dislike insects and they can be pests, they are also essential to our world. In fact, we could not live without them. For instance, dung beetles do a very good job cleaning up dung.

The beetles roll perfect balls of dung in which they lay a single egg. When the egg hatches, the baby eats the dung.

Dung beetle

Apart from honey, what else does a bee produce that we can use?

Useful insects

Here are some other ways that insects are useful to us.

Red food dye: this food colouring is made from the bodies of scale insects.

Silk: believe it or not, the silk you wear is made by silk-moth caterpillars!

Honey: if there were no bees in the world, we would have no honey.

Food: in many cultures around the world, insects such as grubs are a nutritious meal.

Pest control

Sometimes insects, such as aphids, eat huge amounts of our crops. The best way to get rid of them is to introduce another insect that likes to eat them. Ladybirds are often used for aphid pest control.

Aphid

Introducing insects that eat other insects is called biological pest control.

Ladybird

Aphids breed so quickly that it is difficult to control them.

As old as an insect

We know that insects existed 40 million years ago because some were trapped in a tree resin called amber, which hardened and preserved them.

Turn and learn

Other creepy-crawlies:
pp. 142-143
Micro life:
pp. 152-153

Bees produce wax and their venom is used as medicine.

Other creepy-crawlies

There are many creepy-crawlies scuttling around our planet that are not insects. Some live on land, others live in fresh water or the sea. They come in all sorts of weird and wonderful shapes.

Arachnids

Spiders, scorpions, ticks, and mites belong to a land-dwelling family called arachnids. All arachnids have eight legs and two body parts.

The worm family

Segmented worms, such as earthworms, are simple animals that have a head at one end, a tail at the other, and lots of segmented body parts in between. They live on land or in water.

Tarantula

Despite their reputation, most spiders are harmless to humans.

A tarantula has hairs on its legs that can cause irritation to humans. When the spider is annoyed, it flicks them out at the enemy.

How big can spiders grow?

Odd sea creatures

The sea contains some very strange animals. Here are a few:

Sponge: these animals were once thought to be plants.

Starfish: most starfish have five arms to crawl across the sea floor.

Anemone: these flower-like sea animals have no brains.

Snail

Snails are found on land and in the sea.

Molluscs

Slugs, snails, squid, and oysters are molluscs. Some live on land and some live in water.

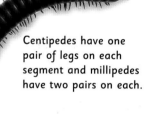

The octopus, which is also a mollusc, is a very intelligent creature.

Centipede

Millipede

Centipedes have one pair of legs on each segment and millipedes have two pairs on each.

Centipedes and millipedes

If you try counting the legs on an insect and you find there are too many, the chances are you have found a centipede or millipede. They have lots and lots of legs.

Crustaceans

Most crustaceans, such as lobsters, crabs, and shrimps, live in water. Only woodlice live on land. They often have a shell and their eyes are on stalks.

Lobster

Some spiders can grow as big as dinner plates!

The world of fish

Fish have been around for 400 million years! They live in seas, rivers, and lakes. Wherever you find water, you can bet there are plenty of fish swimming around.

Types of fish
There are over 30,000 types of fish, which fall into three groups.

Bony fish: 95 per cent of the fish in the world are bony fish with hard skeletons.

Cartilaginous fish: rays, skates, and sharks make up this group.

Jawless fish: only hagfish and lampreys fall into this small group.

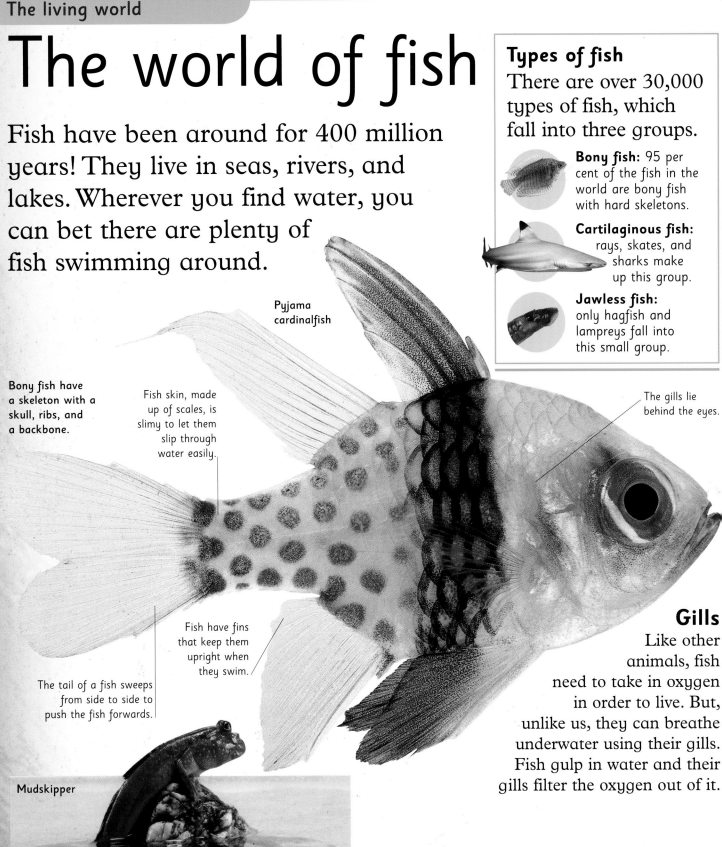

Pyjama cardinalfish

Bony fish have a skeleton with a skull, ribs, and a backbone.

Fish skin, made up of scales, is slimy to let them slip through water easily.

The gills lie behind the eyes.

Fish have fins that keep them upright when they swim.

The tail of a fish sweeps from side to side to push the fish forwards.

Mudskipper

Gills
Like other animals, fish need to take in oxygen in order to live. But, unlike us, they can breathe underwater using their gills. Fish gulp in water and their gills filter the oxygen out of it.

Fish out of water
Mudskippers are one of the few kinds of fish that can survive out of water. They have special gills that take oxygen from air or water. They skip along mudflats using their fins as elbows.

144

Which fish is the slowest in the sea?

The art of swimming

Many fish swim like snakes slide – they wriggle in an "s" shape. Their whole bodies move from side to side and their tails flick to push them forwards. Their fins help to steer them.

Scales

Most fish are covered in hundreds of scales that overlap like roof tiles. Tiny animals can get under the scales and harm them, so fish let others give them a regular clean.

Mandarin fish

Colours can be used for camouflage or to attract a mate.

Some fish can turn on their sides and roll right over. A few can even swim upside down!

Carp

Colour

Fish come in all colours and patterns. Freshwater fish and those living in cooler waters tend to be duller in colour. Tropical fish are sometimes incredibly bright and beautiful.

Eels are found in fresh water and sea water.

Living together

Fish sometimes live in huge groups called shoals. When so many swim together they look like one big fish so they are less likely to be attacked.

Fishy features

Most fish look like the pyjama cardinalfish on the left. Some however have a different appearance. This eel looks more like a snake with fins. Like a snake, it has sharp teeth.

The seahorse is the slowest fish that lives in the sea.

What is a plant?

Plants make their own food from the Sun's rays. Most have leaves that reach outwards to capture sunlight, and roots that dig deep for nutrients and stability.

Seaweed
Seaweed looks like a plant, but is an alga. It doesn't have roots, so it has to stick to rocks or float with the tide.

Plant parts
There are lots of different plants. But most are made of the same vital parts – roots, stems, leaves, and flowers.

The petals attract insects and birds that collect pollen.

The stamen and carpels form the reproductive organs of a plant.

Stems
Stems support the leaves and flowers, and allow water and food to flow from the roots to the leaves.

Flowers
Flowers are key to plant reproduction. They make pollen, and develop seeds and fruit.

Roots
These are the foundations of the plant. They dig deep into the soil, providing stability, as well as sucking up nutrients.

Leaves
These are the work factories of the plant and capture the Sun's energy.

weird or what?
The Venus flytrap doesn't get its energy just from the Sun. It also lures and feeds on unsuspecting insects. Yum!

Water lily
The water lily's flat leaves float on the pond surface, as its roots sink into the pond bed.

What plant has the largest leaves?

Types of plant

Have a look around you. Not all plants are the same. But some plants are more similar than others.

Most conifer trees keep their leaves all year round.

Fern leaves unfurl as they grow.

Ferns

Ferns love damp and shady areas. They have prong-like leaves and spread using spores.

There are about 12,000 species of moss.

Conifers

Conifer trees grow cones that store their seeds. Most conifers have needle-shaped leaves.

The sequoia is the largest tree in the world.

Moss

Mosses love moisture and grow in clumps. They don't have roots or grow flowers.

Leaves

You can identify a tree by the shape of its leaves. In most plants, leaves are broad and flat.

Ash leaf

Maple leaf

Scarlet oak leaf

Flowering plants

This is the biggest group of plants. They produce flowers, fruits and seeds, which mainly grow in seasonal cycles.

Rainforest

These warm and wet forests are home to nearly half the world's plant species.

Deciduous

Deciduous plants shed their leaves to survive drier seasons.

The raffia palm has leaves that grow up to 24 m (79 ft) long.

How plants work

Plants have an amazing system for making and transporting food to all their different parts.

The Sun's energy is trapped in the leaves, and helps make food.

Photosynthesis

Leaves have a green pigment called chlorophyll, which absorbs energy from sunlight. This energy is used to change water and carbon dioxide into sugar.

Cross-section of a leaf vein

Food is moved from leaves to roots and growing tips along a set of tubes called phloem vessels.

A waste product of photosynthesis is oxygen, which animals need to survive.

Some water evaporates through tiny holes, called stomata, on the surface of the leaf. This process is called transpiration.

Tiny tubes, called xylem vessels, carry water up the stem from the roots to the leaves.

Cross-section of a stem

Veins carry water around the leaf.

Roots suck water up from the ground.

Are plants the only organism to use photosynthesis?

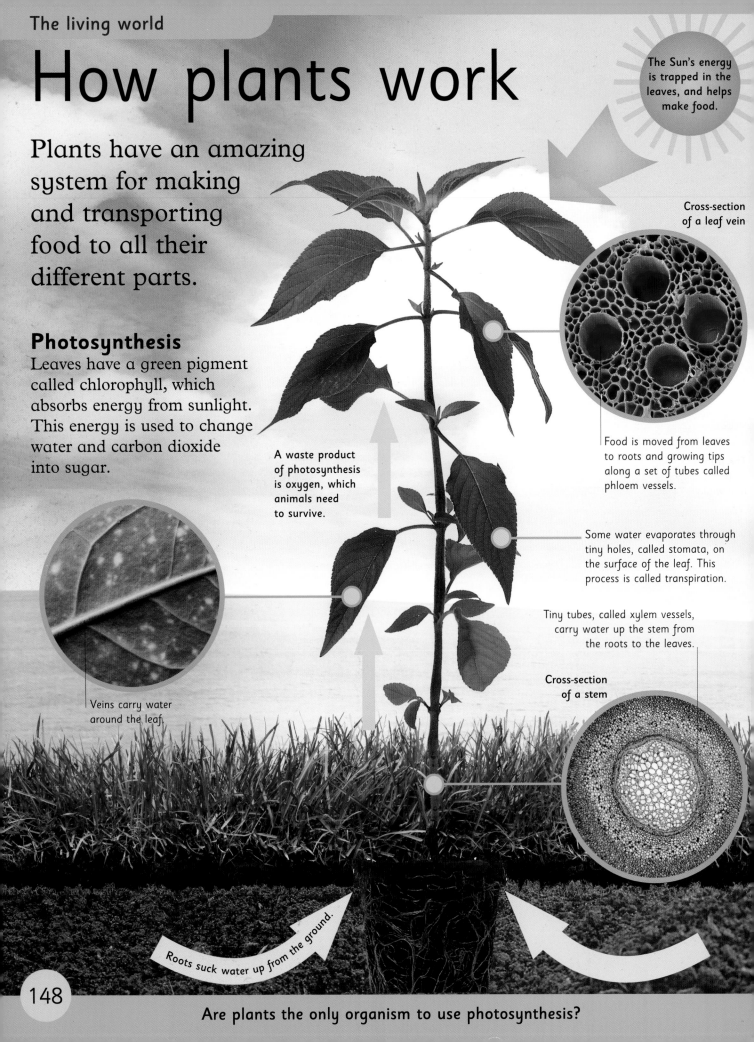

New growth

Plants use sugar and starch as fuel. The fuel is transported to cells where it is burnt to release energy, which is used to grow new cells and repair old ones.

Wilting leaves

On warm, sunny days, plants lose a lot of water from their leaves. If they lose too much, their leaves collapse. This is called wilting. If plants don't get enough water, their leaves will shrivel and die.

Desert plants

Plants that live in dry areas such as deserts have to save their water. Many have leaves that are thick and covered in wax to stop transpiration. Cacti have spines rather than leaves, and thick stems in which they can store water.

Storing food

Spare food is stored for future use. Plants such as hyacinths store food in the base of their leaves. This makes the leaves swell and form a bulb. The bulb survives the winter and in spring it sprouts new leaves.

The fruit acts as a store of sugar and water.

Root

Carrot plants store food in their roots.

Bulb

weird or what? The sea slug *Elysia chlorotica* uses photosynthesis. The slug eats algae that it doesn't fully digest. The remains in its system continue to photosynthesize the food and provide energy.

No, many bacteria also make food by photosynthesis.

Fungi

Mushrooms, toadstools, yeasts, and moulds are kinds of fungi. Fungi are neither animals nor plants. They feed on living or dead animals or plants, and absorb their nutrients.

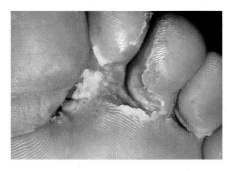

Bread mould

Warm, moist bread

Moulds

Moulds are microscopic fungi which grow in long strands called "hyphae". They feed on dead organic matter – like our food – by making it rot.

Mushrooms

Many fungi are hidden in the soil, or inside food sources like trees. They only become visible when they grow mushrooms. Mushrooms scatter spores, which will grow into new fungi.

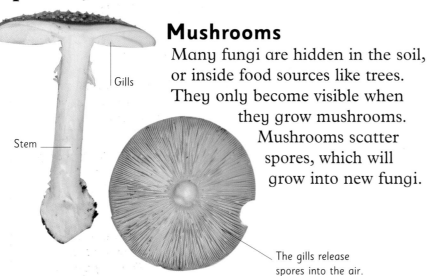

Gills

Stem

The gills release spores into the air.

Athlete's foot

Athlete's foot is a disease caused by ringworm fungi growing on human feet. It makes the skin between your toes turn red and flaky.

Picking wild mushrooms

Many wild mushrooms are not only edible, but also delicious. However, some are highly poisonous! Harmful mushrooms are often called toadstools. They sometimes have bright colours that warn animals not to eat them.

Wood blewit mushroom

Penny bun mushroom

Fly agaric mushrooms

Jelly antler fungus

How big is the world's largest fungus?

Penicillin

In 1928, the Scottish scientist Sir Alexander Fleming made an important discovery. He realized that the mould *Penicillium notatum* makes a chemical that kills bacteria. That chemical, called penicillin, is used today as a medicine to treat many illnesses.

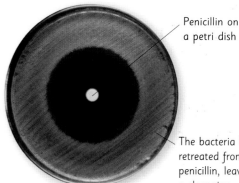

Penicillin on a petri dish

The bacteria have retreated from the penicillin, leaving a clear ring.

Sir Alexander Fleming (1881–1955)

Truffles

Truffles are strong-smelling fungi that grow underground. They are a delicacy used in cookery. Truffle hunters use pigs and dogs to sniff them out.

White truffle

Black perigord truffle

Pig sniffing out mushroom

Yeast

Yeast are microscopic, single-celled fungi. When they feed, they turn sugar into the gas carbon dioxide and alcohol. Yeast plays an important part in bread-making. As it releases gas, it makes bread rise.

Uses of fungi

Fungi have many uses in the home and in industry.

Medicinal fungi can be used to cure many diseases that were once fatal.

Wine is made from grape juice when yeast turns the sugar in the juice into alcohol.

Blue cheese is made with a mould called *Penicillium roquefortii*.

Soy sauce is made by adding fungi and yeast to soy beans and roasted wheat.

Pesticidal fungi can be an environmentally friendly way of killing insects or weeds.

Shaggy parasol mushroom

Shaggy cap mushroom

Common chanterelle mushroom

Chicken of the woods mushroom

A mushroom in the Malheur National Forest, USA, covers 8.9 sq km (3.4 sq miles).

Micro life

Most living things are made up of just one cell, and are too small to see. To study them, we must use powerful microscopes.

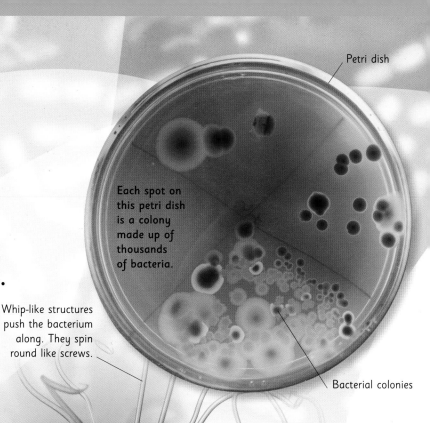

Petri dish

Each spot on this petri dish is a colony made up of thousands of bacteria.

Bacterial colonies

Bacteria

Bacteria are single-celled life forms. They are found in the ocean, in the air, and even in our bodies. They can reproduce very quickly by splitting into two. Some bacteria can make energy from sunlight. However, most feed on dead plants and animals.

Whip-like structures push the bacterium along. They spin round like screws.

Thin hairs attach the bacterium to a surface.

Model of a bacterium

Harmful bacteria

Some bacteria can cause serious illnesses such as cholera and tetanus. Good sanitation and antibiotic drugs help fight diseases caused by harmful bacteria.

The cell is full of a jelly-like substance that helps it to work and grow.

DNA inside the bacterium acts like a control centre.

The cell wall holds the bacterium together and protects it.

Bacteria may be shaped like rods, spirals, or spheres.

Good bacteria

Some bacteria are helpful to humans. Bacteria in our guts protect us from illnesses. Other bacteria are used to make foods such as yoghurt and cheese.

How many copies can a single bacterium make of itself in 24 hours?

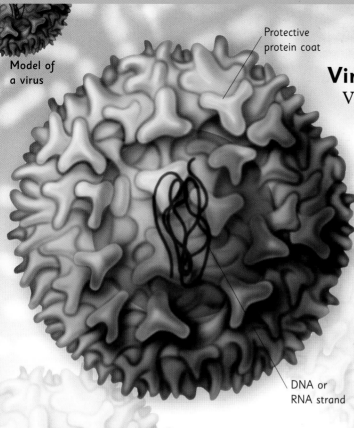

Model of
a virus

Protective
protein coat

DNA or
RNA strand

Viruses

Viruses are much, much smaller than bacteria. They are shaped like spheres or rods. Viruses are not really alive, because they are not made of cells. They only become active when they invade a cell. They copy themselves by taking over the cell and turning it into a virus factory.

Plant viruses

Plant viruses can change the way that plants develop. For example, one virus affects the pigment in tulips' petals. It stops the pigment from working in some places. This makes the petals look stripey.

Vaccinations

Vaccinations can help to protect people from harmful diseases. A person is injected with a weakened form of a virus or bacterium. This prepares the immune system for the real thing.

A virus has made light patches appear on these leaves.

The streaked patterns on this tulip are caused by a virus.

Harmful viruses

Viruses can cause different illnesses.

Chickenpox is easy to catch. The main symptom is itchy spots.

Rabies is a fatal virus that is common in animals such as dogs.

Colds are viruses and can bring on a sore throat, runny nose, and cough.

Model of eukaryotes

Other tiny cells

Apart from bacteria, there are two other kinds of single-celled organisms – eukaryote and archaea. Some eukaryotes are similar to fungi, animals, or plants. Archaea is found in several kinds of habitat, particularly in oceans.

It can make 4,000 million million million copies.

Food chains

Everything in the living world needs food to survive. And everything must feed on something else. This is called a food chain. Each species is part of several different food chains.

5 Decomposers

At the start and end of every food chain there are decomposers, such as earthworms, fungi, and dung beetles. They help break down dead animals and plants, releasing the nutrients back into the soil.

1 Producers

Plants, such as acacia trees and grasses, get their energy from the Sun. They are known as producers.

2 Herbivores

Herbivores, such as impala or zebra, eat the plants. They do not eat meat.

What carnivorous plant catches and eats flies and spiders?

4 Scavengers

Dead meat is known as carrion and is eaten by scavengers such as hyenas, vultures, and bald eagles. These creatures rarely kill for food – they find animals that have died of natural causes and eat other animals' leftovers.

3 Carnivores

Carnivores only eat meat. On the African plains, carnivores include lions, leopards, and cheetahs.

A Venus flytrap.

Sea food

The further you go up the chain, the fewer animals there are. So, in the sea, there are countless plankton, fewer fish, just a few seals, and fewer polar bears.

Polar bear

Seals

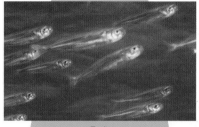

Fish

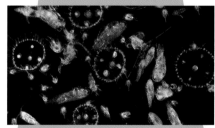

Zooplankton

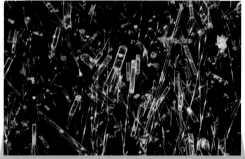

Phytoplankton

155

Ecosystems

All over the world, living things exist in distinct kinds of places called ecosystems. Each has its own climate, soil, and complex community of plants and animals. Oceans and deserts have their own ecosystems.

Natural variety

There are different ecosystems all over the world, and the animals and plants in each one are adapted to its conditions.

Homes, sweet homes

One ecosystem contains a number of habitats. A habitat is the natural home of a particular plant or animal. A tree, or even a leaf, can be a habitat.

Trees offer shelter for animals, and food in the form of leaves and fruits.

Forests

Wherever there is enough rain, forests grow, and they provide homes for a huge range of plants and animals.

Oceans

More than 70 per cent of the Earth's surface is covered by oceans, which contain many different habitats.

Rivers and lakes

Freshwater ecosystems exist in pools, lakes, rivers, and streams. They are found over most of the world's land surface.

Polar and tundra

The freezing polar lands are at the far north and south of the Earth, in the Arctic and Antarctic. At the edges farthest away from the poles, they merge into warmer tundra areas.

156

Mountains

Climate conditions change as you go up a mountain, so different ecosystems can exist here.

Seashores

Seashore ecosystems are half land and half sea. They change as the tide comes in and out.

Grasslands

Humans evolved in grassland habitats. Today, the largest and fastest land animals live here.

Deserts

They can be hot or cold, but deserts are always dry, with little rain. Only a few animals and plants survive here.

Living together

A group of living things in a habitat is called a community. Each one contains plants, animals, and other organisms that all rely on each other.

Ferns grow and absorb nutrients from the soil.

Snails feed on the leaves of plants, and provide food for other animals.

Frogspawn hatches into tadpoles. Some of these are eaten by other water creatures.

Rotting leaves and wood are home to fungi and small animals, such as beetles and slugs.

Frogs, which eat insects, live both on land and in the water.

Picture detective

Look through the Ecosystems and Habitats pages and see if you can find the pictures below.

Turn and learn

Food chains **pp. 154-155**
Carbon cycle: **pp. 222-223**

Tropical rainforests, deciduous woodlands, and cold, coniferous forests.

Polar regions

Polar regions are often dark, blasted by freezing winds, and receive little rain. Only the toughest can survive.

Polar bears have thick blubber under their skin to help keep the cold out.

Although their fur is white, polar bears have black skin.

Polar giants

Large animals lose heat more slowly than small ones, so many Arctic animals are big. A male polar bear can be 2.5 m (8 ft) long and weigh 400–720 kg (881–1,587 lb).

Let's stay warm

Some penguins huddle together to stay warm. The adults and chicks on the outside of the huddle aren't so well protected from the cold, so they take turns standing in the middle.

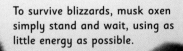

To survive blizzards, musk oxen simply stand and wait, using as little energy as possible.

Musk oxen may look like cattle, but they are actually a type of goat!

A walking coat

The musk ox looks like a small, shaggy haired buffalo. Its coat, said to be eight times warmer than sheep's wool, is made of coarse hairs as long as your arm.

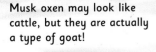

What is the world's largest bear?

One big cover up

Many polar animals have thick coats. The snowy owl has feathers on its body that grow long enough to cover its legs and its bill.

Snowy owl

A fine fur coat

The Arctic fox's luxurious fur even covers the soles of its feet. This fox is dark in the summer, and white in the winter. In the summer, it is very busy collecting and storing food for the winter.

Cushion growth

It's not just animals that need to wrap up warm – plants do too. Purple saxifrage has lots of tiny, overlapping leaves that completely cover the short stems.

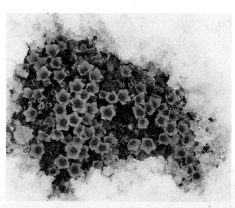

Purple saxifrage is one of the first Arctic plants to flower when the snow melts in June.

The snowy owl's talons are perfectly shaped for gripping a lemming.

Polar regions remain dark from September to March.

Turn and learn

The Arctic: **pp. 8-9**
Antarctica: **pp. 56-57**
Desert regions: **pp. 170-171**

It's best to stay under!

Lemmings cope with the cold by staying in tunnels below the snow, where they search for plant roots to nibble. If they emerge, they may well be caught by a passing snowy owl.

The polar bear.

Deciduous forests

Deciduous trees lose their leaves for part of the year. They mainly grow in regions with warm summers, and lose their leaves in winter.

Layer on layer

Deciduous forests have two or three layers – a canopy (treetops), sometimes a layer of shrubs, and then the low-lying plants such as mosses, ferns, and spring flowers.

If conditions are right, mosses will grow on the bark of forest trees.

Springing to life

A forest appears to sleep in winter, but in spring it bursts into life. Buds open and ferns spread out to soak up the light.

Land of plenty

A forest floor is littered with dead leaves and wood, and there are often plenty of nuts and berries – it's a perfect hunting ground for squirrels.

The grey squirrel will collect and store hazelnuts and other seeds.

What is a squirrel's bushy tail used for?

Links in a chain
Food chains connect a species with what it eats.

Leaves act like solar panels to gather sunlight to make food.

Caterpillars – and many other insects – chew on leaves. That's their food.

Birds hunt caterpillars, especially in spring when they have chicks to feed.

Foxes prey on birds, small mammals, and other creatures.

Maple leaf

A leaf is a tree's food factory. In autumn, it begins to shut down.

Autumn colours
In the growing season, deciduous leaves appear green because of a chemical called chlorophyll. In autumn, the leaves turn yellow, brown, or red as the chlorophyll is destroyed.

Woodpeckers have thick skulls to protect against the shock as they hammer into wood.

Woodpecker

Making an entrance
Woodpeckers use their beaks to dig out grubs and to make nest holes. They have amazingly long tongues to probe and seek out insects.

When mature, a fern bud unrolls and the leaflets open out.

Trees as homes
Woodpeckers take two to three weeks to dig out a nest hole, in which the female lays several eggs. The hole is usually in a dead tree.

A squirrel's tail helps it to balance as it leaps from tree to tree.

Rainforests

Tropical rainforests are rich habitats for a huge variety of plants and animals. Enter a hot, damp, and leafy world.

Parakeet

Time for the umbrella

A rainforest is warm and humid, with frequent downpours. The trees take up much of the rain, but water vapour soon evaporates from their leaves, filling the air with moisture.

A female Queen Alexandra birdwing butterfly

Orang-utan

Bursting with life

Tropical rainforests cover just seven per cent of the Earth's land, yet contain over half of the world's species.

One scientist found 18,000 species of **beetle** in one small area of rainforest.

Around 300 **trees** can grow in a patch of rainforest the size of a football pitch.

New types of **orchids** sare continually being discovered in rainforests.

Of the Earth's 9,000 known **bird** species, one third can be found in the Amazon alone.

Slipper orchid

Which is the largest rainforest in the world?

Emergents are the high tree tops that poke out above everything else.

Rainforest layers

A rainforest is like a block of flats, with different residents at different layers. There are four main levels.

The **canopy** is made up of the majority of the tree tops. It is a forest's leaky roof.

The **understorey** is made up of short trees, shade-loving plants, and lianas (vines).

The **forest floor** is a thick carpet of dead leaves, ferns, and the buttresses of tree roots.

Who lives there?

All sorts of animals make the rainforest their home.

Bushbaby

Bushbabies venture out at night. Their huge eyes help them see in the dark.

Cloud forest

In mountainous areas, rainforests may be so high that they're shrouded in clouds. The constant moisture encourages lush plant growth.

It is likely that these frogs get their poison from the insects they eat. Their colourful patterns let other animals know that they are dangerous to eat.

Blue poison dart frog

Yellow-banded poison dart frog

Eastern rosella

Miltonia Goodale Moir orchid

Turn and learn

Ecosystems: **pp. 156-157** Deciduous forest: **pp. 160-161**

Constrictors don't have fangs or venom. They kill prey by squeezing it to death.

Boa constrictor

The Amazon rainforest in South America.

A sea of grass

Most plants grow from the top, but grass grows from the root. This means it can grow back if it's eaten, or if it is flattened by being trampled.

Grass clump

Grass is resistant to being trampled by hooves.

Grass seed

Grass plants use the wind to spread their pollen (the fine dust that passes from male flowers to female flowers) and their seeds.

In summer, clouds of grass pollen give some people hay fever.

The cycle of life

Tropical grasslands have wet and dry seasons. In the dry season, the grass turns straw-coloured and dies. With the rainy season, it springs back to life.

Cheetah

How old are the baobab trees in Africa?

The grass we eat

Grass doesn't just provide food for animals, but for us too. In fact, most people's main food comes from grasses.

Sugar is produced from sugar cane, a giant tropical grass.

Maize is used for all sorts of food products, including tortillas.

Wheat is used for flour to make bread and cakes, and for pasta.

Rice is an important food in Asia, and is also eaten around the world.

Rye is mixed with wheat to make a heavy flour that is used for bread.

A field of Texas bluebonnet

Spring flowers

While tropical grasslands burst into life in the rainy season, northern grasslands burst to life in the spring. The fields often contain colourful flowers.

Hitching a ride

Many other plants may grow among the grass. Some, such as cleavers, have seeds with tiny hooks that work like Velcro. These cling to animal fur and clothes helping the plant spread its seeds.

Cleavers seeds

Grassland trees are often pruned into an umbrella shape by nibbling animals.

Acacia tree

Giraffe

Baobab trees

In Africa, the baobab tree survives the blistering heat of the dry season by storing water in its enormous trunk.

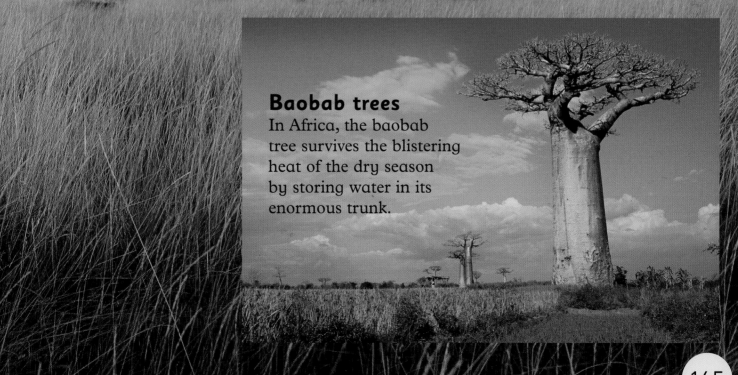

Some of them started growing more than 1,000 years ago.

Weeds and wildflowers

Wildflowers are pretty, but some spread so rapidly they can be troublesome to farmers.

Ragwort is immensely poisonous to horses, ponies, donkeys, and cattle.

Thistle fruits have "parachutes". The seeds can be carried far and wide.

Daisies hug the ground and do well in short grass – such as on a lawn.

Cowslip is found in clearings, at the edge of woodland, as well as in meadows.

Musk mallow produces pretty flowers from June to September.

Lady's bedstraw produces tiny, star-shaped flowers.

Field scabious can produce some 2,000 seeds per plant.

Clover is useful to farmers as it helps fertilize the soil. It is one of the pea family.

Dandelion has many tiny petals, which are later replaced by seeds.

Wood cranesbill is a woodland flower, but grows in hay meadows.

Buttercups spread by scattering parts of the root and bulb, as well as the seeds.

Life in a meadow

In summer, a healthy grass meadow is like a jungle in miniature. It is packed with different plants and animals.

Hidden away

A meadow may be inhabited by moles – almost blind creatures that remain below the ground.

European mole

Under the surface

Moles are capable miners, tunnelling long passages through the soil and producing tell-tale mounds of earth.

Campion flower

Watch out!

Crab spiders are powerful enough to catch bees and butterflies. They hide among the flowers, pouncing when prey comes close.

Crab spider

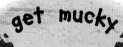
get mucky
Make yourself a miniature meadow inside a jar. Sprinkle a few seeds onto damp soil. Put the jar on a windowsill, keep it watered, and watch as the seeds grow.

166

How long can a slow worm live?

From flower to seed

Dandelions are frequently seen in meadows because they have a way of spreading their seeds that is incredibly successful. Each seed has a "parachute", to carry it far away.

The flower is ready to be pollinated by an insect.

The petals have died and the parachutes are forming.

A breeze lifts the parachutes. They can travel far.

Dandelion seeds

Bubble blower

Froghopper nymphs create damp bubbles of sticky fluid to stop themselves from drying out. The bubble also protects the nymphs from being eaten.

Tiny monkeys

Harvest mice climb along the stems as ably as monkeys climb up trees. They build tennis ball-sized nests.

Harvest mouse

A harvest mouse weighs no more than a teaspoonful of sugar.

There are many different types of snails and a meadow is a good place to find a selection.

Slow but steady

The slow worm is not actually a worm; it's a type of lizard! But it has no legs. This one is hunting for a tasty worm or a snail.

Slow worm

It can live for more than 50 years.

167

At the water hole

Meet my companion

Large animals often appear at a water hole with accompanying oxpeckers. These birds help the animal keep pests at bay, picking off ticks and lice. Besides pest-control, oxpeckers clean up any wounds the host animal may have.

During the dry season in the savannah, the only reliable place to find water is at a water hole. It can be a busy place.

Impala

Although they control parasites, oxpeckers often open up wounds on their host, and feed on blood. This is why they are also considered pests.

That's better!

When a warthog takes a bath, it ends up dirtier than ever. However, the mud helps it to cool down and may help get rid of fleas and other nasty insects that infect the animal's skin.

Red-billed oxpecker

Guinea fowl

How high can impalas jump?

Water birds

Birds are often seen wading in water holes, looking for fish and frogs to eat. There are many different types, and a few are shown here.

Yellow-billed storks stir the water with their foot to disturb fish and frogs.

Saddle-billed storks are the tallest storks, with a height of up to 1.5 m (5 ft).

Crowned cranes are the only cranes able to perch on trees.

Wattled cranes surround their large nests with moat-like water channels.

Stuck in the mud

Some water holes dry up in the dry season. The African lungfish buries itself in mud and lies dormant until the rains come back.

A never-ending thirst

Animals visit a water hole frequently, especially elephants. Elephants have to drink about 200 litres (53 gallons) a day.

African elephants are the largest land mammals.

African elephant

Impala

Turn and learn

Food chains:
pp. 154-155
A sea of grass:
pp. 164-165

An impala can jump up to a height of 10 m (33 ft).

Desert regions

Deserts are the Earth's driest places, with hardly any rainfall. Many of them are boiling hot – but deserts can also be very cold places, such as Antarctica.

Sonoran Desert

Sahara Desert

Gobi Desert

Atacama Desert

Kalahari Desert

Great Sandy Desert

Antarctica

Deserts of the world

A quarter of our world is made up of hot deserts, the biggest one being the Sahara Desert in northern Africa.

Weird weather

During the day, many deserts are scorchingly hot. At night, they can get surprisingly cold. They often have huge sandstorms – or snow storms.

Animal survivors

Few plants can survive in the desert, and so, many animals are meat eaters. Also, many deserts are so hot that a large number of animals retreat underground during the day, hunting at night. Animals also have to develop ways to keep cool and retain water.

Grey-banded king snake

How tall is the tallest cactus on record?

Desert records

Hot and cold deserts are full of extremes, so they hold quite a few impressive records.

Biggest hot desert: the Sahara Desert covers one third of Africa.

Driest hot desert: the Atacama Desert in South America is the driest.

Coldest desert: Antarctica is the coldest desert.

Hottest desert: the Sahara Desert is the hottest in the world.

Most rainfall: the Sonoran Desert in North America receives up to 63 cm (25 in) of rain every year.

Night hunters

During the day, salamanders hide in deep, underground burrows. They come out at night and feed on worms, insects, or other salamanders.

Tiger salamander

Cactus

Some cacti have spines instead of leaves and some have hairs. Spines protect the cactus from being eaten by animals, and also prevent loss of water.

A camel's hump contains fat that con be broken down to release water.

Plant survivors

It is very difficult for plants to survive without much rainfall. The cactus is a clever plant because it collects water during the rains and stores it for dry periods.

Big thirst

A camel can survive for about three weeks without water. When it does drink, it can take in a huge amount.

One Peruvian apple cactus measures 33 m (105.8 ft) in Karnataka, India.

Life in thin air

Walk up a mountain and you'll find that the habitat begins to change the higher you go. It also gets harder to breathe.

Turn and learn
Ecosystems: **pp. 156–157**
Deciduous forests: **pp. 160–161**
Life in a meadow: **pp. 166–167**

Mountain zones
A mountain has distinct zones, each with its own type of wildlife.

A rare sight
There are thought to be fewer than 900 wild mountain gorillas. Although they look fearsome, gorillas are peaceful vegetarians.

Mountain gorilla

Alpine zone
In some parts of the world, mountain peaks have a permanent coating of snow. Nothing grows at this height.

Alpine meadows
In the spring, as the snow begins to melt, lush meadows come alive with flowers. This zone is above the treeline (the limit for tree growth).

Conifer trees
Conifers are adapted for surviving. Even their shape protects them against the weight of the snow.

Deciduous trees
Deciduous trees grow below the conifers. Hence, the air gets a little warmer.

Alpine marmot

Time to wake up!
Mountain meadows are covered with snow in winter. Some animals, like marmots, survive this period by hibernating in burrows.

What is the meaning of the word "alpine"?

Mountain gardens

When the snow melts in spring, the grassy meadows on high mountains are ablaze with flowers.

Mountain daisies bloom in their thousands across alpine meadows.

Creamy-white **rock spirea** form dense mats over rocky areas.

Low, thick clumps of miniature **thyme** make a colourful appearance.

The hardy **saxifrage** comes in many different colours.

In many places, **edelweiss** is now protected – you can't pick it.

Tiny bell-shaped **alpine snowbell** push their way up in early spring.

Gelada baboons

Who needs a tree!

Some monkeys prefer cliffs to trees! Gelada baboons actually sleep on cliffs, perched on the narrowest ledges.

Ibex

This is my home

Ibex are goats. They can scramble up the steepest slopes and leap about without losing their footing.

Alpine chough

Life in thin air

Mountain air is so thin that mountaineers use oxygen tanks. However, birds like the chough have no problem breathing here. A chough once accompanied a climbing expedition to the summit of Mount Everest.

Above the treeline and below permanent snow.

Cool caves

A large cave will take thousands of years to form. From insects to bats, many animals find a cave a good place to live.

A dripping start
Caves are often damp, if not wet. Stalactites form drip by drip as minerals are deposited by water dripping from the roof.

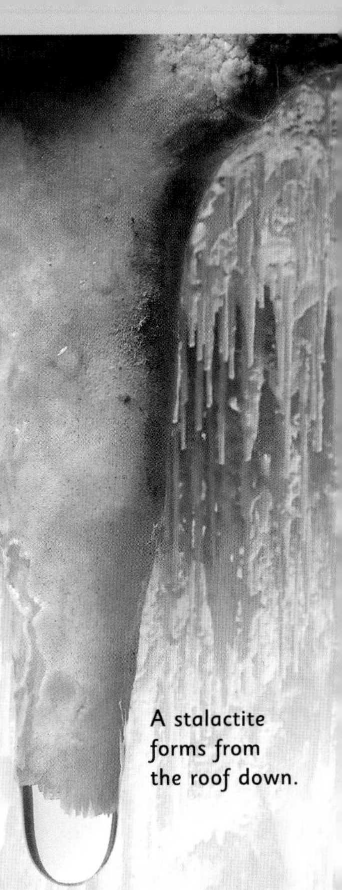

A stalactite forms from the roof down.

Long-eared bat

I hear you!
Many bats have poor sight, but incredibly good hearing. They hunt by making squeaks and clicks – sounds that bounce off prey, telling the bat the prey's location.

Webbed skin for flight

Cave spider

Feel the way
Like bats, cave spiders cannot see well. To compensate, they have a strongly developed sense of touch to help them move around and catch prey.

Which is the largest cave in the world and when was it discovered?

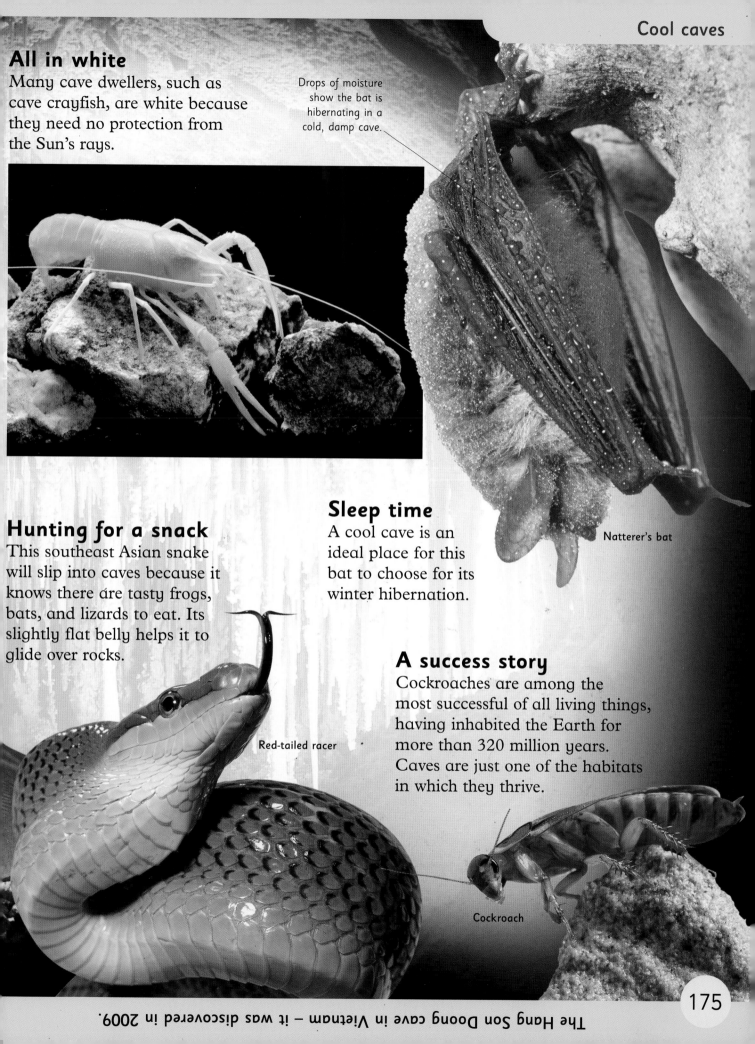

All in white
Many cave dwellers, such as cave crayfish, are white because they need no protection from the Sun's rays.

Drops of moisture show the bat is hibernating in a cold, damp cave.

Hunting for a snack
This southeast Asian snake will slip into caves because it knows there are tasty frogs, bats, and lizards to eat. Its slightly flat belly helps it to glide over rocks.

Sleep time
A cool cave is an ideal place for this bat to choose for its winter hibernation.

Natterer's bat

A success story
Cockroaches are among the most successful of all living things, having inhabited the Earth for more than 320 million years. Caves are just one of the habitats in which they thrive.

Red-tailed racer

Cockroach

The Hang Son Doong cave in Vietnam – it was discovered in 2009.

The flowing current

From foamy white, cascading torrents to slow, but ever-moving waters, rivers provide a rich habitat for a wide variety of wildlife.

The food chain begins

As leaves and dead animals fall into the waters, bacteria multiply. This brings food for aquatic larvae such as the caddisfly.

Caddisfly larva

Caddisfly

From small beginnings

Many rivers start life as fast-flowing streams. It is often a barren beginning, but plants and animals soon thrive.

Mosses often grow on riverside rocks and trees and provide shelter for many tiny bugs that need damp conditions.

Stop that water!

Beavers sometimes build dams to create lakes, slowing the flow of water and so changing their habitat. They also create lodges to live in.

Fallen trees can provide pathways for animals and insects to cross a fast-flowing stream.

Beaver

Which is the world's longest river?

Changing the landscape

Over millions of years, rivers cut channels through the land. A notable example of this is the Colorado River and the Grand Canyon.

The Colorado River

A brown bear is drawn to the river by the presence of fish.

Brown bear

The bird's dagger-like beak holds the fish.

Got it!

Many birds make a slow-moving river their hunting ground, snatching small fish from the water. The kingfisher is a colourful inhabitant of many European rivers.

Against the flow

Adult chinook salmon, also known as king salmon, travel long distances to lay their eggs in the same area where they were born. To get there, they have to swim against strong river currents. It's a dangerous trip!

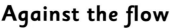

The kingfisher will dive to about 25 cm (10 in) to grab a fish.

177

The Nile, in Africa, at 6,695 km (4,160 miles).

Still waters

A freshwater lake is a large body of standing water. Lakes support a wide variety of life, especially at their edges.

Water hyacinth

Just floating around

Plants that float do well in still water, but they can take over. Water hyacinth looks pretty, but it is a fast-growing weed and can choke other life forms under a thick mat.

Floating plants such as water lettuce provide shade for a lake's creatures.

Water lettuce

Cat in the water

Catfish are named for their barbels – cat-like whiskers that allow them to feel their way in murky water.

Bullhead catfish

Some species of catfish can grow to be more than 3 m (10 ft) in length.

Barbels help the fish to seek out prey. In the case of a large catfish, this may be a duck.

Medicinal leeches

Horse leech

Is it a sucker?

Paddle in a muddy lake and you may emerge to find a leech on your foot. Some, but not all, leeches suck blood.

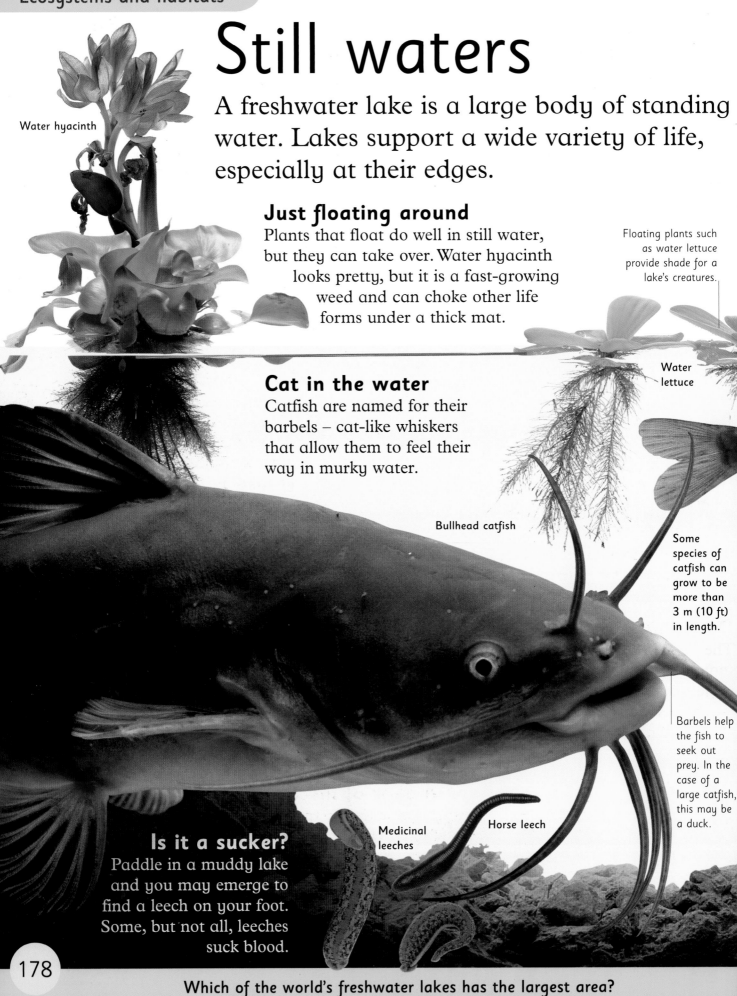

Which of the world's freshwater lakes has the largest area?

Is it a lake?

Lakes form in hollows, but not all are natural. A reservoir is a man-made lake, formed by a dam.

Ospreys are large birds of prey, reaching 1.7 m (5½ ft) wingtip to wingtip.

A bulrush's flowers bloom on spikes and attract insects.

Attacks from above

Ospreys are found on all continents except Antarctica. They will nest near a lake or river, and swoop down to pluck fish from the water.

Life on the edge

Bulrushes and reeds often form a thick bed at a lake's edge. Known as emergents, they grow up from the lake floor and out into the air.

Pike

Dragonflies are frequently seen on the plants at a lake's edge.

The ambush specialist

Pike are adept at ambushing their prey, lying in wait and nabbing passing frogs, fish, and insects.

Don't mess with me!

The fearsome looking alligator snapping turtle is the world's largest freshwater turtle. Some have weighed in at more than 100 kg (220 lbs).

A slice of history

Birds similar to the common loon lived on the Earth some 37 million years ago. This red-eyed bird can dive to an incredible 27 m (89 ft) in search of food.

Lake Superior in North America.

179

A pufferfish sucks
in water to swell
its body.

The BIG escape!
If threatened, a pufferfish may
blow itself up with water to stop
it being swallowed by a predator,
but most predators know to
avoid these highly toxic fish.

Jellyfish protect themselves
with stinging cells on their
tentacles, but these don't
stop a turtle!

Swim for my supper
Sea creatures such as the leatherback turtle
will travel thousands of miles in search of
jellyfish. If the food doesn't come to you,
you have to go and find it!

The lion's mane
jellyfish is one of the
largest of all jellyfish.

Turn and learn
Water mammals:
pp. 132-133
The world of fish:
pp. 144-145

Velvet crab

It's a production line
Many sea creatures produce hundreds
or even thousands of eggs to ensure
some will survive. Turtles will lay 100
eggs at once, while a velvet crab may
produce 180,000 eggs!

Which of the creatures on this page has the longest history on the Earth?

Survival in the sea

The ocean can be a dangerous place and sea creatures have developed a number of clever techniques to increase their chances of staying alive.

On guard!
Some sea creatures will sting or attack if threatened. Lionfish spines contain venom that can stop a fish moving or kill it. Divers are careful not to touch lionfish.

Lost in the crowd
Many smaller fish gather together in large schools. They then move as one unit to look larger than they would as a single fish. It can confuse a predator and so protect them.

Blending in
Many of the ocean's inhabitants are masters of disguise.

Stonefish have lumpy, mottled skin that blends perfectly with the sea floor.

Pipefish swim upright, making them almost invisible amongst seagrass.

Leopard sharks have a patterning on their skin that helps them to hide.

Jellyfish are survivors. There were jellyfish in the oceans 650 million years ago.

Age of the dinosaurs

The Earth has an incredibly long history, as it formed about 4,600 million years ago. Geologists divide the passage of time since into huge chunks called eras. The giant dinosaurs lived in the Mesozoic Era.

Eoraptor was a Triassic dinosaur.

A question of time

Different dinosaurs lived at different times, and many of the best-known dinosaurs never actually met. For example, no *T. rex* ever tried to kill a *Stegosaurus* because their existence was separated by about 80 million years.

MESOZOIC ERA

Coelophysis

Plateosaurus

Brachiosaurus

Stegosauru

Eoraptor

Triassic: 252 to 201 million years ago   Jurassic: 201 to 145 million years ag

How do we know what dinosaurs looked like?

The Mesozoic Era

This era is divided into three time spans, or periods.

 The **Cretaceous** period was ruled by an amazing variety of dinosaurs.

 The **Jurassic** period saw the emergence of massive plant-eating dinosaurs.

 The **Triassic** period, the oldest, saw the appearance of the Earth's first dinosaurs.

Geological time is always shown with the oldest period at the bottom of the list. It reflects the sequence in which rocks are laid down.

Picture detective

Look through the Age of the Dinosaurs pages to identify each of the picture clues below.

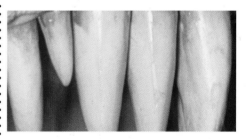
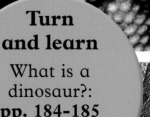

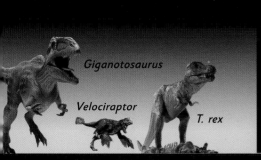

Giganotosaurus

Velociraptor

T. rex

Human beings (*Homo sapiens*) didn't appear until very recently in the Earth's history.

Cretaceous: 145 to 66 million years ago

Homo sapiens

Turn and learn

What is a dinosaur?: **pp. 184-185**
What happened?: **pp. 208-209**

183

We know a lot about their size and appearance from fossil evidence.

What is a dinosaur?

Two legs or four? Meat-eater or plant-eater? What made a dinosaur? They all had four limbs, though many walked on two. There were a number of other features they had in common.

Long tails

Scientists believe dinosaurs held their tails above the ground as there is no evidence of drag marks where trackways have been found.

Scaly skin

Impressions of dinosaur skin are rare, but palaeontologists have found enough to know that many dinosaurs had scaly skin, rather like lizards today.

Cold-blooded lizards have to warm up in sunlight; they cannot control their temperature.

Meat-eating dinosaurs, such as *Giganotosaurus*, were known as theropods.

Were dinosaurs warm-blooded?

It's likely that the meat-eating dinosaurs were warm-blooded, like us, but scientists are not sure if the biggest plant-eaters were, too. Warm-blooded animals use food as fuel to stay warm, so the giant plant-eaters may not have managed to eat enough to do this.

Are dinosaurs lizards?

Giganotosaurus skulls had huge "windows".

Skull holes

Dinosaur skulls had large holes, or "windows". These made them lighter, which was necessary as some of the largest skulls were almost as long as a car.

Meat-eaters had sharp claws.

Plant-eaters had blunt toenails.

Clue in the claws

Meat-eating dinosaurs were known as theropods, which means "beast-footed", because they had sharp, hooked claws on their toes. Plant-eating dinosaurs (sauropods) tended to have blunt hooves or toenails.

Walking tall

Dinosaurs walked on their toes with their legs directly under their bodies.

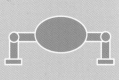

Dinosaurs walked on upright, pillar-like legs.

Crocodiles stand with their knees and elbows slightly bent.

Lizards sprawl, with their knees and elbows held at right angles to their bodies.

Egg layers

All dinosaurs laid eggs – some in nests, just as birds do today. The baby developed in the egg until it was ready to hatch. About 40 kinds of dinosaur eggs have been discovered.

No. They are related, but the two groups are different.

A hip question

Dinosaurs can be split into two groups, according to their hip bones: the saurischians (lizard-hipped) and the ornithischians (bird-hipped).

Most lizard-hipped dinosaurs had a pair of hip bones that pointed forwards or down.

Bird-hipped dinosaurs had two pairs of hip bones pointing back.

186

Did *T. rex* and *Triceratops* ever meet?

T. rex

Triceratops

Saurischians

All meat-eating dinosaurs were lizard-hipped, but some plant-eaters were also lizard-hipped. *T. rex* was lizard-hipped, but so was the mighty plant-eating *Diplodocus*, whom you will meet on page 50.

Ornithischians

These were all plant-eaters. The swept-back bones allowed more room for the digestive organs, and meant their bellies could be carried well back. This made them more stable, and allowed some to walk or run away from danger on two legs.

I'm in this group!

Saurischians can be divided into two main groups.

Theropods, the meat-eaters, such as *Dilophosaurus*.

Sauropodomorphs, such as *Brachiosaurus*, with their small heads and long necks.

I'm in that group!

Ornithischians can be divided into three main groups.

Thyreophorans, the four-footed, armour-plated dinosaurs (e.g. *Stegosaurus*).

Marginocephalians, who had heads with bony frills or horns (e.g. *Triceratops*).

Ornithopods, the two-legged plant-eaters (e.g. *Iguanodon*).

Yes. There's evidence that *T. rex* preyed on *Triceratops*.

Find a friend

Many male animals today compete to win a mate. Stags crash their antlers together, while birds display colourful feathers. Scientists believe dinosaurs had to compete in similar ways.

How did they court?
Dinosaurs may have used their head crests to show off, just like a peacock uses its colourful tail feathers.

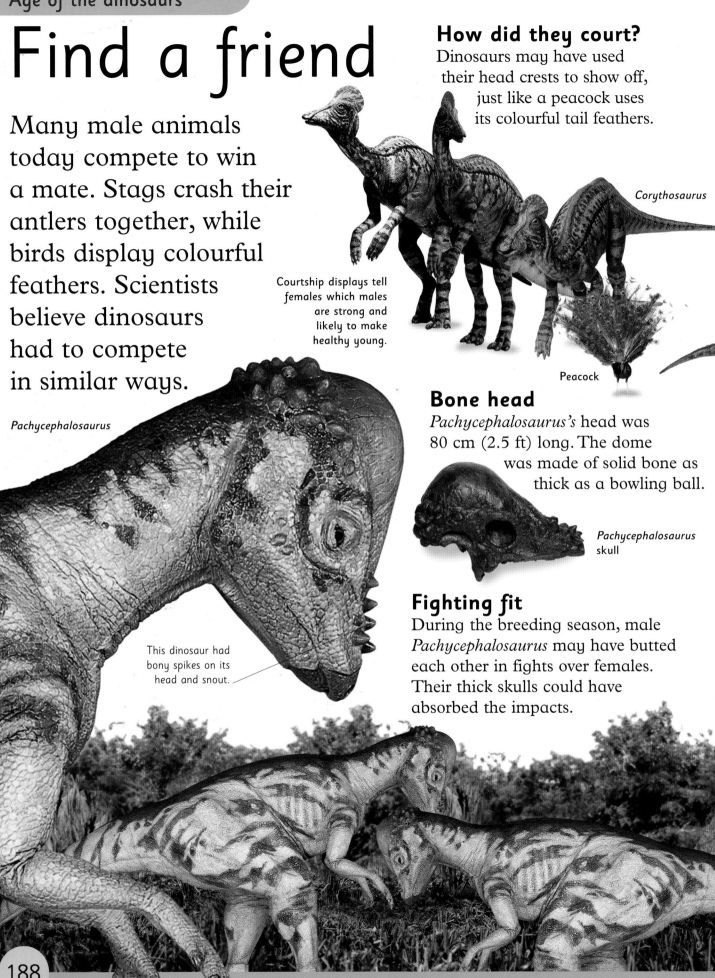

Corythosaurus

Courtship displays tell females which males are strong and likely to make healthy young.

Peacock

Pachycephalosaurus

Bone head
Pachycephalosaurus's head was 80 cm (2.5 ft) long. The dome was made of solid bone as thick as a bowling ball.

Pachycephalosaurus skull

Fighting fit
During the breeding season, male *Pachycephalosaurus* may have butted each other in fights over females. Their thick skulls could have absorbed the impacts.

This dinosaur had bony spikes on its head and snout.

188

Did they talk?

Nobody knows if dinosaurs made sounds, but we suspect they did. *Parasaurolophus,* a hadrosaur (a duck-billed dinosaur), may have done this by blowing air through its crest.

Crest

Parasaurolophus skull

Lambeosaurus skull

Hypacrosaurus skull

Other hadrosaurs had different-shaped crests, suggesting they made different sounds.

Parasaurolophus

Turn and learn

Cretaceous cows: **pp. 194–195**

Crest

Brachylophosaurus

Talk like a frog

Brachylophosaurus had a short, solid crest. It may have had an inflatable pouch on the outside of this that could be used to make noises, a bit like a frog's throat pouch.

Throat pouch

Extraordinary eggs!

Scientists have been lucky enough to find lots of fossilized dinosaur eggs, and even nests. There is a huge variety of sizes and shapes – from small, circular eggs that would fit into the palm of your hand, to eggs the size of cannonballs.

Large scale

This massive egg was found in China and is thought to have been laid by a *Therizinosaurus*. There were larger eggs – the largest was laid by a dinosaur called *Macroelongatoolithus*.

This dinosaur egg fossil is from Mongolia.

A muddy home

Some eggs were laid in mud, which proved a perfect base for fossilization. These are *Maiasaura* eggs from Montana, USA.

Many shapes

Some dinosaur eggs were round, but others were elongated, rather like a loaf of bread.

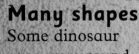

This is a hen's egg. It shows just how large the *Therizinosaurus* egg was.

Oviraptor nest from China, showing the eggs laid in a spiral pattern. Each egg is approximately 16 cm (6 in) long.

Were dinosaur egg shells soft and leathery like those of snakes?

I'm making a break for it!

A tiny dinosaur hatchling would break out of its egg casing. While some dinosaurs were probably ready to look after themselves after hatching, others would have depended on parental help for food and protection.

Model of *Parasaurolophus* hatchling

Fossilized dinosaur egg

Egg care?

Did dinosaurs sit on their eggs, like birds today? Some did; this *Citipati* died and was fossilized sitting on her eggs some 80 million years ago.

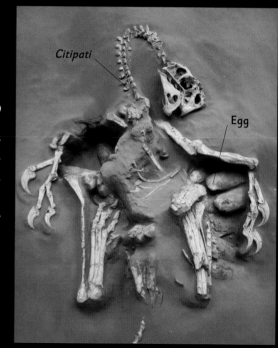

Citipati

Egg

Turn and learn

How was it made?: **pp. 206-207**

Citipati

Nest is dug out of sand or earth.

Bringing it back to life

This model recreates the fossilized scene above, showing the *Citipati* shielding her eggs. These dinosaurs had odd-looking beaked snouts. They may have raided other nests for food for themselves and their young.

191

No. They had hard, brittle shells, like the eggs of birds.

Sauropods

Sauropods were the heaviest, longest, and tallest animals ever to walk on land. They were herbivores, and would have had to graze continually.

Around the world

Sauropods have been found all over the world.

Mamenchisaurus grew to 22 m (72 ft) in length in Jurassic China.

Camarasaurus reached a monstrous 23 m (75 ft) in Jurassic North America.

Barapasaurus grew to lengths of 18 m (59 ft) and roamed Jurassic India.

Vulcanodon was just 6.5 m (21 ft) when it prowled Jurassic Zimbabwe.

Tiny-brained eating machines

Sauropods had tiny heads compared to their bodies. Peg-shaped teeth were used to gather vegetation.

Diplodocus skull

Peg-shaped teeth

Diplodocus's neck and tail made up most of its length.

Look at the size of it!

Imagine a dinosaur that was as long as a tennis court – an adult *Diplodocus* was!

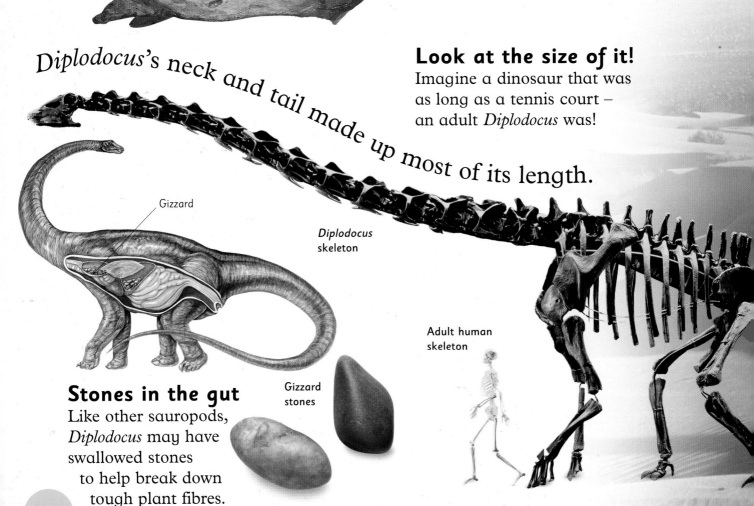

Gizzard

Diplodocus skeleton

Adult human skeleton

Stones in the gut

Like other sauropods, *Diplodocus* may have swallowed stones to help break down tough plant fibres.

Gizzard stones

How many neck vertebrae did the *Diplodocus* have?

It's like a giraffe!

Brachiosaurus had longer forelimbs than hind limbs, so its back sloped down to its hindquarters – rather like a giraffe. But *Brachiosaurus* could reach two or three times higher than a giraffe.

Join hands with eight friends and stretch out your arms. That's about the length of *Brachiosaurus*'s neck!

Sauropods had long tails that helped to balance their bodies.

Up high

Brachiosaurus nibbled leaves at the tops of trees. Its long neck may have helped the *Brachiosaurus* to feed where other plant-eaters could not reach.

Cretaceous cows

Hadrosaurs, which grazed on all fours, were basically the cows of the Cretaceous. They would have been a familiar sight in North America.

All sorts of crests
Those striking crests came in all sorts of different shapes.

 Corythosaurus had a plate-like crest.

 Tsintaosaurus's crest may have been covered in brightly coloured skin.

Lambeosaurus had a helmet-like crest.

Hadrosaurs had stiff tails. It is unlikely these were swung from side to side.

Parasaurolophus

Male hadrosaurs probably had larger crests than the females.

What a sight!
Hadrosaurs are known for having some of the strangest heads of all dinosaurs; many of them had a crest.

Turn and learn
Find a friend:
pp. 188-189
Horns and frills:
pp. 196-197

Can you think of any crested animals today?

A hadrosaur had more than 1,000 teeth (though not all were in use at the same time).

What did they eat?

One hadrosaur fossil contained the remains of its last meal – bark, pine cones, conifer needles, and branches. Such tough plant matter is particularly hard to digest.

Corythosaurus

Did they have teeth?

The beaky jaws contained tightly packed rows of teeth to grind vegetation.

Fossilized hadrosaur teeth

Chew and move on

A hadrosaur such as *Corythosaurus* would have roamed in huge herds, grazing on leaves, pine needles, and ferns.

A number of lizards and birds have crests.

Horns and frills

Built like a rhinoceros, *Triceratops* is one of the best-known of all dinosaurs. It belongs to a group known as the "horned face" dinosaurs or ceratopsians.

That's one hefty plant-eater!

In the big league
Triceratops was one of the largest of all the horned faces, reaching about 10 m (33 ft) in length when fully grown.

196

What does the name *Triceratops* mean?

Other ceratopsians

There were a number of different dinosaurs with horns and frills.

Protoceratops had a head frill but lacked a horn.

Styracosaurus, or "spiked lizard", had a fancy, horned frill.

Pentaceratops had an enormous neck frill and three long horns.

Sheep of the Gobi

Protoceratops roamed the Gobi Desert in Asia rather as sheep roam today. In fact, they were about the size of sheep.

Like all the horned-face dinosaurs, *Protoceratops* had a parrot-like beak.

That's not a fighter

Protoceratops lacked any protection. Its small size would have made it the ideal prey for a number of meat-eaters.

Here you can see the growth of a *Protoceratops* skull, from baby to a fully grown adult.

Fully developed skull

A big graveyard

The Gobi Desert is littered with the remains of *Protoceratops*, and they show all stages of growth.

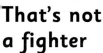
Hatchling's skull

197

T. rex

The mighty *T. rex* roamed North America in the last couple of million years that dinosaurs ruled the planet.

T. rex's eyeballs were the size of a clenched fist.

Titanic teeth

T. rex had awesome curved teeth, each as long as a human hand. Altogether, it had 58 of these pointed weapons.

T. rex preyed on plant-eaters such as *Triceratops*.

T. rex walked on its powerful hind limbs.

When teeth broke, new ones grew to replace them.

Was it a killer?

We don't really know if *T. rex* was a hunter or a scavenger. It may have attacked and killed, or it may have picked at dead or dying dinosaurs. It may have done both.

T. rex is short for *Tyrannosaurus rex*. What does it mean?

Lighten up

With its massive skull that was 1.5 m (5 ft) long, this beast could swallow small dinosaurs whole! Spaces between the skull bones made it lighter.

A *T. rex* had tiny serrations on its teeth. Its bite would have torn into a victim's flesh.

Guanlong was just 1.1 m (3.6 ft) tall, but most of that was tail and neck!

My ancestor

One of the oldest members of the tyrannosaur family was recently found in China. *Guanlong* prowled Earth some 100 million years before *T. rex*.

What a whopper!

Meet Sue, the world's largest and most complete *T. rex* skeleton. She was sold to an American museum in 1991 for a jaw-dropping £5.3 million ($8 million).

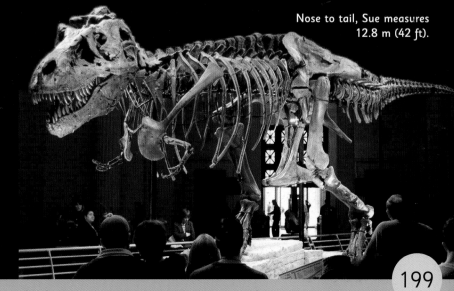

Nose to tail, Sue measures 12.8 m (42 ft).

Tyrannosaurus rex means "King of the tyrant lizards".

Big and bold

Giganotosaurus means "giant southern reptile", and this dinosaur was big. In fact, it may have been larger than *T. rex*. However, the two never met as *Giganotosaurus* was roaming some 10 million years before *T. rex*!

It's a new find!

Giganotosaurus bones were first unearthed in Argentina in the early 1990s, but no complete skeleton has ever been found.

Giganotosaurus would have had a keen sense of smell and excellent eyesight.

weird or what?
It's difficult to imagine just how big and heavy a fully grown *Giganotosaurus* really was. It's thought to have been as heavy as about 125 adult humans. That's a lot of people!

Where did *Giganotosaurus* live?

Let's get it!

A huge sauropod, *Argentinosaurus*, lived alongside *Giganotosaurus*. It's thought this monster may have reached 43 m (140 ft) in length. So one *Giganotosaurus*, which was 13.5 m (45 ft) long, couldn't have brought it down, but these predators may have hunted in packs.

Argentinosaurus

Turn and learn

Age of the dinosaurs:
pp. 182–183
Sauropods:
pp. 192–193

Awesome arms

Giganotosaurus had larger and more powerful forearms than *T. rex*, and they were three-fingered. The fingers would have been used to grasp prey and food.

That's some tooth!

Giganotosaurus had large, serrated teeth that helped in stabbing and gripping prey, and slashing through the meat. The largest teeth were about 20 cm (8 in) in length.

In the warm swamps of Cretaceous Argentina.

Meet the raptors

Velociraptor

The narrow jaws contained about 80 sharp teeth.

The feathers would have been used for warmth, not flight.

Aggressive and speedy, *Velociraptor* was a formidable predator in late Cretaceous Asia. Although small, it was armed with razor-sharp teeth and terrifying dagger-like claws.

Bambiraptor

A feathered dinosaur?

Some dinosaur fossils have been found with traces of a feather-like covering, and it's thought that *Velociraptor* may have had feathers, though no *Velociraptor* fossil has been found with them.

Experts believe that *Deinonychus* were one of the more intelligent dinosaurs. They had a lightweight body and long hind legs.

The killer claw

Deinonychus had a vicious killer claw on each of its hind legs. It held the claw off the ground, and slashed its victims with it.

Deinonychus foot fossil

What does the name *Velociraptor* mean?

This skeleton has been mounted to show *Deinonychus* leaping towards a victim, claws ready.

Deinonychus skeleton

Jump and grab

Velociraptor and its relations, such as the larger *Deinonychus*, may have hunted in packs and jumped onto the back of their prey, all four limbs extended.

Deinonychus means "terrible claw".

"Speedy thief". Scientists believe it may have reached 65 kph (40 mph).

Monsters of the deep

There may have been no marine dinosaurs, but an astonishing variety of toothed giant reptiles ruled the seas while the dinosaurs ruled the land.

Ichthyosaurus

Its neck was as long as its body.

Elasmosaurus was air-breathing, and just like whales today, it had to come to the surface to breathe.

Ichthyosaurs had large eyes.

Swim away...

An *Ichthyosaurus* used to move swiftly to avoid being eaten. The swimming ichthyosaurs, including *Ichthyosaurus* itself, were perfectly suited for chasing fast-moving prey, such as squid. However, they were vulnerable to attack from larger marine reptiles.

... from danger!

Watch out! A *Liopleurodon* is attacking the ichthyosaurs from below. Perhaps the largest sea-based predator of all time, *Liopleurodon* was a short-necked plesiosaur.

What did *Liopleurodon* eat?

Elasmosaurus

What's that?

Elasmosaurus was also a plesiosaur, but it was long-necked. Its four paddle-shaped limbs propelled it easily through the water. It grew up to 14 m (46 ft) in length.

I recognize that!

Many Mesozoic occupants of the Earth's seas would have been familiar to us.

 Jellyfish have been around for about 400 million years.

 Corals are fragile animals, but they have managed to survive since the dinosaurs.

 The **great white shark**'s ancestors date back to the Cretaceous period.

 Squid were on the menu for ichthyosaurs, shown by fossil evidence.

 Snails are also present in fossil form, showing they too are great survivors.

The remains of the largest-known specimen of *Liopleurodon* indicate a maximum length of about 10 m (33 ft).

Liopleurodon

The dagger-like teeth were twice as long as those of *T. rex*.

weird or what?

Some people think the "monster" in Loch Ness, a Scottish Lake, is a plesiosaur that was trapped there when the sea receded millions of years ago!

Anything it could catch, including pterosaurs who flew too close to the water's surface.

How was it made?

Fossils may form when animal or plant matter is buried, soon after death, under mud or sand. However, that's just the beginning of a process that takes millions of years.

70 million years ago
A *T. rex* has died and is washed downstream. It rests on layers of soft mud and is rapidly buried.

Five years later
The creature's soft flesh has slowly rotted away, leaving the bones. Over time, these begin to move apart.

50 million years ago
A sea has now spread over the area once occupied by the river. Heavy pressure is slowly turning the sand to sandstone.

Can you name some of the things that fossilize?

Two million years ago

The passing of millions of years has seen mountain ranges rising above the fossilized *T. rex*, but gradually they are being worn down by extreme weather.

Last year

The area around the fossil is now a desert. Two walkers investigate further when they see the exposed tip of a fossilized bone.

Today

Palaeontologists are now hard at work, uncovering the rest of the *T. rex*. The bones will be removed one by one. The skeleton may end up in a museum.

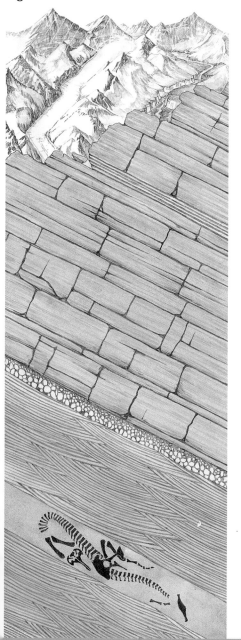

Fossils include bones, teeth, skin impressions, and footprints. Plants also fossilize.

What happened?

Sixty-six million years ago, the giant dinosaurs died out, along with the pterosaurs and most marine reptiles. It was a mass extinction, but what caused it? Many believe it was a meteorite.

What changed?
Scientists now believe a massive meteorite hit the Earth, creating a dust cloud of noxious fumes that screened out the Sun and changed the climate.

Who died?
Huge numbers of animals became extinct. Some are listed below.

Pterosaurs had once filled the skies with their airborne acrobatics.

All the different types of **dinosaur** that had evolved died out.

Huge reptiles disappeared from the oceans.

The rock would have hit the Earth's crust with terrific force, sending shock waves around the world.

It was a big one!
In the early 1990s, geologists found the remains of a massive crater in Mexico. It was 180 km (112 miles) wide. They believe it was caused by a meteorite smashing into the Earth 66 million years ago.

How big were the animals that survived the extinction?

Was that all?

The meteorite hit at a time of immense volcanic activity in an area that is now western India. This activity would have sent up clouds of ash and dust that would have blocked the Sun's light – just like the effect of the meteorite hitting the Earth. The extinction may well have been a combination of both these events.

The rock that created the Mexican crater was 10 km (6 miles) in diameter.

An exploding volcano sends up clouds of lethal dust.

No land animal heavier than a large dog survived.

Living dinosaurs

You may think that reptiles are closely related to dinosaurs, but dinosaurs may have more in common with birds!

A hidden link?
The link between dinosaurs and birds is clear when you look at *Caudipteryx*, one of the many feathered dinosaurs.

Caudipteryx, a turkey-sized Cretaceous creature, would not have been able to fly as its wings were too small.

The first bird?
The earliest-known bird is *Archaeopteryx*, which first appeared in the Jurassic period. It had the toothed head, clawed fingers, and long bony tail, like that of a dinosaur, but it also had feathers.

Fossilized
Archaeopteryx

Archaeopteryx means "ancient wing".

What size do you think *Archaeopteryx* reached?

Why feathers?

Feathers protect birds from water and from temperature changes, and they may have served the same purpose on the feathered dinosaurs.

Hoatzin are found in parts of South America.

Feathers provide good insulation from cold.

Caudipteryx had clawed hands.

We have claws

Some modern birds have clawed wings. Hoatzin chicks have two tiny claws at the end of each wing. The adults do not use them, but the chicks do to clamber through trees.

weird or what?
The evidence that birds are directly descended from dinosaurs is getting stronger all the time. This means that dinosaurs are not extinct! They are living all around us, right now.

Caudipteryx was about the size of a turkey.

Pieces of a puzzle

More and more "dino-birds" are being discovered, and each discovery helps our understanding. This model is based on feathered fossils found in China.

Sinosauropteryx

It was small – about the size of a pigeon.

What is science?

Science is the search for truth and knowledge. Scientists suggest explanations of why things are as they are, and then they test those explanations, using experiments. Some of what science discovers can be applied to our everyday lives.

From atoms to space

Scientists study a huge variety of things – from the tiniest atoms that make up everything around us to the mysteries of space.

Everything you see is made up of minuscule atoms.

Life science

How do living things survive and grow, where do they live, what do they eat, and how do their bodies work? Life science seeks to answer such questions about the living world, from microscopic bacteria to plants and animals – including you!

The scientific study of plants is called botany.

Physical science

This science looks at energy and forces. There are different types of energy, including light, heat, and sound. Forces are the things that hold everything in place in our world. Without the force of gravity, for example, you would fly off into space!

The study of electricity is part of physical science.

Life science studies the living world around us.

The Earth

What is the study of animals called?

Look through the Planet Earth pages and see if you can identify each of the picture clues below.

Earth and space science

The Earth is a dot in a vast Universe filled with planets and moons, stars and galaxies. As far as we know, the Earth is special because it is the only place that supports life. Earth and space science is the study of the structure of our planet – and everything that exists beyond it.

Volcanology is the scientific study of volcanoes.

Materials science

Our Universe is filled with atoms and molecules, which make up elements, compounds, and mixtures. Materials science is the study of these things, how they behave, how we use them, and how they react with one another.

One branch of science studies how materials can change.

Pictures of the Earth from space help scientists understand the Earth better.

Turn and learn

Our world:
pp. 6-7
Our place in space:
pp. 272-273

213

Advances in science

Great scientists are thinkers who understand the world around us, provide solutions to problems, and create new things. This has led to many great inventions and discoveries.

A falling apple probably inspired Newton to think about gravity.

Johannes Gutenberg (c.1398–1468)

Gutenberg played a key role in printing. Experts believe he invented metal-type printing in Europe. Gutenberg's press was quick, accurate, and hard-wearing, compared to earlier woodblock printing.

In a rainbow, white light breaks up into seven colours.

Gutenberg's first printed book was the Bible in 1455.

Isaac Newton (1642–1727)

Newton investigated forces and light. He realized there must be a force that keeps the planets in orbit around the Sun. This force is known as gravity. Newton also discovered that white light is a mixture of lots of different colours.

1400   **1500**   **1600**

Wooden replica of da Vinci's Ornithopter

Leonardo da Vinci (1452–1519)

Da Vinci was a painter and inventor. He drew plans for helicopters, aeroplanes, and parachutes. Unfortunately, the technology of the time was not good enough to build a working model for any of these.

Galileo Galilei (1564–1642)

Galileo proved that the Earth moves around the Sun by looking at the solar system through a telescope. A few wise thinkers had always suspected the truth, but most people at the time believed that our Earth was the centre of everything.

Replica of a 17th-century telescope

Who invented the bifocal lens?

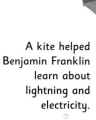

A kite helped Benjamin Franklin learn about lightning and electricity.

did you know?
More than 2,000 years ago, Greek thinker Aristotle recommended that people study nature, and carry out experiments to test the accuracy of ideas.

Super inventions!

Inventions and discoveries have changed the course of our history.

The first known **wheel** was used in Mesopotamia around 3500 BCE.

Paper was invented in China around 105 CE, but kept secret for many years.

The magnetic **compass** was first used by the Chinese. It was invented around 247 BCE.

The **parachute** was first tested in 1617 by Faust Vrancic, centuries after da Vinci made his drawings.

The **steam engine** was invented in 1804. The earliest successful model reached 48 kph (30 mph).

The **colour photo** was first produced by physicist James Maxwell in 1861.

Benjamin Franklin (1706–1790)

American scientist Benjamin Franklin experimented with lightning and electricity. His work in the 1700s laid the foundations for today's electrical world.

Louis Pasteur (1822–1895)

Pasteur is known for discovering pasteurization – a process that uses heat to destroy bacteria in food, particularly milk. He also discovered that some diseases were caused by germs and encouraged hospitals to be very clean to stop germs spreading.

Franklin risked his life flying a kite – he could have been struck by lightning.

1700

1800

William Herschel (1738–1822)

Herschel is well known for his work in astronomy (he was the first to identify the planet Uranus). He also discovered infrared radiation – this technology is used today for wireless communications, night vision, weather forecasting, and astronomy.

Wilhelm Conrad Röntgen (1845–1923)

Röntgen discovered electromagnetic rays – today known as X-rays – on 8 November, 1895. This important discovery earned him the first Nobel Prize for Physics in 1901.

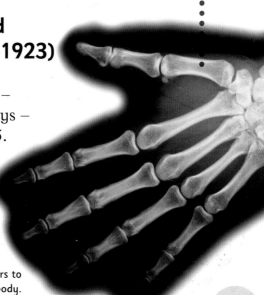

X-rays allow doctors to look inside the human body.

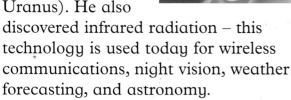
Benjamin Franklin.

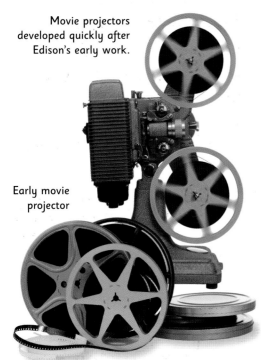

Movie projectors developed quickly after Edison's early work.

Early movie projector

Karl Landsteiner (1868–1943)

Austrian-born physiologist Landsteiner discovered that human blood can be divided into four main groups – A, B, AB, and O. This laid the foundation of modern blood groupings.

Orange juice is a good source of vitamin C.

Albert Szent-Györgyi (1893–1986)

The Hungarian scientist Albert Szent-Györgyi is best known for discovering vitamin C. He also pioneered research into how muscles move and work. In 1937, he won the Nobel Prize for physiology and medicine.

Blood transfusions play an important part in modern medicine.

Red blood cells

You inherit your blood type from your parents.

Thomas Edison (1847–1931)

Thomas Alva Edison produced more than 1,000 inventions, including long-lasting light bulbs, batteries, and movie projectors.

1800

1850

Albert Einstein (1879–1955)

German-born physicist Albert Einstein's famous equation $E=mc^2$ explained how energy and mass are related. It helped scientists understand how the Universe works.

$$E=mc^2$$

Einstein's equation

Earthquakes destroy homes and office buildings.

Charles Richter (1900–1985)

Richter developed a way to measure the power of earthquakes. He worked on his scale with fellow physicist Beno Gutenberg.

A "great" earthquake (8–9.9 on the Richter scale) strikes on average once a year.

Epicentre (an earthquake's point of origin)

Who was the father of the frozen food industry?

Alan Turing (1912–1954)

During World War II, Alan Turing, a brilliant mathematician, helped develop code-breaking machines that eventually led to the invention of modern computers.

The English used Turing's machine to break German codes that were sent through the Enigma machine during World War II.

Tablet

An Apple smartphone

Mobile phones and tablets (1980s)

The first mobiles were large and heavy, weighing about 35 kg (77 lb). Tablet technology has also improved drastically since its invention in the late 1980s.

Modern inventions

Imagine the world without these fantastic inventions!

The first **antibiotic**, penicillin, was discovered accidentally.

Modern **cars** are driven by internal combustion engines that run on petrol or diesel.

Nuclear power is efficient, but some people think it could harm us.

Plastics technology is used to make many of the things in your home.

Compact discs are small and light, and they store lots of information.

Energy-efficient light bulbs help save energy in your home.

Computers (1941)

The first computers were huge machines. They couldn't cope with complicated tasks, but worked on only one thing at a time.

Today's laptops can be lightweight and portable. Early computers filled whole rooms.

900

1950

DNA profiling (1986)

The discovery of DNA (which holds information in human cells) led to DNA profiling, a huge help to the police – criminals can now be identified by a single hair or spot of blood.

Nuclear bombs (1945)

The USA dropped two nuclear bombs on Japan in World War II, killing nearly 300,000 people. It is the only time nuclear weapons have been used in war.

The Internet (1990s)

With its roots in the 1960s, the Internet (short for internetwork) became public during the mid-1990s, and is now used for fun and education by about 2.5 billion users – 70 per cent of whom are online every day.

Before DNA profiling, police identified criminals by their fingerprints. This system was developed in the 1890s.

217

Clarence Birdseye, who started a frozen food company in 1924.

Being a scientist

Scientists study the world around us. They look for gaps in existing knowledge and try to find the answers. Not all scientists study the same things – they specialize in different areas.

Experiments can involve toxic fumes or chemicals that might explode, so scientists wear protective goggles.

Testing, testing

Scientists explore their ideas and theories using tests called experiments. In this book, there are lots of experiments you can try out for yourself.

Mixing it up

Experimenting with chemicals and their reactions can produce some mixed results. Some mixtures can be dangerous, while others can be the answer the scientists are after.

218

A closer look

The microscope was developed by two Dutch spectacle makers in around 1610, and then refined by Robert Hooke in England. Early models revealed tiny organisms in water, while modern versions can look inside a single cell.

Hooke's microscope

Modern microscope

Inside view

When you go to a hospital, the doctor may send you for a body scan. Using a powerful machine, the medical team can see what's going on inside you.

hands on

Fill a cup or vase with water, and add a few drops of food colouring. Cut the end off the stem of a flower and put the flower in the water. The petals turn the colour you mixed in the water.

Experiments allow scientists to observe and theorize how things work and why. It has been found, for instance, how plants take up food and water from the soil and transport it up the stem.

Types of scientist
Almost everything in the world is the subject of study by a scientific specialist.

Zoologists study animals of all kinds except human beings.

Biologists are interested in everything about life and living organisms.

Paleontologists are experts on fossils, and try to learn about organisms from them.

Botanists learn about the world of plants, plant types, and plant groups.

Chemists study elements and chemicals, and they help make new substances.

Astronomers are experts on space, planets, stars, and the Universe.

Entomologists are a special kind of zoologists who learn about insects.

Geologists find out about our Earth, particularly by studying rocks.

Archaeologists are interested in the remains of past peoples and lives.

Ecologists study the relationship between living things and their environment.

Oceanographers know all about oceans and ocean life.

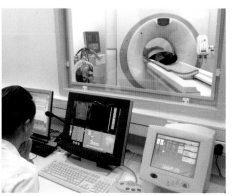

Some microscopes can magnify objects up to 2,000 times!

Science and everyday life

Science is not just used by experts working in laboratories. It is part of all our lives. From brushing your teeth to setting your alarm, science is with you all day, every day, in the form of technology.

Teflon

Iron

Invented in 1938, Teflon was used in space suits. In everyday life, it stops stuff from sticking to hot surfaces.

Teflon pan

Plastic fantastic

Look around you and you will see dozens of things made of plastic. From containers to toys, plastic is a versatile and hard-wearing material. Many plastics can now be recycled.

Electricity

Electricity lights up the world and gives us the energy to run machines and gadgets with which we can cook, travel, work, and play.

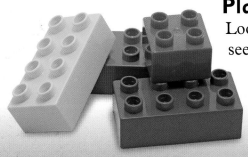

Plastic building blocks

Some medicines come in plastic bottles. Sometimes tablets are contained in plastic packets, and sold in strips.

Cities at night are bright places, lit up by offices, houses, and street lights.

What was the first satellite in space?

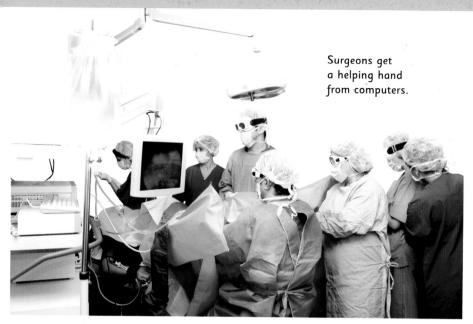

Surgeons get a helping hand from computers.

Masks, aprons, and gloves help doctors keep operation rooms free from infection.

Satellite orbiting the Earth

In the best of health

Long ago, people relied only on herbs to cure diseases. Thanks to modern science, many illnesses, including those that were once untreatable, can now be cured or prevented.

Communications

Satellites orbit the Earth, beaming back all sorts of information. They send TV signals, supply weather information, and help us look into space.

Clothing technology

Advances in sports-clothing technology have impacted everyday clothes. Breathable fabric, stretchy spandex, and thermal underwear were developed from specialized sportswear.

From here to there

Science and technology make it much easier to get around. Trains, planes, and cars make the world a smaller place and allow us to visit exotic destinations. They are also useful for getting to school on time.

Bullet trains in Japan travel up to 300 kph (186 mph).

Turn and learn

Health:
pp. 40-41
Electricity:
pp. 76-77

Sputnik 1, launched by the Soviet Union in 1957.

Carbon cycle

Every living thing contains carbon. Human beings take in carbon through carbohydrates, fats, and proteins in food, and release it as carbon dioxide gas when breathing out. It is also released from dead matter, sometimes quite soon, sometimes millions of years later in fuels such as oil and coal.

An animal's droppings also contribute to the carbon cycle.

It's in the air

Green plants take in carbon dioxide from the air and use it to make food, converting it into things such as carbohydrates. Animals take in some of the carbon when they eat plants.

CARBON DIOXIDE

Plants take in carbon dioxide from the atmosphere

Animals

Animals, such as these sheep, contribute to the carbon cycle by eating grass, breathing in air, and dropping waste. They take in carbon from the plants they eat, and release it when they breathe out. Their bodies will release more carbon when they die.

Animals eat plants and take in some carbon. They breathe out carbon dioxide.

CARBON

CARBON DIOXIDE RELEASED

In particular circumstances, carbon forms a hard crystal. What is it called?

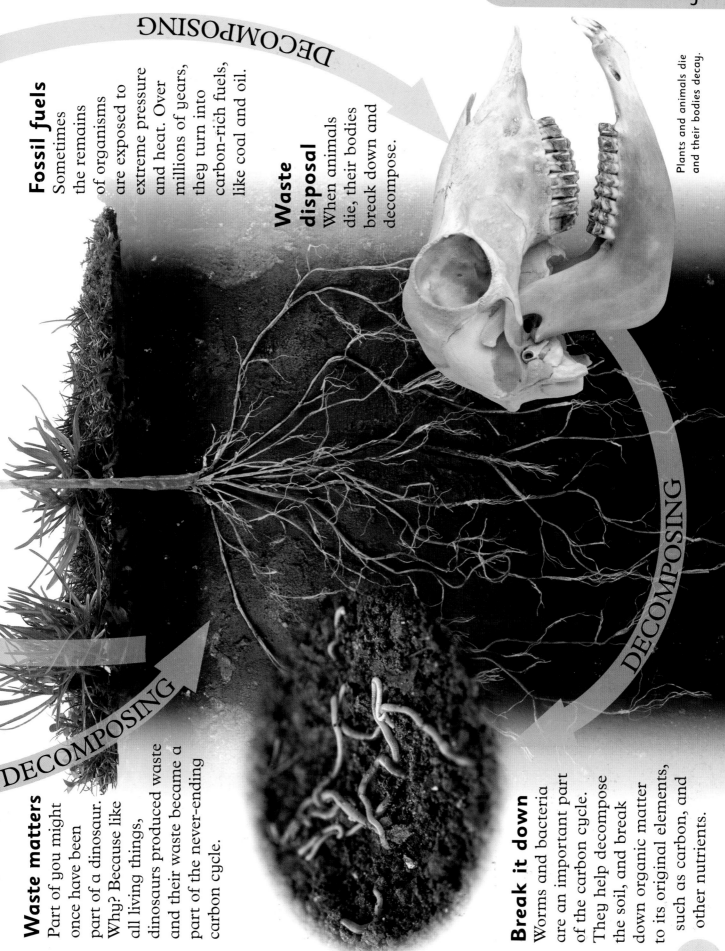

DECOMPOSING

Fossil fuels
Sometimes the remains of organisms are exposed to extreme pressure and heat. Over millions of years, they turn into carbon-rich fuels, like coal and oil.

Waste disposal
When animals die, their bodies break down and decompose.

Plants and animals die and their bodies decay.

DECOMPOSING

DECOMPOSING

Waste matters
Part of you might once have been part of a dinosaur. Why? Because like all living things, dinosaurs produced waste and their waste became a part of the never-ending carbon cycle.

Break it down
Worms and bacteria are an important part of the carbon cycle. They help decompose the soil, and break down organic matter to its original elements, such as carbon, and other nutrients.

A diamond.

223

Properties of matter

Main properties
There are many different properties of matter.

 Boiling point is the hottest a liquid can get before becoming a gas.

 Freezing point is the temperature at which a liquid becomes a solid.

 Plasticity is how well a solid can be reshaped.

 Conductivity is how well a material lets electricity or heat travel through it.

 Malleability is how well a solid can be shaped without breaking.

 Tensile strength is how much a material can stretch without breaking.

 Flammability is how easily and quickly a substance will catch fire.

 Reflectivity is how well a material reflects light. Water reflects well.

 Transparency is how well a material will let light pass through it.

 Flexibility is how easily a material can be bent.

 Solubility is how well a substance will dissolve, such as salt in water.

Some materials are hard and brittle, while others are flexible. Some materials are colourful, while others are transparent. These kinds of features are called "properties".

A cork floats on oil. Oil floats on water.

A plastic building brick sinks through oil but floats on water.

An onion sinks through oil and water, but floats on syrup. Syrup sinks below water.

Does it float?
It's easy to learn about some properties, such as the ability to float. The amount of matter in a certain volume of an object is called its density. Objects and liquids float on liquids of a higher density and sink through liquids of a lower density.

A good insulator
Heat cannot easily pass through some materials. These are known as insulators. For example, aerogel can completely block the heat of a flame. But don't try this at home!

Is diamond harder than quartz?

Broken glass

Brittleness

Some materials, such as window glass, are particularly brittle. They will break when pushed out of shape even a small amount.

Hardness

A scientist called Friedrich Mohs created a scale using ten minerals to compare how hard they are. Many materials are graded on this scale.

Compressibility

Gases can be squashed, or compressed, by squeezing more into the same space. This is what happens when you pump up a tyre.

Gas can be compressed because its particles are far apart. A bicycle pump pushes the particles closer together.

Foot pump

Gas particles

Diamond is the hardest mineral.

9 Corundum

10 Diamond

5 Apatite

4 Fluorite

6 Feldspar

7 Quartz

8 Topaz

Talc is the softest mineral

1 Talc

2 Gypsum

3 Calcite

hands on

Collect some different pebbles and put them in order of hardness. A pebble is harder than another if it scratches it. This is how Mohs worked out his scale.

A smooth flow

Some liquids flow more easily than others. It depends on their "stickiness", or viscosity. Hot lava from a volcano flows slowly because it is sticky.

Yes, diamond is the hardest mineral of all. It can scratch quartz.

Liquid metal
Many substances melt and boil at particular temperatures (its melting and boiling points). Most metals are solid at everyday temperatures because they have a high melting point. But mercury has such a low melting point that it is liquid even at room temperature.

Changing states
Many solids melt, to become liquids, when they become hot enough. When liquids get cold enough, they freeze and become solid. This is called changing states and it happens to all kinds of substances.

Changing states of water
Water exists as a solid, liquid, or gas. You can find all three forms of water in your home. They are ice, water, and water vapour.

Condensation
As water vapour in the air is cooled, it changes into liquid water. This is called condensation. You can see it on the outside of a cold bottle.

When water vapour in the air touches a cold bottle, it condenses into tiny drops of liquid.

Ice is solid water. It forms when liquid is cooled until it freezes. Each piece of ice has a definite shape.

When ice is warmed, it melts and becomes liquid and takes on the shape of the container holding it.

As water is heated, bubbles water vapour (gas) form. They escape from the surface and condense to form a mist of liquid droplets called steam.

Rivers of iron
Iron must be heated in a furnace to make it melt. Molten iron is so hot it glows yellow. It is poured into a mould and left to harden to make solid iron objects.

Why does chocolate become soft and gooey in your mouth?

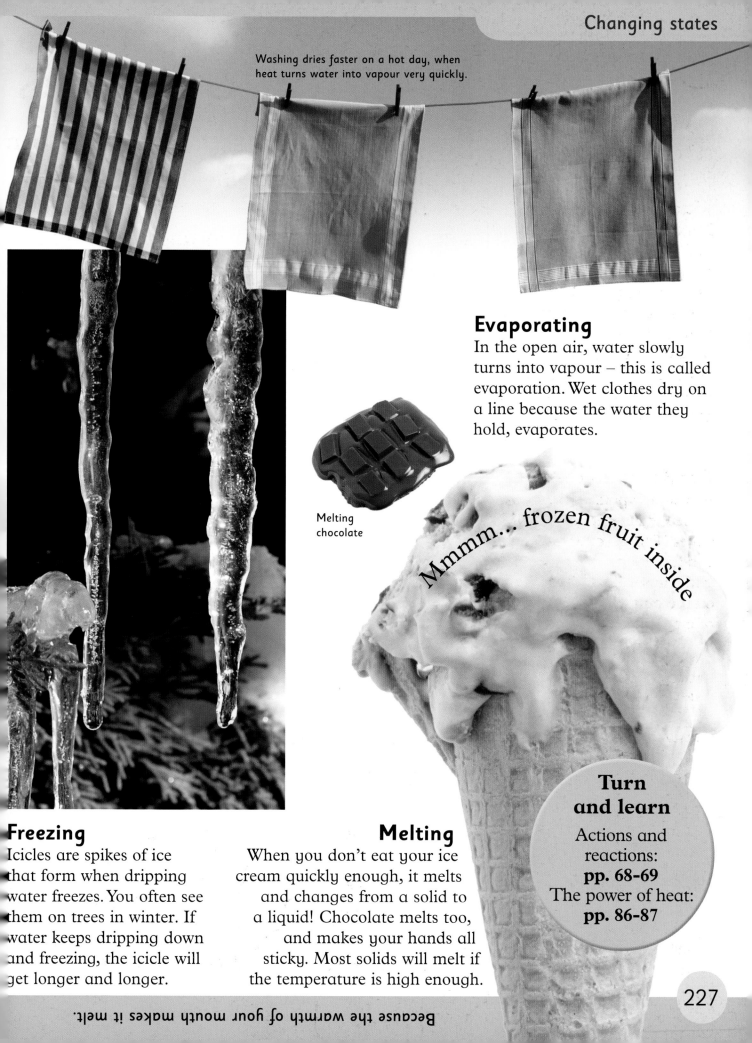

Washing dries faster on a hot day, when heat turns water into vapour very quickly.

Evaporating

In the open air, water slowly turns into vapour – this is called evaporation. Wet clothes dry on a line because the water they hold, evaporates.

Melting chocolate

Mmmm... frozen fruit inside

Freezing

Icicles are spikes of ice that form when dripping water freezes. You often see them on trees in winter. If water keeps dripping down and freezing, the icicle will get longer and longer.

Melting

When you don't eat your ice cream quickly enough, it melts and changes from a solid to a liquid! Chocolate melts too, and makes your hands all sticky. Most solids will melt if the temperature is high enough.

Turn and learn

Actions and reactions: **pp. 68-69**
The power of heat: **pp. 86-87**

Because the warmth of your mouth makes it melt.

Amazing atoms

Atoms are tiny particles that make up everything around us. Each atom of a substance contains the chemical properties the substance is made up of.

Electrons whizz around the nucleus of the atom.

Neutron

Proton

Electron

Inside an atom
Inside an atom are three tiny types of particle: protons, neutrons, and electrons. Protons and neutrons make up the atom's nucleus (core). The electrons are outside this.

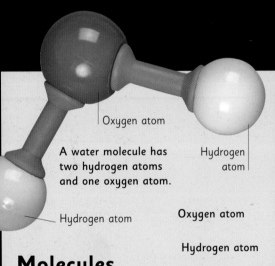

Oxygen atom

A water molecule has two hydrogen atoms and one oxygen atom.

Hydrogen atom

Oxygen atom

Hydrogen atom

Hydrogen atom

Molecules
Substances are made from little groups of atoms called molecules. The molecules of water have three atoms.

Au

GOLD

79

Golden number
An atomic number is the number of protons in an atom. The atomic number of gold is 79. This means that each gold atom has 79 protons.

How many atoms are there in a drop of water?

Sunflower oil comes from the seeds that grow in the middle of a sunflower.

Oxygen atom

Hydrogen atom

Carbon atom

Big molecules

In natural substances like vegetable oil, the atoms are often joined in chains to make very large molecules. The molecules in sunflower oil contain 50 atoms each.

weird or what?

An atom is mostly empty space. If an atom were the size of a sports stadium, the nucleus would be the size of a marble in the middle.

The explosion of a nuclear bomb can create a spectacular "mushroom cloud".

The mighty atom

When the nucleus of an atom is split, it releases a huge amount of energy. Nuclear bombs use this "atomic energy" to create huge explosions. Nuclear power stations use the energy to produce electricity.

About 5 sextillion (5,000,000,000,000,000,000,000).

Molecules

In most materials, atoms are joined in tiny groups called molecules. The shapes of molecules and the way they pack together can help explain how different materials behave.

Steaming ahead

Molecules are always jiggling about. When they get hot, they move further and faster. When water heats up, the molecules may start moving so fast that they escape into the air as water vapour.

Frozen solid

Cold molecules move slowly, allowing them to pack together more easily. When water freezes, the molecules line up in neat rows, forming ice crystals.

Snow may look like white powder, but if you look closely you can see thousands of tiny crystals as clear as glass.

Steam appears when water vapour cools down and becomes liquid again. The steam from this train is made of millions of tiny liquid droplets.

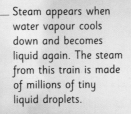

Melt: As a solid heats up, its molecules move faster until they break free from each other and move separately, turning the solid into a liquid.

Solidify: As a liquid cools, its molecules lose energy and move more slowly. Eventually, they start sticking together, turning the liquid into a solid.

Solid

Liquid

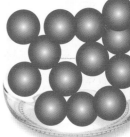

If a liquid is poured into a jar or bottle, it takes the shape of its container and stays in place.

Are diamonds impossible to destroy?

Diamond is made into jewels that are almost indestructible.

Diamond molecule

Diamond is the hardest natural substance known. Its hardness comes from the way the carbon atoms in diamond are arranged. Each atom is joined by strong bonds to four neighbouring atoms.

Each group of five atoms in diamond forms a pyramid shape. This shape makes diamond amazingly strong.

Turn and learn

Changing states:
pp. 56-57
Minerals:
pp. 104-105

Graphite molecule

Graphite, like diamond, is also made of carbon atoms, but the atoms are arranged in a different way, making graphite very soft.

Each carbon atom in graphite is joined to only three neighbours. The atoms form layers that slip over each other, making graphite soft.

Graphite is used to make the soft lead in pencils.

Evaporate: As a liquid heats up, its molecules speed up until they move fast enough to float away as gas.

Condense: When gas molecules lose energy and slow down, they stick together and form liquid.

Gas

A gas can fill any container it's put in. If there's no lid to seal the container, the gas will escape into the air.

No, you can burn them.

Reactions and changes

Materials change as a result of physical processes or chemical reactions. In a chemical reaction, atoms join with or break away from other atoms, forming different compounds. Chemical reactions often lead to a dramatic change.

Melting is not a chemical reaction.

Chemical change

Burning is a chemical reaction involving oxygen (O). Wood is made of compounds containing carbon (C) and hydrogen (H). When it burns, the carbon and hydrogen react with oxygen to produce carbon dioxide (CO_2) and water (H_2O).

Physical change

Not all dramatic changes are caused by chemical reactions. When ice lollies melt, the atoms in the water molecules do not get rearranged into new molecules – they remain water molecules. Melting is simply a physical change.

Burning is a chemical reaction.

Escaping energy

Chemical reactions can release energy as heat and light. A sparkler contains chemicals that release a lot of energy and light to create a dazzling shower of sparks

What chemical reaction makes silver objects slowly turn grey and dull?

Speeding up reactions

Cooking makes carrots softer because the heat causes a chemical reaction. Chopping carrots into small bits speeds up the reaction because it increases the area of contact between the carrots and the hot water.

Sliced carrots cook faster than whole carrots.

Glow in the dark

Light sticks glow in the dark thanks to a chemical reaction that releases energy as light. You can slow down this reaction by putting a light stick in a fridge, which makes it last longer.

hands on
Ask an adult to boil some red cabbage and save the coloured water. Let the water cool. Then add acid (vinegar) or alkali (bicarbonate) and watch for a spectacular change of colour!

Soda volcano

vIf you drop mints into a bottle of fizzy drink, the drink turns to foam and explodes out in an instant. This is a physical change rather than a chemical reaction. The rough surface of the mints helps gas, dissolved in the drink, to turn into bubbles much more quickly than it normally would.

Tarnishing. It happens when silver atoms react with the oxygen atoms in air.

What is energy?

Energy is what makes everything happen. Your body needs energy so that you can move, grow, and keep warm. We also need energy to power our cars, light our homes, and do thousands of other jobs.

Sunshine

We get nearly all our energy from the Sun. Plants absorb the energy in sunlight and store it as chemical energy. The stored energy enters our body through food and is released inside our body's cells. Sunlight absorbed through our skin is also necessary to produce certain vitamins and minerals in our body. The Sun is the ultimate source of energy for all plants and animals.

Only a tiny fraction of the Sun's energy reaches the Earth.

A bow stores energy by bending. When you let go, the bow springs back into shape and releases the stored energy.

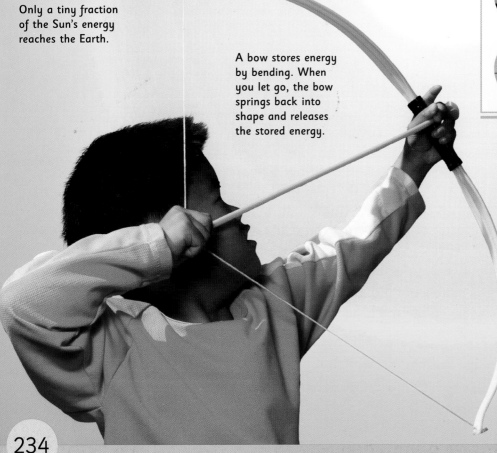

Sources of energy
Energy comes from lots of different sources.

 Wind drives wind turbines, which convert movement energy into electricity.

 Geothermal energy is heat from deep underground.

 Dried plants can be burnt to provide energy for cooking, heating, and lighting.

 Waves can be used to generate large amounts of electricity.

 Dams harness the energy in rivers flowing downhill to make electricity.

 The **Sun**'s energy can be captured by solar panels to make electricity.

 Fossil fuels, such as oil, are used to power cars and to make electricity.

Stored energy

An object can store energy and release it later. When you wind up a clockwork toy, energy is stored in a spring. A bow and arrow uses stored energy to shoot the arrow. Stored energy is also called potential energy because it has the potential to make things happen.

Is energy destroyed when we use it?

Movement energy

Rollercoasters start from the top of a hill, where their height gives them a lot of potential energy. As they move downhill, the potential energy turns into movement energy (kinetic energy), making them go faster and faster.

Nuclear energy

Matter is made up of tiny particles called atoms. The centre of an atom, called a nucleus, stores huge amounts of energy. This nuclear energy is used in power stations to make electricity.

Electrical energy

Lightning is caused by electrical energy in a storm cloud. The electrical energy turns into the heat and light energy of lightning and the sound energy of thunder.

Chain reactions

Changing energy from one type to another is called "energy conversion". The steps can be linked to make an energy chain.

Coal contains chemical energy.

Burning coal produces heat energy, which is used to boil water. Boiling water creates steam.

Moving steam is a form of kinetic (motion) energy, which operates turbines.

The kinetic energy produced by the moving turbines creates electricity.

Electrical energy used by television sets changes into light, sound, and heat energy.

Energy cannot be destroyed. It turns into another form of energy when it's used.

Electricity

Have you ever thought about what powers your television, your computer, or the lights in your bedroom? A flow of electricity makes all these things work.

Power supply

Electricity travels to your home along wires above and sometimes below the ground. The wires above the ground hang on metal towers called pylons.

Making electricity

Electricity is a form of energy. It can be made using any source of energy, such as coal, gas, oil, wind, or sunlight. On a wind farm, wind turbines use the energy of moving air to create electricity.

Everyday electricity

We use electricity in all sorts of ways in our everyday lives.

Electricity is used to **heat** up household appliances such as irons and cookers.

Electricity is used to **light** up our homes, schools, offices, and streets.

Electricity helps in **communication** by powering telephones and computers.

Electricity helps in **transportation** by powering certain vehicles, such as trains.

What's the name of a small object that can store electricity?

Circuits of power

An electric circuit is a loop that electricity can travel around. An electric current moves through the wires in this circuit, and lights up the bulb.

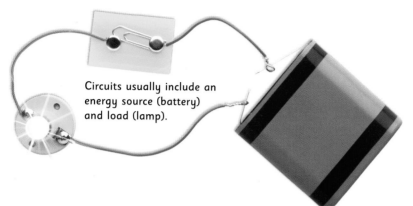

Circuits usually include an energy source (battery) and load (lamp).

Electrical cables

Electrical cables are made of metal and plastic. Electricity flows through the metal (which is called a conductor). The plastic (which is called an insulator) stops electricity escaping.

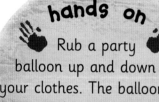

hands on

Rub a party balloon up and down on your clothes. The balloon will now stick to the wall. This is because rubbing it gives the balloon an electric charge.

Lightning strikes

Electric charge building up in one place is called "static electricity". Lightning is an electric current caused by static electricity building up in thunderclouds.

High voltage

Electricity can be very dangerous. This triangle is an international warning symbol. It means "Caution: risk of electric shock".

Food battery

Food that contains water and weak acid will conduct electricity. In a food battery, a chemical reaction between the metal and the acid in the food creates an electric current.

A conductor attached to food (containing acid) forms an electric circuit.

A battery.

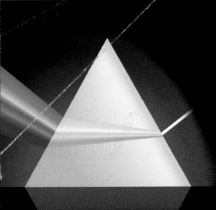

Light

Light is a form of energy that our eyes can detect. It comes in all the colours of the rainbow, but when the colours are mixed together, light is white.

Where does light come from?

Light is produced by electrically charged particles in atoms – especially negatively-charged electrons.

Candlelight is produced by hot atoms in tiny particles of soot inside the flame.

Casting shadows

Light can only travel in straight lines. If something blocks its path, it casts a shadow – a dark area that the light cannot reach.

Fireflies

Some animals create their own light. Fireflies flash a yellowish-green colour from their abdomen at night to attract mates.

Using light

We can use light for many different things.

 CDs and **DVDs** store digital information that can be read by laser beam.

 Cameras capture light in a split second to create photographs.

 Telescopes collect the light from stars and planets, and produce magnified images of them.

 Mirrors reflect light so we can see images of ourselves.

 Periscopes bend the path of light so we can see around corners.

 Torches shine a beam of light to help us see in the dark.

What's the fastest thing in the Universe?

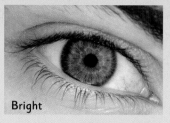

Bright

Dark

Light enters your eyes through your pupils (the black circles in the middle). Pupils can change size. When it's dark they get bigger to let more light in, and when it's bright they shrink so you don't get dazzled.

How your eye works

The human eye works like a camera. The front parts of the eye focus light rays just as a camera lens does. The focused rays form an upside-down image in the back of your eyeball.

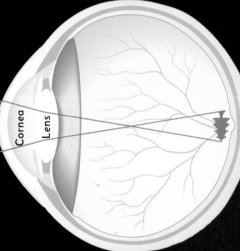

1. Light rays from the tree enter your eye.

Cornea

Lens

Tree

2. The cornea (front of eye) and lens focus the rays.

3. An image forms on the back of the eye. Light-sensing cells send the image to the brain.

4. The brain turns the image the right way up.

Reflecting light

When light hits a mirror, it bounces straight back off. If you look into a mirror, you see this bounced light as a reflection.

Convex mirrors bulge outwards. They make things look smaller but let you see a wider area.

Concave mirrors bulge inwards. They make things look bigger but show a smaller area.

Light beams

Unless it enters your eyes, light is invisible. The beam of light from a lighthouse can only be seen from the side if it catches mist or dust in the air, causing some of the light rays to bounce off towards you. Lighthouse beams sweep round in circles and can be seen from far out at sea.

Light. It travels at a billion kph (620,000,000 mph).

Sound

Every sound starts with a vibration, like the quivering of a guitar string. The vibration squeezes and stretches the air, sending its energy out in waves in all directions. This is a sound wave.

<h2>Measuring sound</h2>
Loudness is measured in decibels.

 Leaves rustling nearby make a sound of only 10 decibels.

 Somebody **whispering** close by measures about 20 decibels.

 City traffic reaches approximately 85 decibels.

 Drums being played nearby makes a sound of around 105 decibels.

 Road-drills measure about 110 decibels from a close distance.

 A **lion's roar** would measure 114 decibels if you were close enough.

 Fireworks can measure 120 decibels or more.

 The sound of **jet engines** sometimes hit 140 decibels if heard from nearby.

Sound notes

When you blow across a bottle, the air inside vibrates. Small air spaces vibrate more quickly than large spaces, making higher notes. So partly empty bottles produce lower notes than fuller ones.

Silent space

Sound can travel through solids, liquids, and gases, but it can't travel where there is no matter. There is no sound in space because there is no air.

Sound waves travel through air like a wave along a coiled spring.

How hearing works

When a sound reaches your ears, it makes your eardrums vibrate. The vibrations are passed to your inner ear through tiny bones. From here, nerves send messages to your brain that allow you to recognize the sound.

Do all animals hear sounds in the same way?

Speeding sound

Sounds travel through air at about 1,200 kph (750 mph). It travels faster through solids and liquids than through gases. Supersonic jets fly faster than the speed of sound, so they can pass over you before you hear their sound.

When a supersonic jet breaks the speed of sound, it catches up with the sound waves in front of it and squashes them. As the air is squashed, it produces a sound called a "sonic boom".

The echo effect

Some animals use sound to communicate or to hunt. Dolphins "talk" by making clicks, barks, and other sounds that other dolphins recognize. They also use clicks to find food – the sound bounces back off objects as an echo, so the dolphin can establish their shape and position. This is called echolocation.

When sounds bounce back, the dolphin can tell if the object is a yummy fish or another dolphin!

241

No – dogs and bats can hear higher notes than people.

Forces and motion

It can be difficult to make an object move, but once it is moving, it will go on moving until something stops it. Force is needed to start something moving, make it move faster, and make it stop.

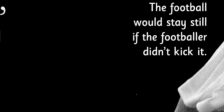

The football would stay still if the footballer didn't kick it.

Newton's laws of motion

In 1687, Isaac Newton presented three important rules that explain how forces make things move. They have become the foundation of physics and work for just about everything, from footballs to frogs.

Newton's first law

An object stays still, or keeps moving in a straight line at a constant speed, if it isn't being pushed or pulled by a force.

Forces make things accelerate. In this case, the force is created by the cyclist's powerful legs.

Newton's second law

The bigger the force and the lighter the object, the greater the acceleration. A professional cyclist with a lightweight bike will accelerate faster than a normal person cycling to work.

Newton's third law

Every action has an equal and opposite reaction. The leaf moves away as the frog leaps in the opposite direction.

242

Speed and velocity

Speed is different from velocity. Speed is how fast you are going and is easy to work out – divide how far you travel by the time it takes. Your velocity is how fast you travel in a particular direction. Changing direction without slowing reduces your velocity, but your speed stays the same.

If you drive 80 km (50 miles) in two hours, your speed is 40 kph (25 mph).

Accelerating is fun, but defining it in scientific terms can be confusing. This is because acceleration doesn't just mean speeding up. It is any change in velocity. So, it is also used to describe slowing down and changing direction.

The golf ball will carry on rolling until friction, gravity, and air resistance slow it down.

Inertia

When things are standing still or moving, they continue to remain in the state they are in (unless force is applied to them to change it). This tendency to be as they are called inertia.

Rescue helicopters balance forces so they can hover above the waves.

LIFT

DRAG/
FRICTION

THRUST

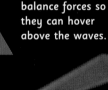

GRAVITY

Turn and learn
Magnetism: **pp. 78–79**
Gravity: **pp. 88–89**

Balanced forces

Forces act on objects all the time. Opposing forces can be balanced out. When this happens, the object won't be pushed in any direction.

The maximum velocity of falling through air is 200 kph (124 mph).

Machines

Machines make tasks easier. They reduce the effort you need to move something, or the time it takes. They work either by spreading the load, or by concentrating your efforts. All the machines you see here are called simple machines.

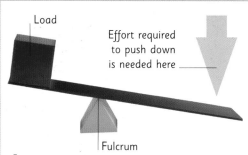
Load

Effort required to push down is needed here

Fulcrum

Levers

A lever is a bar that can turn around a fixed point (fulcrum). If you apply a force (effort) to one part of a lever, another part exerts a force (load).

One type of lever works like a seesaw with the fulcrum between the load and the effort.

Another type places the load between the fulcrum and the effort (as on a wheelbarrow).

A **third type** of lever, shown by tongs, places the effort between the fulcrum and the load.

Axle

Wheel and axle

An axle goes through the centre of a wheel. Together they work as a simple rotating machine that makes it easier to move something from one place to another.

Gears

Gears are wheels with teeth that interlock so that one wheel turns another. They increase speed or force. Gears on a bicycle affect how much you must turn the pedal to spin the wheel.

The pedal turns a wheel, which turns a smaller wheel at a greater speed.

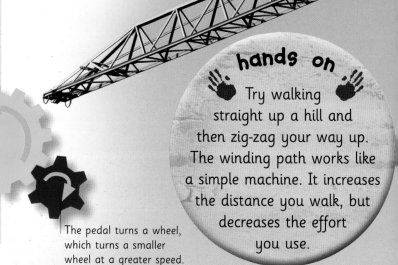

hands on
Try walking straight up a hill and then zig-zag your way up. The winding path works like a simple machine. It increases the distance you walk, but decreases the effort you use.

What is another name for gear?

Wedge

An axe blade is an efficient but simple machine that increases force. When it hits the wood, the wedge forces the wood to split apart between its fibres.

It takes just one man to pull a stone up the slope, but four men are needed to lift a stone straight up.

Inclined plane

It is easier to push or pull something up a slope than lift it straight up. A slope, or inclined plane, therefore increases force. In ancient Egypt, stones were dragged up slopes to build the pyramids.

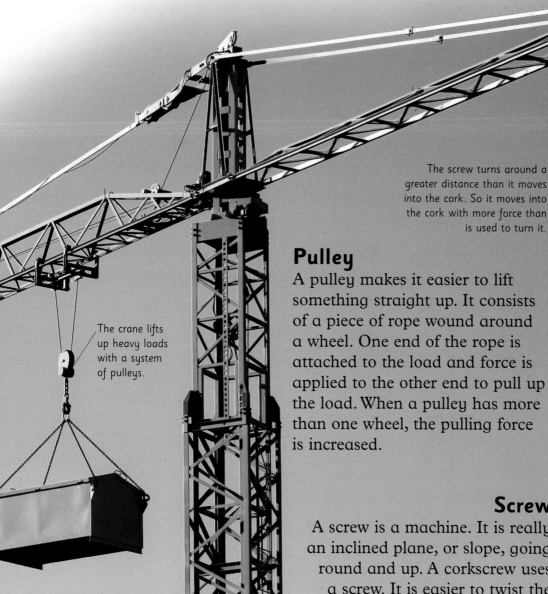

The crane lifts up heavy loads with a system of pulleys.

The screw turns around a greater distance than it moves into the cork. So it moves into the cork with more force than is used to turn it.

Pulley

A pulley makes it easier to lift something straight up. It consists of a piece of rope wound around a wheel. One end of the rope is attached to the load and force is applied to the other end to pull up the load. When a pulley has more than one wheel, the pulling force is increased.

Screw

A screw is a machine. It is really an inclined plane, or slope, going round and up. A corkscrew uses a screw. It is easier to twist the point of a screw into a cork than to push a spike straight in.

245

Cogwheel.

Our planet

The Earth is the planet where we all live. It is a huge ball of very hot rock with a cool surface called the crust. Planet Earth travels in space.

North Pole

The Earth's axis goes through its poles.

The Earth's axis...

...is tilted to one side.

South Pole

Spinning Earth

The Earth slowly spins around once a day. The line it spins around is called the Earth's axis. At the ends of the axis are the Earth's poles.

The Earth's surface

There are seven huge pieces of land on the Earth's surface. They are called continents. They cover about one-third of the surface. Oceans cover the rest.

Earth as a magnet

Have you ever used a compass to find your way? It works because the Earth acts as if it has a giant bar magnet in the middle.

Which is the biggest ocean on the Earth?

Inside the Earth

The Earth's crust is quite thin. Underneath is a deep layer of hot rock called the mantle. In the middle is a heavy core.

Core
Mantle
Crust

The cracked crust

The Earth's crust is cracked into lots of huge pieces called plates. The cracks are called fault lines. Earthquakes and volcanoes often happen where the edges of the plates grind together.

The San Andreas Fault, California, USA

Mountains and valleys

Most mountains are made when rocks are pushed upwards by movements of the Earth's crust. Blowing winds, flowing rivers, and glaciers wear away the mountains.

Sedona, Arizona, southwestern USA

Picture detective

Look through the Planet Earth pages and see if you can identify each of the picture clues below.

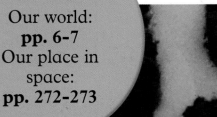

Turn and learn

Our world: **pp. 6-7**
Our place in space: **pp. 272-273**

247

The Earth's structure

Seen from space, the Earth is a mass of blue oceans and swirling clouds.

The Earth is the only planet in the solar system that can support life because it's just the right distance from the Sun. Our amazing world is a huge ball of liquid rock with a solid surface.

Inside the Earth

If you could cut the Earth open, you'd see it's made up of layers. The thin top layer, where we live, is called the crust. Underneath is a layer of syrup-like rock called the mantle, then an outer core of molten (liquid) iron and nickel. At the centre is a solid iron-and-nickel core.

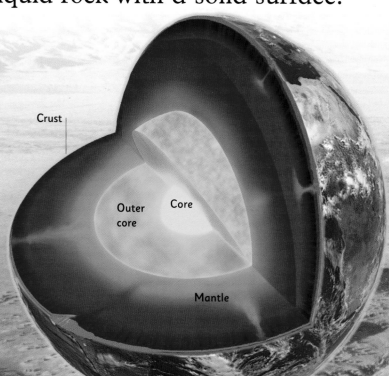

Crust

Outer core

Core

Mantle

Life-support systems

The Earth's atmosphere and its surface water play an important role in supporting life. They help keep our planet at just the right temperature by absorbing the Sun's heat and moving it around the world.

What is the biggest ocean on the Earth?

Volcanoes

Volcanoes are openings in the Earth's crust. Sometimes, magma (melted rock) from just beneath the crust bursts through these openings as a volcanic eruption. Lots of ash and dust shoot out too.

Making mountains

The Himalayas started to form 50 million years ago, when two moving plates collided. The mountains are still growing! Mount Everest, the tallest peak in the world, is a part of the Himalayan range and is growing 4 mm ($^{3}/_{20}$ in) each year.

Fault lines

Earthquakes happen when two plates of the Earth's crust rub against each other. The boundary between the plates is called a fault line.

Earthquakes often occur along the San Andreas Fault.

Drifting continents

The world hasn't always looked like it does now. Millions of years ago, all the land was joined together. Slowly, it broke up and the continents drifted apart.

200 million years ago   135 million years ago   10 million years ago

Cracked crust

The Earth's top layer is made up of giant pieces called "plates". These fit together a bit like a jigsaw, but they're constantly moving. Volcanoes and earthquakes often happen in the weak spots where plates move against each other.

San Andreas Fault

Active volcanoes

The Pacific Ocean.

Rocks and minerals

The Earth's crust is made up of different rocks. Some of these are hard but others are soft and crumbly. They are formed in different ways.

Serpentine is a mineral that stone carvers use to create works of art.

Gabbro is a rock that is used to make kitchen surfaces and floors.

White mica is a mineral that you can find in some kinds of toothpaste.

What is a rock?

A rock is formed from minerals. Most rocks are made up of different minerals, but some contain just one. There are three main types of rock: igneous, sedimentary, and metamorphic.

Fossils in stones

Fossils are the remains or imprints of plants and animals that died millions of years ago, preserved in stone.

The rock cycle

Over many years, the rocks in the Earth's crust gradually change from one type into another. They are transformed by wind, water, pressure, and heat.

Igneous rock

When hot molten magma from the Earth's interior cools and solidifies, it forms igneous rocks. Some harden underground, such as granite. Some erupt first as lava in a volcano.

Sedimentary rock

Wind and water wear rocks away. Small pieces wash into the sea. These settle into layers, which pack together to form sedimentary rocks, such as limestone and sandstone.

Metamorphic rock

Sometimes rocks are crushed underground or scorched by hot magma. Then they may be transformed into new rocks, such as marble, slate, and gneiss.

Which type of rock floats on water?

Rock salt is a mineral that is spread on roads in icy weather. It makes the ice melt.

What is a mineral?

A mineral is a solid that occurs naturally. It is made up of chemicals and has a crystal structure. Minerals are everywhere you look. We use minerals to build cars and computers, fertilize soil, and to clean our teeth.

Minerals in your home

Minerals make up many common objects.

Halite is the natural form of salt, which we add to our food for flavour.

Quartz from sand is used to make the silicon chips in calculators and computers.

Kaolinite is used to make crockery. It is also used to make paper look glossy.

Illite is a clay mineral and is used in terracotta pots and bricks.

Mica is used to make glittery paint and nail polish.

Graphite is the lead in pencils. It is also used in bicycle brakes.

Mineral mixtures

Granite rock is made up of different coloured minerals. The black mineral is mica, the pink is feldspar, and the grey mineral is quartz.

Feldspar is used for glazing ceramics.

Mica is ground up and used in paint.

Quartz can also occur as the gemstone amethyst.

Crystals

Minerals usually form crystals. Crystals have a number of flat surfaces. The largest crystals form when minerals in magma or trapped liquids cool very slowly.

Quartz stalactites form in caves over thousands of years.

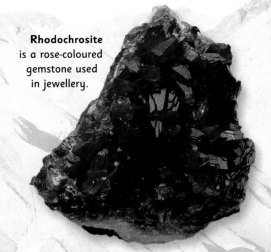

Rhodochrosite is a rose-coloured gemstone used in jewellery.

Pumice – it is filled with air bubbles, so some pieces can float.

Shaping the land

The surface of our planet never stops changing. Over millions of years, land is slowly worn away by wind, rain, and rivers. Floods, volcanoes, and earthquakes can change the shape of the land in just a few hours.

River power
The Grand Canyon formed over millions of years as the Colorado River slowly wore down the rock deeper.

Going underground
Caves form when rain seeps underground and eats away at soft rock such as limestone.

Coastal shapes
Powerful waves shape the coastlines around the world's oceans.

Bays form where waves wear into areas of softer rock along the coast.

Headlands are areas of harder rock that have not been worn away.

Sea arches form when waves open up cracks in headlands.

Sea stacks are pillars of rock left in the sea after an arch collapses.

Glaciers at work
Glaciers are huge rivers of ice that flow slowly off snowcapped mountains. Broken rock sticks to the bottom of the glacier, which then wears away the land like sandpaper, carving out a deep, U-shaped valley.

252

New islands

Some volcanoes are hidden under the sea. When they erupt, they can give birth to whole new islands, like Surtsey in Iceland (left). Surtsey burst out of the sea in 1963.

Before flood

After flood

Floods

Heavy rain makes rivers overflow, causing floods. Floods have enormous power and can wreck buildings and reshape the land.

Worn by wind

Strong winds can lift sand off the ground and blast it hard against rocks. The rock is worn into strange shapes.

Hills of sand

In deserts, winds blow sand into hills called dunes. In some deserts, the dunes stretch for hundreds of miles, forming a "sand sea".

Mount Kilauea in Hawaii.

253

Soil

Soil is the thin layer of loose material on the land. Soil contains minerals, air, water, and decaying organic matter.

Humus

Topsoil

Subsoil

Regolith

Bedrock

Layers in soil

Soil builds up in layers over many years. Plant roots grow in the topsoil, which is generally the richest in plant food. The lower layers are rocky. Plant roots do not reach this far down in the soil.

Healthy humus

Humus is a dark, rich substance made up of rotting plants and animals (called "organic matter"). It contains lots of nutrients, which plants need to grow.

Life underground

Soil is home to thousands of animals, including slugs, ants, beetles, and spiders. Larger animals that spend time underground, such as moles, mix up humus and minerals as they burrow through the soil.

What is a scientist who studies soil called?

Sizing up soil

Different types of soil have different sized particles.

Sandy soils contain particles about 2 mm (0.08 in) across.

Clay soils have very small particles. Water collects between them.

Loamy soils have a mixture of small and large particles.

Soil erosion

When soil is farmed too much, its nutrients get used up. The topsoil blows or washes away. Not many plants can survive in these areas without the rich topsoil.

Ploughing breaks up soil, to stop it getting hard and solid. This helps keep soil fertile and crops grow more easily.

FORD 7740

Important earthworms

Earthworms help to make fertile soil. Their burrows let air into the soil, and create pathways for water to move around more easily. Earthworms also help the remains of plants and animals to decompose. This releases important nutrients into the soil. Earthworm waste is good for soil too!

hands on

Half fill a jar with soil and top it up with water. Put on the lid and shake. Leave for a day. The soil should separate into layers.

A pedologist.

Resources in the ground

The ground holds many useful things, from fuels like coal and oil, to drinking water and building materials. These valuable items are known as resources, and we have dug, drilled, and searched for them for many years.

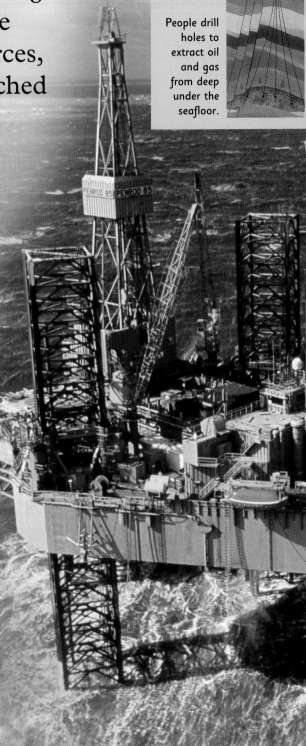

Sea level

Rig

People drill holes to extract oil and gas from deep under the seafloor.

Finding fuels

Oil and gas are often found in pockets deep underground. Sometimes, these are even below the seabed. Coal develops closer to the surface in layers called seams.

Deep drilling

Oil rigs far out at sea use huge drills to extract the liquid oil from the ground. Coal is solid, and is dug out in mines or pits.

In hot water

Water in the ground can get very hot near volcanoes. In Iceland, they use this naturally hot water to heat houses or make steam to turn electricity generators.

Which underground resource are plastics made from?

Getting gas
Gas is only found in certain places. To get it to where it is needed, it is fed through very long pipes, or changed into liquid and put in special ships.

Glass bottles are shaped from molten glass.

Making glass
Glass is made by melting together sand, soda ash, and ground limestone. People blow or machine-press the red-hot mineral mixture into different shapes. These set hard and clear as the glass cools.

Extracting metals
Most metals are found underground as minerals in rocks called ores. Giant machines dig up the ore. The metal is extracted, or taken out, from the ore using heat.

Metal variety
Different metal resources have different uses.

 Aluminium is a soft metal used to make cans, aircraft, and car bodies.

 Gold is rare and looks beautiful, so it is often used to make awards and medals.

 Iron is strong. It is used to make steel for ships, buildings, and pylons.

 Copper prevents barnacles from growing on it, so parts of ships are often coated with it.

Creating concrete
Concrete is an important building material. It is made with water, sand, gravel, and cement. Water, sand, and gravel are found in the ground, while cement is made from limestone, which is also found in the ground.

Oil

Fresh and salt water

The Earth is often called the blue planet because 75 per cent of its surface is covered in water. Most of the Earth's water is salt water in the oceans. Less than one per cent of all the water on the Earth is fresh.

Freshwater sources

People get fresh water from different sources on the Earth's surface, including rivers, streams, lakes, and reservoirs.

Rivers and **streams** flow from mountains down to the oceans.

Lakes are natural dips in the Earth where water collects.

Reservoirs are man-made lakes that are built to store water.

The hydrosphere

The hydrosphere is the name for all the water on the Earth. It includes oceans, rivers, and lakes. It also includes water that is frozen, such as icebergs.

Trapped in ice

Less than 33 per cent of fresh water is usable by humans. The rest is frozen in glaciers or icebergs (below), or as huge sheets of ice at the North and South poles.

Water for life

All living things must have water to survive. In mammals, including humans, water is part of the blood and of organs, such as the skin and brain. There is water in every cell in your body. In fact, cells contain about two-thirds of the body's water!

How much of your body is water?

Salty seas

The world's oceans are salty because they contain a lot of dissolved chemicals that scientists call salts. Drinking water also contains salts, but only in small amounts, so you can't taste them.

The Dead Sea, located in Asia, contains so much salt that people can just float on the surface.

Surviving in salt water

Countless animals live in water. They don't drink, but take water into their bodies in other ways. Fish often absorb water as it washes in and out of their gills. Salt-water fish absorb only a little of the salt.

hands on

Put an egg in a glass of water. The egg will sink. Start stirring in salt until the egg rises. The egg will eventually float because salt water is denser than fresh water.

Estuary life

An estuary is the wide part of a river where it nears the sea. When the tide comes in, salt water flows into the estuary. When the tide goes out, the estuary contains mostly fresh water from the river or stream that flows into it. Mangrove trees, like the ones shown here, are able to live in the changing estuary water.

259

The water cycle

Water is constantly on the move, between oceans, land, air, and rivers. This movement is called the water cycle.

Water falls as rain, snow, or hail from clouds.

When this water vapour floats high in the sky, it condenses and forms clouds.

Sun

Water heated by the Sun evaporates. It changes from liquid to vapour.

Rainwater collects in rivers and streams, and also seeps underground.

Groundwater

Water from rivers and streams flows into the sea.

Sea

Natural recycling

The water cycle is the journey water makes as it moves from the air to the land, and into the seas, and then back into the air again.

On the dry side

Moisture-laden sea air has to rise when it hits a coastal mountain. Since air cools as it rises, all the moisture condenses and falls as rain. So, on the other side of the mountain, no rain falls. This area is called a rainshadow.

What is electricity generated by running water called?

Groundwater

In the water cycle, some water seeps underground, where it collects in rocks and sometimes forms pools in caves. Some groundwater is pumped up and used for drinking or irrigation.

Using water

Fresh water is trapped in reservoirs and then piped to homes, businesses, and farms. When you turn on a tap, the water that comes out has been on a long journey!

Damp ground

Wetlands form on land in areas where fresh water does not drain away. They provide a habitat for many plants, birds, animals, and fish.

Drought

When very little rain falls, experts call it a drought. Droughts do not occur only in deserts – any area that gets much less rain than usual is said to be suffering from drought.

Saving water

There is a limited amount of fresh water on the Earth. If we want to make sure there's enough to go around, it's important that everyone uses less.

Don't keep taps running while you are brushing your teeth or washing.

Flush the toilet only when necessary. Some toilets have two flush controls.

Don't run the dishwasher when it's half empty – wait until it's full.

Take a shower instead of a bath. Showering uses much less water.

Hydroelectricity.

The atmosphere

Planet Earth is wrapped in a thin layer of air called the atmosphere. Without this protective blanket of gases, life on the Earth could not exist.

Gases in air

Air is a mixture of different gases, including nitrogen, oxygen, and carbon dioxide. Oxygen is vital for plants and animals as it allows them to breathe. Carbon dioxide is also vital for plants. They absorb it from the air and use the carbon atoms to help build new leaves and stems.

Shimmering particles

The atmosphere is mainly made up of gases, but it also contains tiny particles of dust, pollen, and water droplets. All particles can cause a haze in the air when the Sun shines through them.

The purple area, where the ozone layer is the thinnest, is called the ozone hole.

The greenhouse effect

If there was no atmosphere, the Sun's warming rays would bounce off the Earth and disappear into space. But the atmosphere traps some of the heat, making the Earth warm enough for us to survive.

Protective layer

A gas called ozone in the atmosphere protects the Earth from harmful rays in sunlight. This ozone layer has become thinner because of chemical pollution. During the spring season (August–October) in the Southern Hemisphere, an area of the ozone layer above Antarctica becomes much thinner than anywhere else. This "ozone hole" occurs every year.

How far up from the ground does space officially begin?

Into thin air

Like everything else, air is pulled by gravity. Most air molecules are pulled close to the ground, where the air is thick and easy to breathe. Higher up, air is so thin that climbers need oxygen tanks.

From space, the atmosphere looks like a blue haze over the Earth.

Layers of the atmosphere

The atmosphere is made up of layers, each with a different name. The bottom layer is the troposphere, where clouds form and planes fly. Above this, the air gets thinner and thinner as the atmosphere merges into space.

Light spectacular

Sunlight can create dazzling effects as it strikes the atmosphere and is scattered by air, water, and dust.

Rainbows form when water droplets reflect sunlight and split it into different colours.

The **sky looks blue** on clear days because air molecules scatter blue light the most.

At **sunset**, only the red and orange light of sunlight make it through the atmosphere.

Moving water

The atmosphere is always swirling around, creating winds. The winds push on the oceans, causing the water to swirl too. These swirling currents carry warmth around the planet.

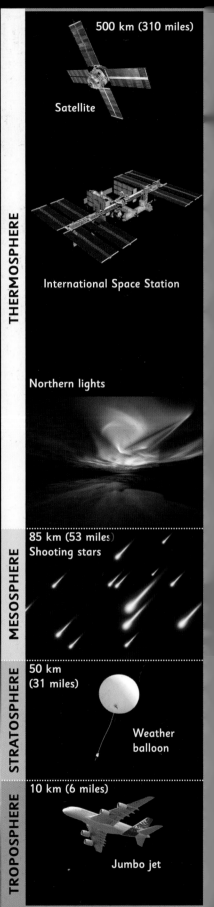

500 km (310 miles)

Satellite

THERMOSPHERE

International Space Station

Northern lights

85 km (53 miles)
Shooting stars

MESOSPHERE

50 km (31 miles)

STRATOSPHERE

Weather balloon

10 km (6 miles)

TROPOSPHERE

Jumbo jet

263

Weather

Is it sunny or rainy? Is there snow on the ground or a thunderstorm brewing? People are always interested in the weather because it affects what we do and what we wear.

Kites stay high in the air by catching the wind.

Weather words

Here are some main features of the weather.

Sunshine gives us heat and light. It warms the air and dries the land.

Clouds are made from tiny water droplets. Dark clouds mean rain is coming.

Hailstones are balls of ice that grow inside thunderclouds.

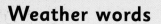
Wind is air moving around. Winds can be a light breeze or a strong gale.

Rain is drops of water that fall from clouds. Rain is very good for plant life.

Snow is made from tiny bits of ice. It falls instead of rain when it is very cold.

Predicting the weather

Weather forecasters look at pictures beamed back from weather satellites. Computers then help forecasters work out what the weather is going to be like over the next few days.

Rainy days

Rain clouds form when warm, moist air rises upwards and then cools. Droplets of water join together until they become so heavy that they fall. Rain clouds look dark because sunlight cannot shine through the droplets.

Which is bigger – a tornado or a hurricane?

Wildfires

Long periods of hot or dry weather can make plants dry out so much that they catch fire easily when struck by lightning. This can lead to a raging wildfire that burns down whole forests.

Stormy weather

Lightning strikes when electricity builds up in clouds. The electricity is created when ice crystals in the clouds rub against each other. A bolt of lightning heats the air around it so quickly that the air explodes, creating the rumbling noise we call thunder.

The brightest bolts of lightning travel upwards from the ground to the clouds.

Winds on the move

Wind is moving air. Warm air rises and cool air sinks. This movement is what makes the wind blow.

Twisters

Tornadoes (twisters) are whirling funnels of wind that form beneath massive thunderclouds. The fierce wind can do enormous damage, and the funnel can suck up debris like a gigantic vacuum cleaner.

weird or what?

Hailstones can grow to be enormous in certain conditions. The biggest hailstone weighed nearly 1 kg (2 lb) and was 20 cm (8 in) across!

A hurricane is thousands of times bigger than a tornado.

The energy crisis

People around the world use energy for many different purposes – from powering cars to heating homes. Most of this energy comes from burning coal, oil, and natural gas (fossil fuels). But these fuels won't last forever, and their fumes are damaging the atmosphere.

Nuclear power stations generate energy by splitting atoms.

Global warming

Burning fossil fuels fills the air with greenhouse gases, which trap some of the Sun's heat in the atmosphere. If the Earth becomes too warm, polar ice caps will melt, the sea level will rise, and deserts will spread.

Alternative energy

We need to find sources of energy other than fossil fuels – sources which cause less pollution and will not run out. Nuclear power is one option. Others possibilities include energy from sunlight, wind, and waves.

Heat from the Sun enters through the atmosphere.

Greenhouse gases trap heat, although some escapes back into the atmosphere.

The wind provides a limitless supply of non-polluting energy. However, wind turbines are large and can be costly to set up.

What are fossil fuels made of?

Cleaner cars

Ordinary petrol cars use a lot of oil, and produce harmful fumes. Now car makers are looking for alternatives to petrol. Electric cars do not give off any kind of fumes. Hydrogen engines burn hydrogen gas, and only give off water.

To recharge an electric car, you just plug it in.

Rising energy needs

As the world's population grows, we are using more and more energy. But to stop global warming, we may have to reduce the amount of energy we all use.

Energy-saving homes

This house saves energy by using solar panels and wind turbines to generate its own non-polluting electricity. The walls are thick, so that less energy is needed to heat the house.

To reduce the energy used in manufacturing, it's a good idea to use recycled building materials.

Making a difference

There are lots of small things we can all do to save energy.

 Start growing your own vegetables and fruits, even if they're only in pots.

 When planning a holiday, remember that trains, boats, and cars use less energy than aeroplanes.

 Instead of buying new clothes, swap with a friend or buy them second-hand.

 Eat local food that hasn't travelled miles, because transporting food costs energy.

 Don't throw away glass, plastics, metal, or paper – reuse or recycle them.

 Take your own bags when you go shopping. Making plastic bags takes energy.

 Don't leave your TV or laptop on standby – this wastes lots of electricity.

 Hang your laundry outside to dry. Don't waste electricity running a dryer.

 Ask your parents about **insulating the roof** to prevent heat from escaping.

 If you get cold, **put on a jumper** instead of turning up your heating.

The remains of plants and animals that lived millions of years ago.

What is space?

Space holds many secrets. It contains places where human beings can be stretched into different shapes, and their body fluids can be boiled, or frozen solid. That's why astronauts wear protective clothing in space. Welcome to a mysterious – and endlessly fascinating – universe.

What is space?

When people think of space, they think of the following.

 Astronauts feel **weightless** and float around.

 Vast areas of space are **completely empty**.

 Every **star** is a burning ball of gas. Our Sun is a star.

 Astronauts, or **cosmonauts**, are people who travel into space.

 Space probes and **artificial satellites** are what scientists use to explore space.

 There is no air in space, so there is **absolute silence**.

Is that space?

On a cloudless night, you can see thousands of stars. Space is the name we give to the huge empty areas in between the atmospheres of stars and planets. Apart from the odd rock, space is sprinkled only with dust and gas.

Too big to imagine

Astronomers measure distance in space in light years. One light year is the distance light travels in one year – that's about 10 million million km (6 million million miles).

A planetary nebula forms when a dying star creates a cloud of dust and gas. This is the Helix Nebula, about 650 light years away, seen from NASA's Spitzer Space Telescope.

How old is the Universe?

Why is space so dark?

Space is dark because there is nothing there to reflect light. From space, the Earth looks lit up because light from our Sun reflects off sea and land, and the particles in our atmosphere.

US astronaut Michael Gernhardt went on four separate space missions, and spent more than 23 hours walking around in space.

Picture detective

Look through the What is Space? section and see if you can identify the pictures below.

Turn and learn

The Milky Way: pp. 274-275
Rockets: pp. 276-277

Experts believe it's just under 14 billion years old.

Where does space begin?

The Earth is cloaked in a thin layer of gases – the atmosphere. Outside this atmosphere is space, where there is no air to breathe, or to allow wings to fly, and where nobody can hear you scream.

Fading away
Our atmosphere does not just end suddenly – it fades gradually into space.

View from *Mir*
The Russian *Mir* space station was in orbit for 15 years. Here, it has been photographed by the US shuttle Atlantis.

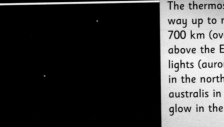
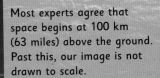
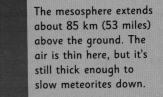
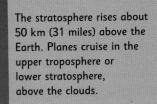

EXOSPHERE

THERMOSPHERE

MESOSPHERE

STRATOSPHERE

TROPOSPHERE

The exosphere is the outer layer of the atmosphere, extending about 10,000 km (6,000 miles) above the ground. From here, lighter gases drift into space beyond.

The thermosphere reaches way up to more than 700 km (over 400 miles) above the Earth. The polar lights (aurora borealis in the north and aurora australis in the south) glow in the thermosphere.

Most experts agree that space begins at 100 km (63 miles) above the ground. Past this, our image is not drawn to scale.

The mesosphere extends about 85 km (53 miles) above the ground. The air is thin here, but it's still thick enough to slow meteorites down.

The stratosphere rises about 50 km (31 miles) above the Earth. Planes cruise in the upper troposphere or lower stratosphere, above the clouds.

The troposphere extends between 6 and 20 km (3½–12 miles) above the ground. All our weather takes place in the troposphere.

What is the mix of gases that makes up our atmosphere called?

Space badge
The US space agency NASA (National Aeronautics and Space Administration) awards astronaut wings to service personnel and civilians who have flown more than 80 km (50 miles) above the Earth's surface. Shown here are civilian astronaut wings.

If you could drive a car straight up, it would take only about an hour to reach space.

Gaia, a European satellite, launched in 2013

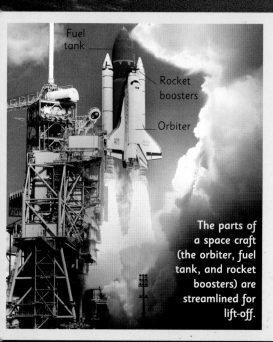

Fuel tank

Rocket boosters

Orbiter

The parts of a space craft (the orbiter, fuel tank, and rocket boosters) are streamlined for lift-off.

Slipping through air
A spacecraft has to be streamlined to move easily and safely through air. Where necessary, an extra part, called a fairing, is added to achieve this effect. A nose cone – the front end of a rocket, or aircraft – is an example of a fairing.

Space hat-ellite
Up in space, satellites can be any shape at all. They don't need to be streamlined, because there's no air there.

271

It is called air.

Our place in space

The Earth seems huge to us – after all, it can take you a long time just to travel to school! But the Earth is only a very tiny part of space. So where exactly does it belong in the Universe?

The Earth looks like a swirly blue marble suspended in space.

The Earth and its moon

The Earth, our home in space, has one natural satellite, or moon – called the Moon. It is about one quarter of the size of the Earth and, on average, orbits about 384,000 km (240,000 miles) away from us.

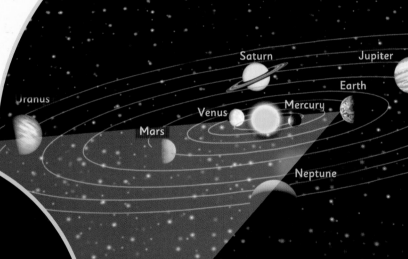

Saturn

Jupiter

Uranus

Earth

Mercury

Venus

Mars

Neptune

This picture shows where the planets are located. None of them, or their orbits, are drawn to scale.

Astronauts who have seen the Earth from space, are struck by its beauty. One described it as looking like a Christmas-tree decoration.

The solar system

The Earth is the third planet from the Sun at just the right distance from it to support life. The eight planets that orbit the Sun (plus moons, comets, asteroids, meteoroids, dwarf planets, dust, and gas) make up our solar system

Which was the ninth planet of the solar system, now classed as a dwarf planet?

In a spin
Our galaxy has long curved arms that spiral out from a central bulge.

The Milky Way

Our Sun and the solar system

The Local Group
The Milky Way is one of the largest galaxies in a cluster known as the Local Group. Millions of galaxy clusters make up the Universe.

The Milky Way
Our solar system is located in a galaxy called the Milky Way, a collection of billions of stars. It lies on the edge of one of the spiral arms.

Our home in space supports trillions of living things.

Pluto.

The Milky Way

Our solar system is a tiny part of a gigantic barred spiral galaxy, the Milky Way. This is made up of billions of stars, which look as if they have been sprinkled thickly onto the night sky.

Scientists think there are about 400,000 million stars in the Milky Way galaxy, but there may be even more.

Why is it milky?

Before the invention of telescopes, people could not see the stars very clearly – they were blurred together in a hazy white streak. The ancient Greeks called this streak a "river of milk". This is how our galaxy became known as the Milky Way.

Turn and learn

Our place in space: **pp. 272-273**
A star is born: **pp. 290-291**

Milky myths

Many myths have developed about the formation of the Milky Way.

Native American stories tell of a dog dropping corn as he fled across the sky.

Hindu myth sees the milkiness as the speckled belly of a dolphin.

Kalahari bushmen say it was created by hot embers thrown up from a fire.

The **ancient Egyptians** believed the stars were a pool of cow's milk.

A side view

The Milky Way, like al spiral and barred spira galaxies, is flat, with a bulge at the centre, and arms that circle outwards

Where are the oldest stars in the Milky Way?

The time it takes for our solar system to orbit the Milky Way once, is known as a galactic year. It's approximately 230 million Earth years.

We are here!

It takes light 100,000 years to pass from one edge of the Milky Way to the other.

In a sphere of stars surrounding the galaxy, often in giant balls called globular clusters.

Rockets

Rockets carry satellites and people into space. A rocket burns fuel to produce a jet of gas. The hot gas expands rapidly and is blasted downwards causing a force (the thrust) to push the rocket up.

A nose cone, or fairing, reduces air resistance as the rocket takes off.

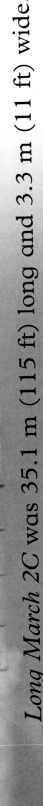

Long March 2C was 35.1 m (115 ft) long and 3.3 m (11 ft) wide.

Birth of the rocket
The first liquid-fuelled rocket was launched in 1926 by an American, Robert Goddard. It reached 12.5 m (41 ft). The flight lasted 2.5 seconds.

Launch of the *Long March 2C* rocket from the Jiuquan Space Centre, China, on 19 August 1983. Its main cargo was a photographic imaging satellite.

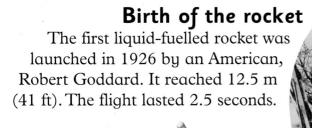

Vostok 1 spaceship

On return, Yuri Gagarin parachuted from the *Vostok 1* capsule 7 km (just over 4 miles) above the ground.

First in space
The first person in space was the Russian cosmonaut, Yuri Gagarin. He was sent up in *Vostok* 1 on 12 April 1961 for a 108-minute flight.

How many tests were needed for the engine that powered the first stage of *Ariane 5*?

To escape the Earth's gravity, a rocket has to reach just over 11 km (7 miles) per second. This is called the escape velocity.

Types of rocket
There are many different kinds of rocket.

Soyuz rockets are used by astronauts to reach the International Space Station.

Saturn V were the largest rockets ever built. They were used to launch all the Moon landings.

Firework rockets are used for celebrations.

Military rockets have been used for hundreds of years.

Experimental rockets provide information about fast and high flight.

Some satellites have small rocket engines to position them once they are in orbit.

Regular launches
Today, rockets such as *Ariane 5* are used to launch satellites into space. A satellite is a rocket's payload, or cargo, whose size determines whether it is sent up by a small or large rocket.

This is the *Ariane 5* launch vehicle. The main tank contains 25 tonnes (27.5 tons) of liquid hydrogen. The tubes on each side are solid fuel boosters that supply extra power for lift-off.

Biggest and best
The *Saturn V* were the largest, and most powerful, rockets ever built. They were used 13 times, between 1967 and 1973, including for the first Moon landing.

Around 300 tests were done.

Moon journey

During the 1960s, there was a race between the USA and the former Soviet Union to put a man on the Moon. The USA succeeded by landing the first humans on the Moon with *Apollo 11* in 1969.

Apollo 11 reached the Moon because of a huge rocket called *Saturn V*. Most of *Saturn V* contained the fuel needed to blast it into space. Three astronauts sat in a tiny capsule at the top of the rocket.

10 The service module is ejected before re-entry into the Earth's atmosphere.

Service and command modules **9**

The journey back

1 Five F1 engines blast the *Saturn V* rocket into space from the Kennedy Space Center.

11 The command module is the only part of the mission to return to the Earth.

Earth

Kennedy Space Center

The journey out

12 Command module

13 Re-entering atmosphere

3 The command and service modules separate from the rocket and perform a 180° turn.

The service module contained the power and life-support systems.

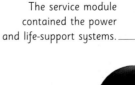

2 The rocket's engines fire to set the craft on a course to the Moon.

What was *Apollo 11*?

Apollo 11 was the first manned mission to land on the Moon. It was made up of three modules, or parts: the tiny command module, the service module, and the lunar module.

How many astronauts have walked on the Moon?

Turn and learn

Men on the Moon:
pp. 280–281
Rockets:
pp. 276–277

5 The rest of the rocket is discarded while the command, service, and lunar modules continue to the Moon.

6 The journey has taken 102 hours, 45 minutes. The lunar module is ready to land.

7 The command and service modules orbit the Moon (one astronaut remains on board) while the lunar module lands. Two astronauts walk on the Moon.

Moon

4 The command and service modules reattach to the lunar module, which is still connected to the rocket.

8 The lunar module joins the command and service modules so the two lunar astronauts can climb through. The lunar module is then abandoned.

The Eagle has landed

The lunar module (the part of *Apollo 11* that landed) was also known as the *Eagle*. It touched down on the surface of the Moon on 20 July 1969.

The three astronauts worked and slept in the command module.

Apollo 11

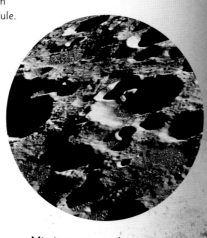

Mission commander Neil Armstrong struggled to find a flat landing site. He succeeded with just seconds to spare.

Men on the Moon

On 20 July 1969, Neil Armstrong became the first person to walk on the surface of the Moon. He was joined by Buzz Aldrin. A third astronaut, Michael Collins, remained in orbit with the command and service modules.

weird or what?
The lunar module computer on *Apollo 11* had approximately 64KB of memory. Some calculators can now store more than 500KB.

The lunar module was nicknamed the *Eagle*.

What did they do?
Armstrong and Aldrin spent almost 22 hours on the Moon. About 2.5 hours of this was spent outside the *Eagle*, collecting rock and soil samples, setting up experiments, and taking pictures.

What was it like?
Buzz Aldrin described the Moon's surface as like nothing on the Earth. He said it consisted of a fine, talcum-powder-like dust, strewn with pebbles and rocks.

Why is there no blue sky on the Moon?

Here comes the Earth

Instead of the Moon rising, the astronauts saw the Earth rising over the Moon's horizon – it looked four times bigger than the Moon looks from the Earth.

How did they talk?

There's no air in space, so sound has nothing to travel through. Lunar astronauts use radio equipment in their helmets to talk to each other.

Neil Armstrong

We have transport!

Three later *Apollo* missions each carried a small electric car, a lunar rover, which allowed the astronauts to explore away from the lander. These were left on the Moon when the astronauts left.

This dish antennae allowed the astronauts to send pictures to the Earth.

Splashdown

The astronauts returned to the Earth in the *Apollo 11* command module. This fell through the atmosphere and landed in the Pacific Ocean. A ringed float helped to keep it stable.

One lunar rover reached a top speed of 22 kph (13.5 mph).

281

Space shuttle

NASA's space shuttle programme was first launched in April 1981, and completed its last mission in 2011. The partly reusable craft taught astronauts an immense amount about working in space.

Ditch the tanks!
The rocket boosters were released two minutes after launch. They parachuted back to the Earth and would be used again. The tank was discarded eight minutes after launch, and broke up in the atmosphere.

Main (external) fuel tank

Which bit is that?
The shuttle had three main components – the orbiter (the plane part, and the only part that went into orbit), a huge fuel tank, and two rocket boosters.

The orbiter carried between five and seven crew members.

Heat protection
Nearly 25,000 heat-resistant tiles covered the orbiter to protect it from high temperatures on re-entry.

United States

NASA

Discovery

weird or what?
Woodpeckers delayed a space shuttle launch in 1995 by pecking holes in the fuel tank's insulating foam. Plastic owls were later used to frighten other birds away.

The orbiter's engines were used once the orbiter reached space.

There were two rocket boosters, one on each side. Once lit, the boosters could not be shut off. They burned until they ran out of fuel.

How long did it take the orbiter to reach space?

Pop it in there!

Each orbiter had a huge payload bay. You could park a school bus in this cavity, which held the satellites, experiments, and laboratories that needed to be taken into space.

The payload's doors opened once the shuttle was in orbit.

The orbiter fleet

Five orbiters were built. Two have been lost in tragic accidents.

Columbia first flew in 1981. It disintegrated on re-entry in 2003.

Challenger was destroyed in 1986, just 73 seconds after launch.

Discovery first flew in 1984. It marked the 100th shuttle mission in 2000.

Atlantis first flew in 1985. It completed 33 missions, the last one in 2011.

Endeavour replaced *Challenger*. It flew 25 missions between 1992 and 2011.

Space shuttle *Endeavour* landing at Edwards Air Force Base, California, USA

A safe landing

Shuttles glided down, belly first. Once the orbiter touched the runway, it released a 12-m (40-ft) drag chute to slow it down.

The future shuttle

NASA tested a new orbiter, called the *Orion Crew Vehicle*, on 5 December 2014. It is supposed to be able to carry up to six astronauts on each mission. This will make it possible for humans to explore asteroids and Mars.

The *Orion Crew Vehicle*

It took just over eight minutes.

Working in space

We have all seen workers on a construction site, hammering and drilling. Imagine a construction site travelling in space high above the Earth's surface. That's what astronauts have to cope with when they are repairing a satellite, or putting together a space station.

International Space Station (ISS)

Illustration of how a sunrise would look from space

Is it warm today?
In orbit, the strong sunshine heats astronauts up. Surprisingly, it's difficult to lose heat in space, so spacesuits have to include a refrigeration unit!

An astronaut may be outside the space station for hours at a time. This one is working on the station's robotic arm.

Between 1998 and 2014, more than 350 individual spacewalks were performed by astronauts outside the International Space Station. Two astronauts always spacewalk together on the ISS.

hands on
Astronauts say that moving their hands in their gloves is difficult. To feel what they mean, put a rubber band around your closed fingers and try to open them. Do this 15 times.

What does EVA stand for?

A piece of history

The first-ever spacewalk was performed by Soviet astronaut Alexei Leonov on 18 March 1965. He was soon followed by American Edward White on 3 June 1965.

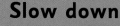

Edward White was the first American to spacewalk.

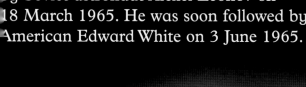

Alexei Leonov became a celebrity in the Soviet Union and around the world.

Slow down

Astronauts have to work slower than construction workers on the Earth. If they twist a bolt too quickly, they will send themselves into a spin.

Make it larger

Space tools are extra large so that astronauts can grab them in their bulky gloves. They also have to be tied to the astronaut to prevent them from floating away.

ExtraVehicular Activity. It means spacewalking!

Exploring Mars

Spacecraft have flown past Mars, orbited it, and landed on its surface. One day, we may even build a base on Mars. It may be cold, barren, and dusty, but it's full of possibilities.

Why study Mars?

At some point in its history, Mars, also called the Red Planet, may have supported life forms. Although it is about half the size of the Earth, it has clouds, weather patterns, and polar icecaps – once it even had active volcanoes. Learning about Mars may help us to understand our own planet.

On the barren surface of Mars, the robotic *Sojourner* rover examines a rock later nicknamed "Yogi".

Seeing red

The landing craft that visited Mars took lots of pictures of its surface. These show a layer of soil that is rich in iron, which gives Mars its red colour – like rusty iron on the Earth.

Looking at Mars

There have been a number of missions to Mars.

 The **Viking landers** were two spacecraft that tested for signs of life in 1976.

 Pathfinder touched down in 1997 and released a small rover called *Sojourner*.

 Mars Express is Europe's first mission to a planet. It has been taking photos from orbit since 2004.

 Mars Reconnaissance Orbiter began orbiting in 2006. It maps and takes detailed images of Mars.

 The car-sized **Curiosity** rover is the latest one to work on Mars. It landed in 2012.

How much did it cost to build, launch, and land the Mars rovers, *Spirit* and *Opportunity*?

What's happening now?

Spirit and *Opportunity* are two rovers that began exploring the Martian surface in 2004. Though *Spirit* stopped working in 2009, *Opportunity* is still operational. They have both sent back a wealth of data about the planet's surface, including evidence that there was once water on Mars.

The NASA rover *Opportunity* holds the off-Earth roving record – it has covered more than 40 km (25 miles) on Martian land.

Cameras mounted on masts give scientists panoramic views of the Martian surface.

The rover is powered by solar panels.

This image shows a 9-mm (0.35-in) hole in Mars' surface drilled and photographed by *Spirit*.

The future on Mars

Scientists are always searching for ways to unlock the secrets of the Red Planet. The suggested ideas include an aeroplane that could travel across its surface (above left) and a thermal probe that would penetrate its ice caps (above right).

In order to explore the potential of a colony in space, eight scientists lived in a self-contained dome, called *Biosphere II*, for two years during the early 1990s.

Living on Mars

If we do establish a base on Mars, it will have to be a self-contained structure that protects its inhabitants from both the atmosphere and the Sun's radiation. Below is an artist's impression of what a Martian base might look like.

Approximately $800 million.

The Sun

Our Sun is a star, but it is closer to us than any other star. Like all stars, it is a massive ball of burning gas, fed by constant explosions in its core. Without it, our planet would be lifeless.

The Sun's colour is best seen when reflected in water. Never look directly at the Sun.

Shimmering lights can light up the skies towards the Earth's polar regions.

Long lived

The Sun was born just under five billion years ago. Although it burns four million tonnes (tons) of fuel each second, it is so big that it will continue to burn for another five billion years.

Solar wind

The Sun sends out a stream of invisible particles, called the solar wind. When these pass the Earth's North and South poles, they can create stunning colours.

Investigating the Sun

Various space probes have been designed to study the Sun.

Ulysses was launched in 1990 to look at the Sun's polar regions.

SOHO was launched in 1995 to observe the Sun and solar activity.

TRACE was launched in 1998 to study the Sun's atmosphere.

A hot spot?

White areas show places where the Sun's surface temperature is higher than elsewhere. Cooler, dark areas, called sunspots, sometimes appear on the surface.

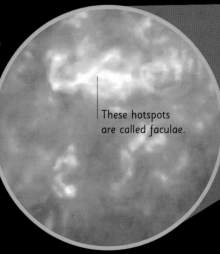

These hotspots are called faculae.

Does the Sun spin?

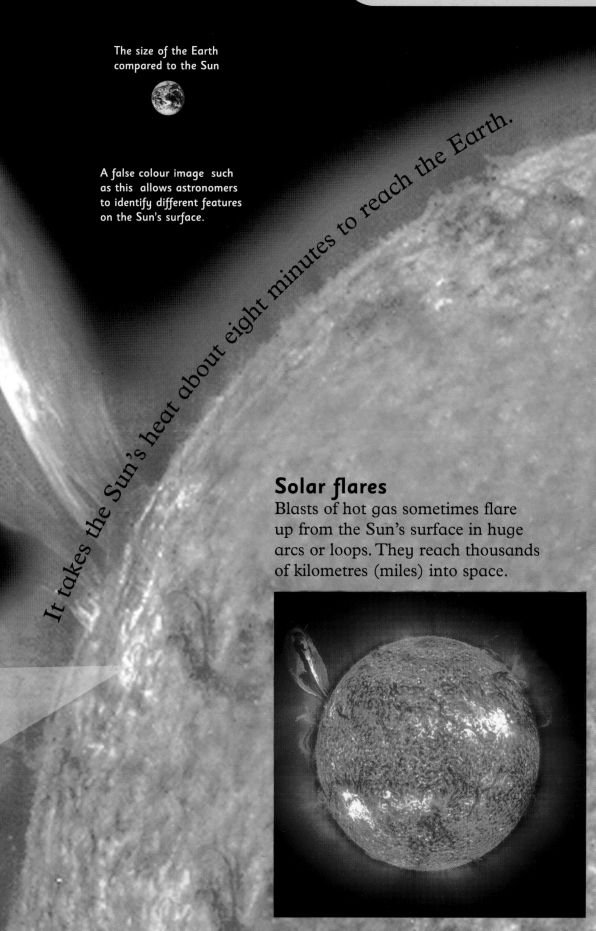

The size of the Earth compared to the Sun

A false colour image such as this allows astronomers to identify different features on the Sun's surface.

It takes the Sun's heat about eight minutes to reach the Earth.

Solar flares

Blasts of hot gas sometimes flare up from the Sun's surface in huge arcs or loops. They reach thousands of kilometres (miles) into space.

289

Yes, it does. It spins on its axis, like the planets of the solar system.

A star is born

Like many space pictures, this image of the Eagle nebula has been artificially coloured so it can be seen clearly.

Clusters of stars are constantly being born from clouds of dust and gas thousands of times the size of our solar system, in a process that can take millions of years.

Born in a cloud
Between existing stars, there are patches of dust and gas. Gradually, these draw in more and more dust and gas to form huge clouds called nebulae.

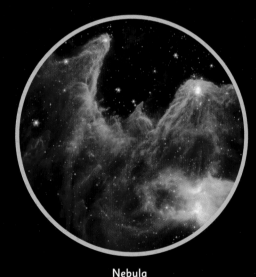

Nebula

Hot colours
As the matter within gets more and more dense, the clouds start to shrink under their own gravity, and eventually break into clumps. This collapse builds up heat, which forms a dense, hot core (protostar) that fills the surrounding nebulae with light and colour. This spectacular effect (right) was captured by the *Spitzer* space telescope.

The process of star formation captured by the *Hubble* telescope

We have fusion!
With enough matter, the process of heating continues. The core gets denser and hotter. Eventually nuclear fusion begins, releasing huge amounts of heat and light – a star is born.

Which star cluster is also called the Seven Sisters?

What's in a name?

Horsehead, Lagoon, Eagle, and Crab... some of the best-known nebulae have popular names inspired by their shape.

Crab nebula

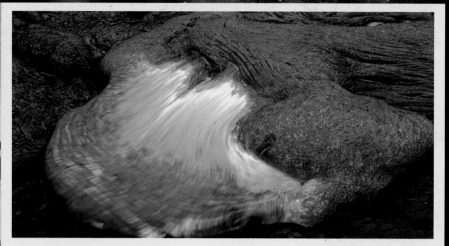

Is that one red?

Some stars shine red, others shine yellow or bluish white. A star's colour depends on its temperature. Red stars are the coolest, while blue stars are the hottest.

Lava also reveals its temperature through its colour. Here, the yellow lava is hotter than the red.

Our Sun is a yellow dwarf star. These stars are medium-sized, and live about 10 billion years.

What type of star?

Stars have different characteristics according to the amount of matter involved in their birth. They differ in colour, temperature, and brightness, and in the length of time they stay alive.

The life of a star

The Universe is home to lots of different types of star.

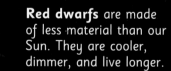

Red dwarfs are made of less material than our Sun. They are cooler, dimmer, and live longer.

Blue giants are among the hottest stars, and live for less than 100 million years.

Supergiants are the rarest stars. They have short lives – under 50 million years.

29

The Big Bang

A Universe is born

What was later termed the Big Bang was first proposed by Georges Lemaître in 1931. Scientists believe it was the beginning of everything, but don't know what caused it to happen.

Georges Lemaitre

Most scientists now believe that the Universe was born from a hot, dense spot more than 13 billion years ago. They call this event the Big Bang.

As the Universe expands and cools, at 300,000 years, matter as we know it starts to form. The Universe is a thousandth of its size today.

The Big Bang – "a day without yesterday".

What happened?

Space and time were brought to life from a minute speck, which was unbelievably hot and heavy. The energy contained in this speck immediately began to spread out, in the form of an ever expanding fireball.

Was the Big Bang an explosion?

ng time coming

er only began to form hundreds
usands of years after the Big
– long after the fireball had
d. The resulting gases would
the stars, planets, and
ies that exist today.

At 9 billion years, the Universe looks much as it does today, if a little bit smaller. Our Sun starts to form.

Stars and galaxies start to form after about 300 million years.

What's that?

Scientists have detected a faint radio signal, present in any direction they look for it in space. They believe it is a faint glow from the Big Bang's superhot fireball. It is called The Cosmic Background Radiation.

The Cosmic Background Radiation was discovered by American physicists Arno Penzias and Robert Wilson in the 1960s.

No beginning, no end

An alternative to the Big Bang, the Steady State Theory claimed there was no beginning or end for the Universe. It's just always been there. Few scientists now believe in the Steady State Theory.

weird or what?
The astronomer who gave the Big Bang theory its name didn't support it. He termed it Big Bang as a criticism and was surprised that the name stuck. He believed in the Steady State Theory.

No – it was an event during which there was an expansion. The Universe is still expan

True or false?

Can you work out which of these facts are real, and which ones are completely made up?

2 The soft lead in pencils is made from quartz.

1 The Sun's light takes 20 minutes to reach the Earth.

3 Rock salt is used to melt ice on roads in cold weather.

4 Triceratops was a plant-eating dinosaur.

5: True 6: False – in the Netherlands 7: True 8: False – it stores water in its trunk

5 Indian dancers use expressions and body movement to tell a story.

6 Wooden clogs were invented in Switzerland.

7 Caecilians are members of the amphibian family.

8 A baobab tree collects and stores water in its roots.

295

Quiz

Test your knowledge
with these quiz questions.

1 The first lunar module to land on the Moon was nicknamed...

A: Vulture   B: Eagle
C: Condor   D: Falcon

2 Which of these is not a continent?

A. Europe   B. South America
C. Antarctica   D. Amsterdam

3 What type of rock is sandstone?

A. Sedimentary   B. Metamorphic
C. Crystalline   D. Igneous

4 Which is the world's most crowded place?

A. Mumbai   B. New York
C. Hong Kong   D. Paris

5 Medieval knights would take part in practice battles known as...

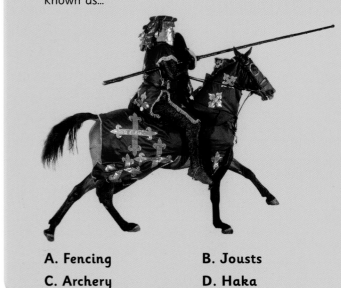

A. Fencing   B. Jousts
C. Archery   D. Haka

6 What is a person who studies living organisms known as?

A. Botanist   B. Biologist
C. Zoologist   D. Ecologist

7 Carrots store food in their...

A: Leaves   B: Spines
C: Roots   D: Fruits

8 What do insects such as caterpillars use for breathing?

A. Spiracles   B. Gills
C. Lungs   D. Skin

9 The nose cone of a rocket helps to make it more...

A. Lightweight   B. Spacious
C. Streamlined   D. Powerful

10 Rainbows can form when sunlight meets...

A: Dust particles   B. Air molecules
C. Pollen grains   D. Water droplets

11 How many bony parts is the human skull made up of?

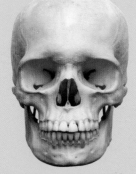

A: 4   B: 2
C: 1   D: 3

12 Which is the coldest desert in the world?

A: Siberia   B: Arctic
C: Himalayas   D: Antarctica

13 In which year was the world's first printed book made?

A: 1455   B: 1645
C: 1665   D: 1595

14 Windmills along the coast of the Netherlands help to...

A: Irrigate crops   B: Drain the land
C: Drill for oil   D: Generate steam

15 What was the Opera House in Sydney designed to resemble?

A. A boat's hull   B. A bird's wing
C. A ship's sail   D. A flower petal

16 Mercury is the only metal that is always liquid because it has a...

A. High freezing point B. Low melting point
C. High boiling point   D. Low boiling point

Who or what am I?

Can you work out who or what is being talked about from the clue?

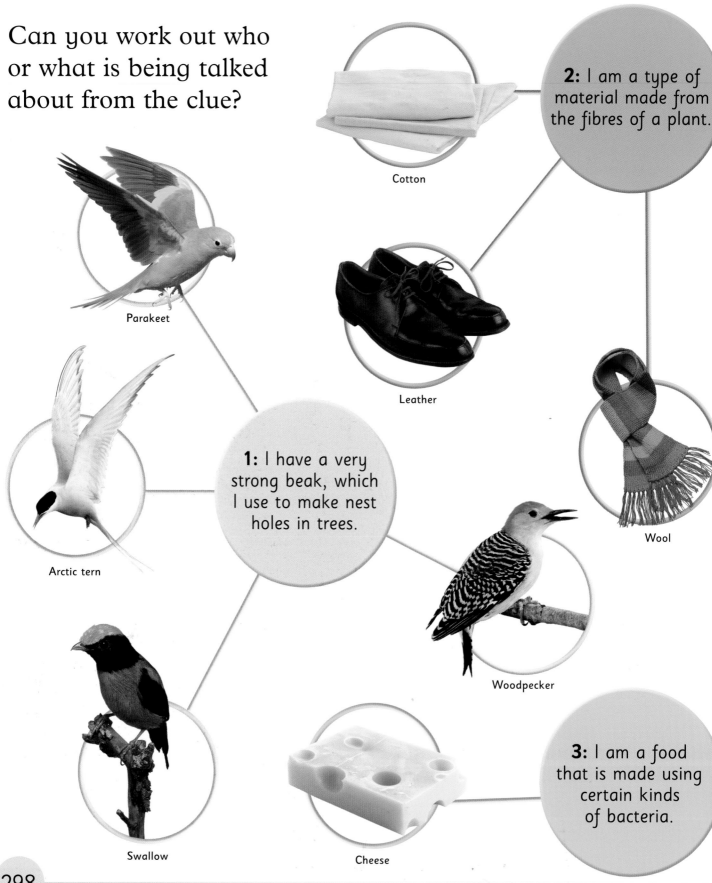

Cotton

2: I am a type of material made from the fibres of a plant.

Parakeet

Leather

1: I have a very strong beak, which I use to make nest holes in trees.

Wool

Arctic tern

Woodpecker

Swallow

Cheese

3: I am a food that is made using certain kinds of bacteria.

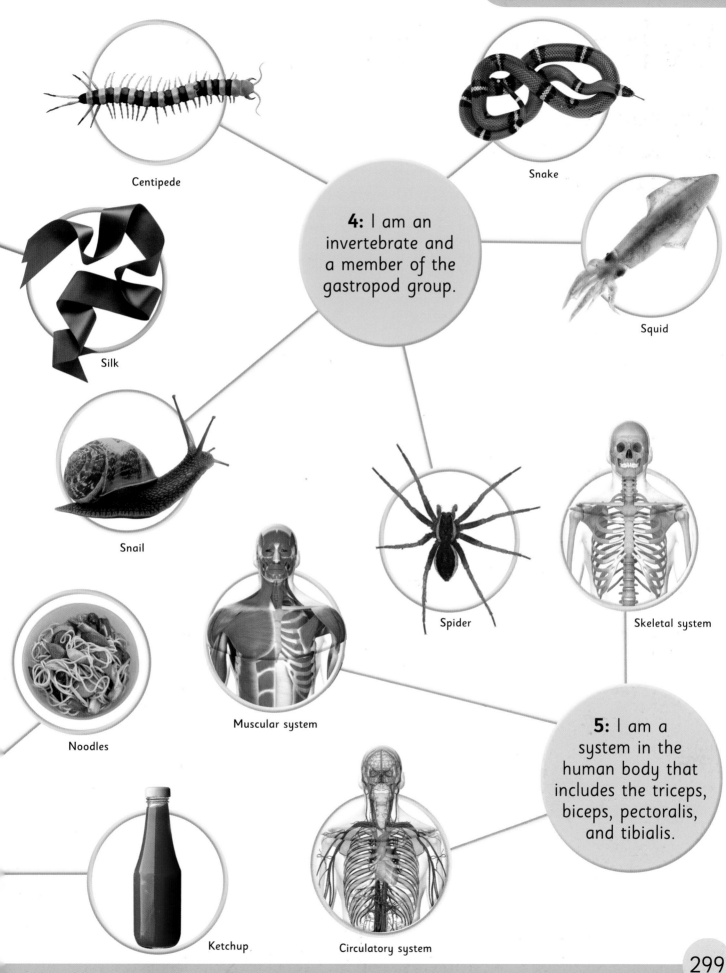

Centipede

Snake

Silk

Squid

4: I am an invertebrate and a member of the gastropod group.

Snail

Spider

Skeletal system

Noodles

Muscular system

5: I am a system in the human body that includes the triceps, biceps, pectoralis, and tibialis.

Ketchup

Circulatory system

1: This US scientist's work in the 1700s laid the foundations for today's electrical world.

4: This tool was developed by two Dutch spectacle makers in 1610.

3: This dinosaur would have been a familiar sight in the forests and swamps of North America.

2: This city, located in the Andes mountains in Peru, was home to the Inca civilization.

Where in the world?

5: This man became the president of South Africa in 1994.

Match the description of each of these people, objects, or animals with the pictures, and discover what part of the world each belongs to.

Corythosaurus

Compass

Jericho

Red-tailed racer

Nelson Mandela

Gingerbread

6: Gingerbread 7: Yoghurt 8: Jericho 9: *Protoceratops* 10: Compass 11: Red-tailed racer 12: Tuatara

6: The Polish town of Torun is well known for this food item.

9: The Gobi Desert in Asia is littered with the remains of this dinosaur.

7: People in Bulgaria eat a lot of this food item because they think it helps them live longer.

10: This tool was first used by the Chinese.

8: This township in Jordan is one of the first cities of the world.

11: This Southeast Asian reptile feasts on frogs, bats, and lizards.

12: This animal from New Zealand is the only survivor of a group of reptiles that lived with the dinosaurs.

Tuatara

Microscope

Machu Picchu

Protoceratops

Yoghurt

Benjamin Franklin

Answers: 1: Benjamin Franklin 2: Machu Picchu 3: Corythosaurus 4: Microscope 5: Nelson Mandela

Glossary

acceleration Change of speed – speeding up or slowing down

alpine Areas on a mountainside that are above the trees but below the permanent snow

alveoli Tiny air sacs inside your lungs

amphibian Animal that can live on land or in water

ancestor Someone you are related to who lived a long time ago

astronaut Person who is trained to travel in space

astronomy Study of the universe

atmosphere Thin layer of gas that surrounds a planet

bacterium (plural: bacteria) Living thing with just one cell. Bacteria are found all over the world – in the oceans, on land, in plants, and in our bodies

carnivore Animal that eats meat. Lions are carnivores

cell Tiny unit that is the basic building block of all living things

chlorophyll Chemical in plants that makes them green. It is essential for photosynthesis

chromosome Rod-shaped strand containing DNA, found in the nucleus of a cell

civilization Way of life of a group of people living in a particular area. For example, the ancient Greek civilization

condensation Changing from a less dense state, such as a gas, into a more solid state, such as a liquid. For example, water vapour condenses into water

continent Large area of land, usually divided into different countries. Europe is a continent

decibel Unit of measurement for sound

deciduous Plant that loses many or all its leaves in one season each year. Oak and maple trees are deciduous

decomposition Breaking down (decaying) of dead animals and plants into smaller pieces, and recycling them into nutrients

dermis Deepest layer of skin, which contains nerves and blood vessels

diaphragm Muscle under your lungs that moves up and down as you breathe

digestion System that breaks down and absorbs food so your body can use it for energy and to make new cells

DNA Chemical inside your body that contains the instructions for making living cells

ecosystem Community of plants and animals living and interacting with each other and their immediate environment

epidermis Top layer of skin that you can see

equator Imaginary line around the middle of the world

era Period of time in history

estuary Place where a river meets the sea

evaporation Changing of a liquid to a gas

evergreen Plant that has leaves on it throughout the year

extinct Animal or plant that has completely disappeared from our world

fault Place where the Earth's crust has cracked and moved

fertilization Joining of a male cell and a female cell to start growing a baby. Also, improving soil by adding nutrients to it

fossil Remains of a plant or animal that has died and been preserved in rock

fossil fuels Fuels, such as coal, oil, or natural gas that was formed underground millions of years ago from the remains of dead plants and animals

friction Force that makes things slow down. When two solids rub against each other, or when a solid moves through liquid or gas, it causes friction

galaxy Large rotating system of stars, gas, dust, and empty space held together by gravity

gene Genes are a part of your DNA, and contain chemical information that controls the way your body develops and works. Genes pass from parents to their children

germ Tiny living things (micro-organisms) found everywhere including inside our bodies. Bacteria are germs. Some germs are good, but some are bad and make us ill

geyser Naturally occurring hot spring, where occasionally the water boils and shoots up in a big spurt

glacier Huge river of ice

gladiator Man trained to fight other men or wild animals in an arena while others watched in ancient Rome

gravity Attraction between everything in the universe. Gravity makes the moon rotate around the Earth, and the Earth and other planets rotate around the Sun

habitat Natural home of an animal or plant

herbivore Animal that eats mainly plants. Giraffes are herbivores

hibernation When animals rest through the winter. They normally find somewhere warm and dry and sleep throughout the cold season

hieroglyphics Ancient Egyptian method of writing that uses symbols

hydrosphere All the water on the Earth's surface, including ice, and water vapour in the atmosphere

immune system Cells and tissues in your body that protect it from infection. If you do get an illness, your immune system often creates special defences so you don't get the same illness again

inertia Tendency everything has to avoid movement or change

infrared radiation Heat energy that is given off by all solids, liquids, and gases

insulator Something that does not let heat or electricity travel through it very easily

invertebrate Animal without a backbone

irrigation Bringing water to land so plants can grow

mammal Warm-blooded animal that has fur and feeds its young with its own milk

mantle Layer of hot, solid rock that lies beneath the Earth's crust and surrounds the Earth's core

marsupial Mammal group in which the female has a pouch for its young

melanin Substance that our body produces to protect our skin from the sun

microchip Tiny electronic device used in computers and machines

mineral Solid with a crystal structure that is found in the ground

monsoon Heavy rain-and-wind storm that occurs in southern Asia

morse code System for sending messages using dashes and dots

mucus Sticky substance inside your airways that traps germs

mummy Dead body that has been preserved by removing some of the organs, treating the body with special chemicals, then wrapping it in long strips of cloth

nucleus Structure inside a cell that contains chromosomes and is essential for making proteins

nutrient Substance taken in by a plant or animal that is essential for its growth.

nymphs Insects that have not yet become adults

omnivore Animal that eats both plants and meat

orbit Path that one object makes around another in space, while under the influence of gravity

ore Mineral that contains a metal

ornithischian Bird-hipped dinosaur

outback Remote, inland areas of Australia

pasteurization Process that uses heat to destroy bacteria in food

percussion Type of musical instrument that is hit or shaken to produce a sound

pharaoh Powerful ruler of ancient Egypt

photosynthesis Process by which plants use sunlight to make food from water and carbon dioxide in the air

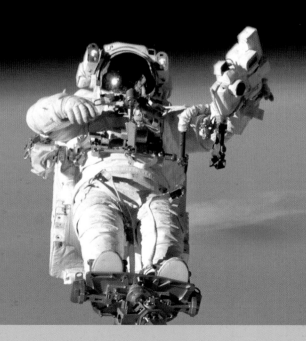

planet Large, round object that orbits a star

population All the people or animals living in an area or country

predator Animal that kills other animals for food

reef Ridge of coral or rock just above or below the sea's surface

reflex action Automatic movement of your body that you can't control

religion Belief in, and worship of, a God or gods; a set of beliefs and way of doing things

reproduction Process by which animals and plants produce young

reptile Cold-blooded animal that usually lays eggs. Reptiles have tough, scaly skin

reservoir Man-made or natural lake where water is stored for use

runes Viking symbols used for writing

samurai Ancient Japanese warrior

saurischian Lizard-hipped dinosaur

savannah Tropical grassland with a few trees, found in eastern Africa and northern South America

scavenger Animal that rarely kills for food, but eats animals that have already died or been killed

space Large, almost empty, places beyond the Earth's atmosphere

spectator Person who watches an event

synthetic Made from man-made materials

transpiration Release of water vapour from a plant through small holes in the leaves

transplant When an organ is removed from someone's body because it is not working very well, and a new one is put in its place

tropical Area of land and sea on either side of the Equator

universe Everything that exists – the Earth, Moon, Sun, all planets and all galaxies, and even those we haven't discovered yet

vaccination Injection that contains a very weak form of the virus or bacterium that you are being vaccinated against

vertebrate Animal with a backbone

virus Very tiny infectious agent that contains DNA and grows on living cells. Viruses cause disease in plants and animals

x-ray Photograph that shows the inside of your body

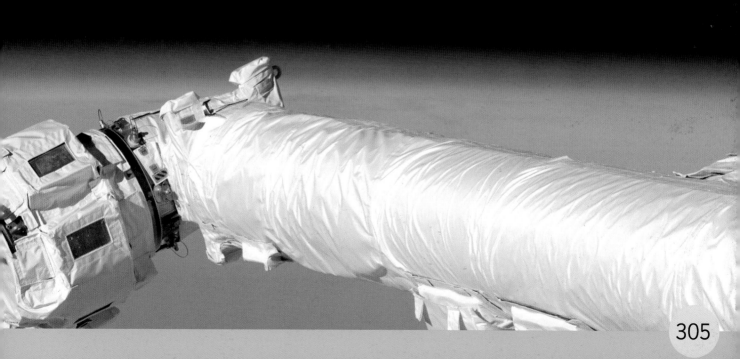

Index

Picture credits

The publisher would like to thank the following for their kind permission to reproduce their photographs:
(Key: a-above; b-below/bottom; c-centre; f-far; l-left; r-right; t-top)

Action Plus: Glyn Kirk 54crb (rugby player); **Aerofilms Ltd:** 89fcrb; **akg-images:** 93tl; **Alamy Images:** Ablestock 105bl; Arco Images GmbH/Thielmann, G. 259tc; Blickwinkel/Baesemann 155fcra; Bryan & Cherry Alexander Photography 55r; Andrew Butterton 267bl; Rosemary Calvert/ImageState 41fcra; Scott Camazine 125fcr, 264c; Nigel Cattlin 149cla; Croftsphoto 257tc; Phoebe Dunn/Stock Connection Distribution 112cra; eye35.com 239bl; Clynt Garnham 235br; Axel Hess 234b; Marc Hill 253tr; Esa Hiltula 20ftr (sauna); D. Hurst 125br; Images of Africa Photobank/David Keith Jones 255tc; ImageState/Pictor 105tc; ImageState/Pictor International 147r, 256bl; Janine Wiedel Photolibrary 101tc; Jeff Morgan Tourism and Leisure 196b; Jon Arnold Images Ltd 37cla; JupiterImages/Comstock Images 105cr (toilet); JupiterImages/Goodshoot 101tr; K-Photos 123c; Paul Andrew Lawrence 265tl; Oleksiy Maksymenko 225ftr; The Natural History Museum, London 153bc, 153fbr; Ron Niebrugge 262tr; Edward Parker 260br; Andrew Paterson 257c; Phototake Inc./Peter Treiber 257c; Rolf Richardson 36br; Robert Harding Picture Library Ltd/Ken Gillham 36clb; RubberBall Productions 104r, 105c, 105cra (boy), 110r; Friedrich Saurer 125tl; Andy Selinger 155cb; Stock Connection Blue/Tom Bean 130-131; Stockfolio 555 217bl, 229br; Jerome Tisne (RF)/JupiterImages/Pixland 113tl; Visual&Written SL/Mark Conlin/VWPics 252cb; WoodyStock/McPhoto 252-253; **Ardea:** Piers Cavendish 14cra; Francois Gohier 190br; Stefan Meyers 176bl; Edwin Mickleburgh 57fbr; Pat Morris 139cr; Valerie Taylor 155fcr, 180clb; Zdenek Tunka 177cb, 177fcla; M. Watson 13clb; **ArenaPAL:** Fritz Curzon 72b; **Atlantide Phototravel:** 88cra; **Auto Express:** 35fclb; **Bryan & Cherry Alexander Photography:** 10bl, 41ca, 159cr; RV0012-13 41fcla; Nogues Alain/Sygma 26fbr; Alan Schein Photography 43fcr; Paul Almasy 10crb (logs), 11tr (logs), 19ftl (boat), 38cr, 41fcl, 47ca; James L. Amos 9ftr; Roger Antrobus 87tc; Archivo Iconografico, SA 27c, 82cla; Tony Arruza 12clb, 23c; Yann Arthus-Bertrand 43clb; Craig Aurness 43fbr; Hinrich Baesemann/EPA 28bcl; Roger Ball 29clb; Anthony Bannister/Gallo Images 141r; Dave Bartruff 50bc; Tom Bean 14cla; Annebicque Bernard/Sygma 26tr; Bettmann 22cb, 56cb, 56fbl, 97tc, 279cb, 281clb, 281fcra; Bettmann/Francis G. Mayer 26fcrb; Bettmann/ Neil Armstrong 280, 280tc; Stefano Bianchetti 214cl; Christophe Boisvieux 21c; Georgina Bowater 43c; Michael Boys 254cl; Tom Brakefield 15bc, 15fbr, 27fbl; Andrew Brown/Ecoscene 253tc; Jan Butchofsky-Houser 37fcra; Car Culture 267tc; Philippe Caron/Sygma 23fbr; Michelle Chaplow 30fcrb; L. Clarke 53cb; Lloyd Cluff 248-249; Dean Conger 46fcra, 47fcla; W. Perry Conway 131tl; Richard Cummins 23cra; Barry Davies/Eye Ubiquitous 54cr; James Davis/Eye Ubiquitous 39cb, 81fcr, 86cra; Tim Davis/Davis Lynn Wildlife 56cla, 57ca; Michael DeYoung 158ca, 177ca; Carlos Dominguez 20bc; Laura Doss 100; Robert Dowling 28cr; EPA 263fcl; Ric Ergenbright 40fbr; Douglas Faulkner 132-133c; Sandy Felsenthal 14cr; Ales Fevzer 76l; David Forman/Eye Ubiquitous 10cra (drill), 11tr (drill), 13fclb, 13fclb (drill), 43bc, 44tl; Owen Franken 47fclb (house); D. Robert & Lorri Franz 129r; Free Agents Limited/Dallas and John Heaton 29c, 34bc, 35cla, 48bl; Michael Freeman 38ftr, 44fcra, 50c; Fukuhara, Inc./ Richard Fukuhara 51fcla; Paul Funston/Gallo Images 140cl; Jose Fuste Raga 28bc, 34clb; Colin Garratt/Milepost 92½ 23tr, 27tl; Raymond Gehman 10-11b; Todd Gipstein 32ca; Philippe Giraud/Sygma 18-19t; Darrell Gulin 14c (pelican); Dan Guravich 40fcra; Martin Harvey 131br; Jason Hawkes 23cr; Lindsay Hebberd 73cl; Chris Hellier 42b, 43ftl; John Holmes/Frank Lane Picture Agency 46crb, 47fcla (flower); Jeremy Horner 44ftr, 48fcrb; Scott Houston/Sygma 11cb; Carol Hughes/ Gallo Images 140-141b; Peter Johnson 54fbr (albatross), 168l, 169cla (crane); Jose Luis Pelaez, Inc. 101clb; Ray Juno 29r; Wolfgang Kaehler 28fcrb, 41cb, 54cfrb (birds), 57cb; Steve Kaufman 12fcrb (bird), 50ca; Layne Kennedy 198fcl; Thom Lang 104cl (brain); Maurizio Lanini 29cra; Alain Le Garsmeur 49ca; Danny Lehman 42ftr; Charles & Josette Lenars 47br, 89bl; Liu Liqun 49cl; Massimo Listri 28fcra; Yang Liu 49br; Craig Lovell 34br, 35bc, 54cl (train); Christophe Loviny 46cra; Renee Lynn 54cr; William Manning 13fcla; Dennis Marsico 55fbl; Jim McDonald 37bl; Joe McDonald 129bc; Sally A. Morgan/ Ecoscene 27tc; Warren Morgan 54tr; Christopher J. Morris 31cl; David Muench 170c; Francesc Muntada 34tc; NASA 272fcr; NASA/EPA 283fcra (as discovery); NASA/Roger Ressmeyer 272clb; Anthony Nex 19cra (house); Michael Nicholson 37c; Diego Lezama Orezzoli 16fcra; Photo B. D. V. 75tl; Michael Pole 54cr; Rick Price 57cla; Louie Psihoyos 190cl, 190cr, 191cr, 192-193b, 199tr, 202-203, 207t; Louie Psihoyos/Science Faction 190l, 191ftl, 201bl; Carl & Ann Purcell 38crb; Steve Raymer 36crb; Carmen Redondo 18clb, 35ftl; Roger Ressmeyer 23ca, 40fb; Reuter Raymond/Sygma 25c; Reuters/Sue Ogrocki 199br; Arthur Rothstein 38clb; Charles E. Rotkin 256cl; Galen Rowell 15fcra, 16br, 57cl, 57fbl, 57fcl, 129cr; Erik Schaffer/Ecoscene 96-97c; Shepard Sherbell/Saba 257bc; Paul A. Souders 21bl (sculpture), 52cb, 55fcl, 135cra, 164-165; David Stoecklein 29tr; Vince Streano 32tc; Keren Su 46cra, 48cla, 49tc; Paul J. Sutton/Duomo 221c; Sygma 253ftl; Liba Taylor 35cl; Roger Tidman 18cr, 56cra; David Turnley 41bcl; Peter Turnley 28cla, 43ca, 97bc; Van Parys/Sygma 25fcla; Vanni Archive 39r; Brian A. Vikander 49fcl; Uwe Walz 28ca; Kennan Ward 159tr; Patrick Ward 23fcla (blackpool tower), 54l (background); Karl Weatherly 29tc; Chad Weckler 165tc; Robert Weight/Ecoscene 56-57tc; K.M. Westermann 18cb; Nik Wheeler 26tr, 43cla, 43tl; Adam Woolfitt 29tl; Michael S. Yamashita 46tr, 73tl; Jim Zuckerman 26bl, 193tr; **Dorling Kindersley:** Bob Gathany 296ca; The National Music Museum 73cr, The Science Museum, London 97crb, Sydney Opera House Trust 297cb; The American Museum of Natural History 189cla (hypacrosaurus), 189fcla (lambeosaurus), 197br; Bedrock Studios 182bc (plateosaurus); Board of Trustees of the Royal Armouries 81fcr (armour) 95ftr, 95tr; Robert L. Braun - modelmaker 182fbr (stegosaurus), 187cr (dilophosaurus), 187crb (stegosaurus), 197fcla (styracosaurus); The British Library 60cb (books), 66fcra; The British Museum 44fcr, 81bl, 81fcrb, 83cra, 84bl, 84l, 85ca, 85cra, 87cra (book), 89tl, 9cr, 93cra; Centaur

Studios – modelmakers 188tr; John Chase/The Museum of London 66bc, 66cra; Conaculta-Inah-Mex/Instituto Nacional De Antropologia E Historia 14fcr, 15fclb (stone head), 92fbr; Philip Dowell 16cr; Egyptian Museum, Cairo 80tr; Franklin Park Zoo, Boston 128ca; Hasbro International Inc. 77tr; Jonathan Hateley – modelmaker 210r, 211fclb; Graham High at Centaur Studios - modelmaker 182br (brachiosaurus), 183bl (t-rex), 208cra (triceratops); Historiches Museum Der Stadt Wiend, Vienna 71fcl (programme); Jon Hughes/Bedrock Studios 1cl, 183fbl (gigantosaurus), 200cl; Imperial War Museum, London 217ftl; Index Stock/Alamy 240cb; Michael Jackson 25clb, 29cl (beer); Marwell Zoological Park, Winchester 20cr; Mattel Toys 77c; Judith Miller/Elms Lesters 121ftl; Peter Minister 182-183, 185br; Museo Archeologico Nazionale di Napoli 33cla; Museum of the Order of St John, London 94clb; NASA 81c, 213r, 242cr, 271bl, 289tc; National Maritime Museum, London 49fcrb; National Trust 22fcrb; Natural History Museum, London 16cb, 46fcr (oyster), 49crb, 51cl (oyster), 53fcl (opals), 82fcl, 82ftl, 134bl (tail/body feather), 134clb (inner wing), 134clb (outer wing), 134l, 135fclb (crow foot), 162ca, 185c, 185fcr, 189cla (parasaurolophus), 211cla (blue feather), 222br, 226tl, 231cr, 251fbr; The Natural History Museum, London 14ca; Odds Farm Park, High Wycombe, Bucks 22cr; Peabody Museum of Natural History, Yale University 202bl, 203tl; Pitt Rivers Museum, University of Oxford 71fcla (panpipes), 82br, 82cb; Powell-Cotton Museum, Kent 63cl; Luis Rey – modelmaker 183fbl (velociraptor), 202cla, 202ftl (troodon); Rough Guides 156eb (river), 185tr; Royal British Columbia Museum, Victoria, Canada 37br, 37clb, 81cra, 83cb; Saint Bride Printing Library, London 67cla; The Science Museum, London 2bl, 226c, 226cr, 226fcr; Senckenberg Nature Museum, Frankfurt 210bl; Neil Setchfield 12cb (hollywood); St Mungo, Glasgow Museums 63fcr, 65c; Statens Historiska Museum, Stockholm 91fcr; Stephen Oliver 66c, 67bc; University College, London 128fcla; University Museum of Archaeology and Anthropology, Cambridge 93cra (armlets); Wallace Collection 95cla; Barrie Watts 223cl (grass); Weymouth Sea Life Centre 21bc, 52fbl (octopus); Jerry Young 8fcrb, 9c, 15fcl, 38tl, 41cl, 52cra (dingo), 156bl, 184c; **Dreamstime.com:** Lano Angelo 295r, Buriy 71cra, Yuriy Chaban 297cra, Orcea David 66br, Ifeelstock 217ca, Isselee 135br, Jarcosa 298cl, Jose Manuel Gelpi Diaz 109c, Richie Lomba 301br, Richard Moody 68tl, Vladimir Ovchinnikov 217c, Sergiy Palamarchuk 297tl, Scanrail 97, .shock 61tc, Michael Truchon 298cb, Yuri Yakovlev 299bl; **E & E Picture Library:** R. Nathwani 65tr; **ESA:** 286c, 271crb, 277fcr (satellite); **Financial Times:** 67cl, 67r; **FLPA:** Flip De Nooyer/FN/Minden 211fbr, 211tr; Silvestris Fotoservice 162bl; D. P. Wilson 155fcrb; Konrad Wothe/Minden Pictures 173cr, 241b; **Getty Images:** 36cb (bobsleigh), 42cla; AFP 21tr; Altrendo Travel 68ca; Amana Images/Yoshio Otsuka 165br; The Bridgeman Art Library/German School 214c; James Burke/Time Life Pictures 249tr; David Cannon 17fcla; Cousteau Society 145cb; Adrian Dennis/AFP 23fcla; Discovery Channel Images/Jeff Foott 250-251; Robert Frerck 14tl; Gallo Images/Daryl Balfour 164cr; Iconica/Frank Whitney 239r; The Image Bank/Alvis Upitis 20ftr (paper mill); The Image Bank/Antonio M. Rosario 272cr; The Image Bank/Antony Edwards 22fcra (angel); The Image Bank/Doug Allan 257cla; The Image Bank/Flip Chalfant 13c (seers tower); The Image Bank/Frans Lemmens 19c; The Image Bank/Jeremy Woodhouse 25r; The Image Bank/LWA 269ftr, 273cla; The Image Bank/Philippe Bourseiller 252cla; The Image Bank/Thomas Schmitt 52c (truck); The Image Bank/Tyler Stableford 243t; David Kjaer 11fcr; National Geographic/Joel Sartore 233c; National Geographic/Klaus Nigge 200-201 (background); National Geographic/Michael K. Nichols 172bl; National Geographic/ Michael S. Quinton 179crb; Panoramic Images 169fcla (stork); Photodisc 172cb (deciduous); Photodisc/David De Lossy 172c (conifer); Photodisc/Michael Goldman 86crb; Photographer's Choice/Georgette Douwma 122bl; Photographer's Choice/Marco Simoni 252fclb (headland); Redferns/Nicky J. Sims 71bc; Riser/Edwin Remsberg 13fcl; Riser/Georgette Douwma 145r; Riser/John R. Ramey 21bl; Riser/Philip and Karen Smith 248bc; Riser/Sightseeing Archive 280br; Riser/Terje Rakke 21fclb; Robert Harding World Imagery/Chris Rennie 37crb; Guido Alberto Rossi 32cr; Erik Simonsen 221tr; Stone/AEF - Yves Debay 19c; Stone/Anthony Cassidy 53clb; Stone/Art Wolfe 33cla (etna), 33cr (etna); Stone/Brett Baunton 35tr; Stone/Daryl Balfour 19ftl (mountain); Stone/David Sutherland 40c; Stone/Demetrio Carrasco 261tl; Stone/Frans Lemmens 24cla; Stone/Herb Schmitz 54bl; Stone/Hideo Kurihara 55fcla (geyser); Stone/Janet Gill 23tc (big ben); Stone/Joe Cornish 26cra; Stone/John Chard 170-171, 294-295t; Stone/Joseph Devenney 15ca; Stone/Keith Wood 256-257; Stone/Ken Fisher 16c; Stone/Martin Puddy 45r; Stone/Michael Kelley 177tl; Stone/Paul Harris 8bc; Stone/Pete Turner 12fcra; Stone/Siegfried Eigstler 166-167; Stone/ Stephen Frink 13bc; Stone/Steven Hunt 180tl; Stone/Tim Flach 111cla; Stone/Will & Deni McIntyre 15r; Stephen Studd/Photographer's Choice 160cra; Taxi 31cra; Taxi/Brian Kenney 189fclb; Taxi/Doug Corrance 22fcra; Taxi/Gary Bell 160l; Taxi/Getty Images 12fcrb, 16fcrb; Taxi/Jon Arnold 23cra (royal pavillion); Taxi/Michael Freeman 15cl (pyramid); Taxi/Peter Adams 44fcrb; Taxi/Travel Pix 51fcl (mt fuji); The Image Bank/Jeff Rotman 180-181; V. C. L. 93b; Heinrich Van Den Berg 127ca; Zhongda Zhang/IVPP 199c; **Tory Gordon-Harris:** 92cb, 92l; Reproduced by permission of the Henry Moore Foundation: 68cra; **Simon Holland:** Simon Holland and Victoria Waddington 73bc; **Hutchison Library:** Andrew Eames 40cra, 56fcrb; Robert Francis 94fcla (japanese castle); Isabella Tree 9clb; **Images of Africa Photobank:** David Keith Jones 19cla; **Imagestate:** Kord.com/Age Fotostock 51cr; Pictor 15c (flamingos), 33fcl, 44cr, 47cra, 51fbl, 52fcr, 113bl; Pictor/Douglas David Seifert 14fcl; Pictor/Ethel Davies 45clb; Pictor/Randa Bishop 51fcl (geishas); **iStockphoto.com:** ruvanboshoff 300br, Kelly Cline 226bl; Esemelwe 235crb; Mark Evans 231tr; Filonmar 231br; Sergey Galushko 236cr (iron); Péter Gudella 239clb; Michelangeloboy 227cl; NSPImages 238br (torch); Jurga R 235cra; Stephen Strathdee 147tr; Sylvanworks 233clb; **Morten Jensen:** 69cb; **Dr Marcus Junkelmann:** 88bl; **Kokoro Dinosaurs:** 211br; **Lebrecht Music and Arts:** Odile Noel 70l (b/ground); **Courtesy of Lockheed Martin Aeronautics Company, Palmdale:** 241t; **Lonely Planet Images:** Rhonda Gutenberg 38cra; Craig Pershouse 36br (crosses), 36tc; Tony Wheeler 39c; **NASA:** cl, cra, crb, 268b, 268fcl, 268fcl (sun), 268fclb (astronaut), 269cb, 270-271 (b/ground), 276ca, 277ftr (shuttle), 277l, 278tl, 282, 282clb, 283br, 283cl, 283tl, 284-285, 285bc, 285cr, 285tr, 286cr (mgs), 286cr (mpl), 286crb (sojourner), 286tl, 286-287 (b/ground), 286-287b, 287br, 287cla, 287ftr, 287tr, 288fbl (solvn), 288fbl (earth), 291br, 291cfb, 296-297; ESA, H. Weaver (JHU/APL), A. Stern (SwRI), and the HST Pluto Companion Search Team 291tr; Finley Holiday Films 13cb; GRIN 97c; HQ-GRIN br; C. Mayhew & R. Simmon (NASA/GSFC), NOAA/

NGDC, DMSP Digital Archive 6bl; MSFC br; ESA/ASU/J. Hester 291cra, Bill Ingalls 263cra, 277tr, JPL 286cb (Mars Reconnaissance), JPL-Caltech 283br, 284tr, 286cb; **Natural Visions:** Richard Coomber 168cra; The **Natural History Museum, London:** 188cr, 189cl (brachylophosaurus), 191b; **naturepl.com:** Ingo Arndt 17br; Pete Cairns 179tc; Martin Dohrn 16-17cb; Georgette Douwma 145tl; Barry Mansell 175cla; Vincent Munier 50cla; T. J. Rich 41clb; Anup Shah 19r; Lynn M. Stone 44cl; **NHPA/Photoshot:** A.N.T. Photo Library 52fclb (snake), 131c; Laurie Campbell 136bl; Bill Coster 41ftl; Andrea Ferrari 194-195; Martin Harvey 168-169; Adrian Hepworth 162-163; Daniel Heuclin 130fcra (tree-kangaroo), 138cra (caecilian), 139crb, 169tr; Hellio & Van Ingen 159br; Burt Jones & Maurine Shimlock 52fclb (snail); Gerard Lacz 133clb; Andy Rouse 129fbl (dolphin); Jonathan & Angela Scott 129tl; Norbert Wu 133tr; **Nokia:** 97tr (phone); **Photolibrary:** Don Farrall/White 265bl; Fresh Food Images/Amanda Heywood 40clb, 41fcrb; Gallo Images-Anthony Bannister/White 261cl; IFA Animals/IFA-Bilderteam GMBH 173tc; Paul Kay/OSF 146tr; Oxford Scientific (OSF)/Bert & Babs Wells 130fcra (numbat); Oxford Scientific (OSF)/David B Fleetham 52fclb (sea snake); Oxford Scientific (OSF)/Mike Powles 40cb; Oxford Scientific (OSF) / Roger Brown 130fcra (bandicoot); Oxford Scientific (OSF)/Thomas Haider 132l; Photodisc 226bc; Harold Taylor / OSF 155fbr; **Photoshot/World Pictures:** 20ca, 33br; Rudi Pigneter 46bl; **Pictorial Press Ltd:** 77cb; **Pictures Colour Library:** Charles Bowman 20br (geyser); George Hunter 10fbr (skyline); Edmund Nagele 23bl; **Press Association Images:** Associated Press/John Rasmussen 90; Tony Marshall/Empics Sport 76tr; **PunchStock:** Digital Archive Japan 288ftl; **Robert Harding Picture Library:** R. Kiedrowski 64l 17fcl, 34tr, 44br, 75ca, 118c; Mohamed Amin 63ftr; Charles Bowman 24crb, 38tc; Jeremy Bright 62l; V. Englebert 92cr; Alain Evrard 60l; Robert Francis 93c; Miwako Ikeda/Int'l Stock 68-69b; D. Jacobs 53fcl; Roy Rainford 89cl; Luca Tettoni 64cra; Alison Wright 44bc; **Science Photo Library:** 103bc, 150fcr, 262-263, 292tl; Professors P. M. Motta, K. R. Porter & P. M. Andrews 115cla; Samuel Ashfield 152tr; Julian Baum 284cr; John Bavosi 108fclb; Biophoto Associates 117cla; Dr. Tony Brain 121fcla; BSIP/Chassenet 239ftl, 239tl; BSIP/Dr T. Pichard 117cla; Dr. Jeremy Burgess 219tl; Chris Butler 290cl; Custom Medical Stock Photo 114tc; Christian Darkin 118tr, 197tr; David A. Hardy, Futures: 50 Years In Space 274-275; Martin Dohrn 102fcra; John Durham 151tr; Bernhard Edmaier 8cl (background), 9cr (background), 209, 249tl; Eye Of Science 165cr; Vaughan Fleming 251bl; Mark Garlick 237tr, 290br, 290-291, 292-293; Adam Gault 153cl; Carlos Goldin 200tr; Steve Gschmeissner 103br, 103cl, 103fbl, 112cl, 116-117b, 148fcra; Adam Hart-Davis 287cr; Gary Hincks 262bl; JPL-CalTech/STSCI/VASSAR/ NASA 269fbr; Edward Kinsman 233r; Ted Kinsman 215bl; Larry Landolfi 268c; G. Brad Lewis tl, 225b; David Mack 152bl; J. L. Martra, Publiphoto Diffusion 104bl; Maximilian Stock Ltd 79crb; Astrid & Hanns-Frieder Michler 120clb (skin), 122ca; Mark Miller 153bl, 153br, 153cb, 153cl (background), 153cra, 153ftl, 153tl; Allan Morton/Dennis Milon 274cl; Prof. P. Motta/Dept. Of Anatomy/ University "La Sapienza", Rome 114br; Dr. Gopal Murti 102br; NASA 78cr, 208-209b, 262bc, 283fcr (ss atlantis), 286cb; National Cancer Institute 110fcla; Dr. Yorgos Nikas 117tc, 119tl, 119tr; NREL/ US Department Of Energy 224br; David Nunuk 269fcra; Laurie O'Keefe 192clb; David Parker 198-199; David Parker For ESA/CNES/ ArianeSpace 277crb; Physics Today Collection/American Institute of Physics 293cr; Alain Pol, ISM 115bc; Prof. Aaron Polliack 103bl; Philippe Psaila 217cb; Ria Novosti 276cb, 285cla; Paul Robbens & Gus York 279br; Royal Observatory, Edinburgh/AAO 269fcrb; Friedrich Saurer 280cra, 282bl, 284bl, 293bc; Francoise Sauze 238fclb; Karsten Schneider 263bc; Victor De Schwanberg 104fcl (heart), 104fcl (kidney) Science Source 151tl; SOHO/ESA/NASA 289; Andrew Syred 103ca, 112bc, 112crb, 148fcrb; Sheila Terry 255fcla (loamy); US Geological Survey 216fbr; D. Van Ravenswaay 208cclb; Detlev Van Ravenswaay 269fcr; Dr. Mark J. Winter 229cr; Sean Hunter Photography: 12cl, 31ftl, 32cr (pisa), 33clb (pisa); **Shutterstock:** Adfsa 267c; Alle 126ftl; Andres 215fcrb (family); Apollofoto 261bc; Matt Apps 252fbl (arch); Andrey Armygayo 217cra (car), 228bl; Orkhan Aslanov 221tl; Lara Barrett 124fbl (anemone); Giovanni Benintende 213t; Claudio Bertoloni 215fbr; Mircea Bezergheanu 264-265t; Murat Boylu 228bc; Melissa Brandes 250cb; Karel Brož 122br; Buquet 111clb; Michael Byrne 220b; William Casey 212fcr; CBPix 259c; Bonita R. Cheshier 230cr; Stephen Coburn 258-259b; Sahua D 242; Digitalife 212-213b; Pichugin Dmitry 124-125, 212clb, 224fclb (lake), 253cra, 258-259tr; Denis Dryashkin 151cr (pills); Neo Edmund 127fcrb (butterfly); Stasy Eidiejus 242tl; Elen 226-227 (background); Christopher Ewing 217cr (bulb); ExaMedia Photography 266tr; Martin Fischer 265r; Flashon Studio 232bl; Mark Gabrenya 148-149cb; Julien Grondin 213c; Jubal Harshaw 148br; Johann Hayman 154tr; Home Studio 230fbr, 231bc; Chris Howey 266l; Eric Isselée 126br; Jhaz Photography 235bl; Gail Johnson 155fr; Kameel4u 237clb; Sebastian Kaulitzki 216cr; Nancy Kennedy 125fbr; Stephan Kerkhofs 156cb (reef); Tan Kian Khoon 111bl; Tamara Kulikova 265crb; Liga Lauzuma 154-155; Chris LeBoutillier 244cr; Francisco Amaral Leitão 257br; Luchschen 216clb; Robyn Mackenzie 233tl; Hougaard Malan 148-149t; Patricia Marroquin 213clb; Martiin || Fluidworkshop 238ftl; Mashe 122fcr; Marek Mnich 233ca; Brett Mulcahy 235tl; Ted Nad 236cra; Karl Naundorf 234crb (pump); Cees Nooij 230l; Thomas Nord 221b; Aron Ingi Ólason 156bc; Oorka 266cfr; Orla 123tc; Pandapaw 126cl; Anita Patterson Peppers 238tr; Pcross 238bl; PhotoCreate 219cl; Jelena Popić 225ftl; Lee Prince 237cr; Nikita Rogul 224fbl (barbed wire); RPixs 244-245; Sandra Rugina 261br (dishwasher); Kirill Savellev 252fbl (stack); Elena Schweitzer 220c; Serp 147fcrb (maple); Elisei Shafer 259b (coral); Igor Smichkov 260l; Carolina K. Smith, M.D. 226cl; Snowleopard1 123cb; Elena Solodovnikova 147cr, 147fbr (yellow ash); Ng Soo Jiun 147fbl; Specta 127tfbl; James Steidl 216tl; Teekaygee 147l; Igor Terekhov 220cra; Tramper 254br; Ultimathule 229tc; Robert Paul Van Beets 216br; Vnlit 122fcra; Li Wa 216c; Linda Webb 214cra; R. T. Wohlstadter 263fcr; Jurgen Ziewe 214fbr, 258br; **Sony Computer Entertainment Europe:** 77t; **Still Pictures:** 20fcrb; Biosphoto/Klee J.-L. & Hubert M.-L. 130c; John Cancalosi/Peter Arnold. Inc. 191tl; Sergio Hanquet 53r; Andreas Riedmiller 29crb; **SuperStock:** Age Fotostock 31bl, 218-219b; J. Beck 46cr; J. Silver 189b, 189r; Steve Vidler 51fcl (castle); **Warren Photographic:** 196t

All other images © Dorling Kindersley
For further information see: www.dkimages.com